Cooking Light®

fresh food
fast
24/7

Cooking Light

fresh food
fast
24/7

Oxmoor
House®

©2012 by Time Home Entertainment, Inc.
135 West 50th Street, New York, NY 10020

ISBN-13: 978-0-8487-3645-3
ISBN-10: 0-8487-3645-1
Library of Congress Control Number: 2011943946
Printed in the United States of America
First Printing 2012

Be sure to check with your health-care provider before making any changes in your diet.

Oxmoor House

VP, Publishing Director: Jim Childs
Creative Director: Felicity Keane
Brand Manager: Michelle Turner Aycock
Senior Editor: Heather Averett
Managing Editor: Rebecca Benton

Cooking Light® Fresh Food Fast 24/7

Editor: Shaun Chavis
Project Editor: Emily Chappell
Assistant Designer: Allison Sperando Potter
Director, Test Kitchen: Elizabeth Tyler Austin
Assistant Directors, Test Kitchen: Julie Christopher, Julie Gunter
Test Kitchen Professionals: Wendy Ball, RD; Allison E. Cox; Victoria E. Cox; Margaret Monroe Dickey; Alyson Moreland Haynes; Stefanie Maloney; Callie Nash; Catherine Crowell Steele; Leah Van Deren
Photography Director: Jim Bathie
Senior Photo Stylist: Kay E. Clarke
Associate Photo Stylist: Katherine Eckert Coyne
Assistant Photo Stylist: Mary Louise Menendez
Assistant Production Manager: Diane Rose

Contributors

Copy Editors: Jacqueline Giovanelli, Kate Johnson
Proofreader: Dolores Hydock
Indexer: Mary Ann Laurens
Nutritional Analyses: Wendy Ball, RD; Jessica Cox, RD; Susan McIntosh, MS, RD
Interns: Erin Bishop; Mackenzie Cogle; Jessica Cox, RD; Laura Hoxworth; Alison Loughman; Lindsay A. Rozier; Ashley White
Test Kitchen Professionals: Martha Condra, Erica Hopper, Kathleen Royal Phillips
Photographers: Brian Francis, Beau Gustafson, Lee Harrelson, Mary Britton Senseney, Jason Wallis
Photo Stylists: Mindi Shapiro Levine, Anna Pollock

Time Home Entertainment Inc.

Publisher: Richard Fraiman
Vice President, Strategy & Business Development: Steven Sandonato
Executive Director, Marketing Services: Carol Pittard
Executive Director, Retail & Special Sales: Tom Mifsud
Director, Bookazine Development & Marketing: Laura Adam
Publishing Director: Joy Butts
Finance Director: Glenn Buonocore
Associate General Counsel: Helen Wan

Cooking Light®

Editor: Scott Mowbray
Creative Director: Carla Frank
Deputy Editor: Phillip Rhodes
Executive Editor, Food: Ann Taylor Pittman
Special Publications Editor: Mary Simpson Creel, MS, RD
Senior Food Editor: Julianna Grimes
Senior Editor: Cindy Hatcher
Associate Food Editor: Timothy Q. Cebula
Assistant Editor, Nutrition: Sidney Fry, MS, RD
Assistant Editors: Kimberly Holland, Phoebe Wu
Test Kitchen Director: Vanessa T. Pruett
Assistant Test Kitchen Director: Tiffany Vickers Davis
Recipe Testers and Developers: Robin Bashinsky, Adam Hickman, Deb Wise
Art Directors: Fernande Bondarenko, Shawna Kalish
Associate Art Director: Rachel Cardina Lasserre
Junior Designer: Hagen Stegall
Photo Director: Kristen Schaefer
Assistant Photo Editor: Amy Delaune
Senior Photographer: Randy Mayor
Senior Photo Stylist: Cindy Barr
Photo Stylist: Leigh Ann Ross
Chief Food Stylist: Charlotte Autry
Senior Food Stylist: Kellie Gerber Kelley
Food Styling Assistant: Blakeslee Wright
Copy Chief: Maria Parker Hopkins
Assistant Copy Chief: Susan Roberts
Research Editor: Michelle Gibson Daniels
Editorial Production Director: Liz Rhoades
Production Editor: Hazel R. Eddins
Assistant Production Editor: Josh Rutledge
Administrative Coordinator: Carol D. Johnson
CookingLight.com Editor: Allison Long Lowery
Nutrition Editor: Holley Johnson Grainger, MS, RD
Production Assistant: Mallory Brasseale

To order additional publications, call 1-800-765-6400 or 1-800-491-0551

For more books to enrich your life, visit **oxmoorhouse.com**

To search, savor, and share thousands of recipes, visit **myrecipes.com**

Cover: Sautéed Tilapia Tacos with Grilled Peppers and Onion, page 270 and Shredded Chicken Tacos, page 271; **Front flap:** Dark Chocolate–Cherry Almond Bark, page 342; **Back cover:** Cinnamon-Apple–Stuffed French Toast, page 75; White Cranberry–Peach Spritzers, page 250; Grilled Halibut with Hoisin Glaze and Grilled Baby Bok Choy, page 298; **Page 2:** Balsamic Peach Melba Parfaits with Spiked Mascarpone, page 326

welcome

Enjoy fresh, fast food every meal of the day. This latest cookbook in the *Cooking Light* Fresh Food Fast series makes it even easier to celebrate a healthy lifestyle 24 hours a day, 7 days a week. We often hear from readers and parents who are eager to feed their families good food around the clock. There's a growing national movement focused on healthy lunches for schoolchildren, and recent research confirms that breakfast truly is the most important meal of the day. *Cooking Light Fresh Food Fast 24/7* helps you make fresh, healthy, and delicious food a bigger part of how you eat.

In this new collection of 280 5-ingredient, 15-minute recipes, we've created flavorful, easy dinners fit for sharing with family and friends. You'll also find ideas for breakfast and lunch on the go, brunch, and fun snacks, plus appetizers and cocktails for entertaining. Each Test Kitchen–rated recipe meets at least one of two criteria: It calls for 5 ingredients or fewer (excluding water, flour, cooking spray, oil, salt, pepper, and optional ingredients), or it can be prepared in 15 minutes or less. Many accomplish both!

Plus—we've made life easier with a new section: Market to Meal Planners. Each planner gives you one shopping list for nine recipes, including three dinners. Recipes in each planner share common ingredients, so you can make the most of the food you buy.

Cooking Light Fresh Food Fast 24/7 includes other new features, such as:
- "Feed Four for $10 or Less" helps stretch your dollar with budget meals. (Prices were derived from midsized-city supermarkets in Summer 2011. Side dishes are included in the cost of the meal. Salt, pepper, and cooking spray are freebies.)
- "To-Go Tips" offer ways to pack a portable meal so it stays fresh.
- "Switch It Up" shows you how to turn a salad recipe into a sandwich, or a sandwich recipe into a salad—essentially giving you a new dish to try!

All the recipes are designed to get you in and out of the kitchen in minutes. It's never been easier to enjoy good food every day!

The *Cooking Light* Editors

contents

45

127

210

249

285

368

market to meal
planners

We're skeptical of full-week meal planners because that's just not realistic for most people. Some of us spend evenings chauffeuring carloads of kids to soccer practice and play dates. Others cook just for two. Instead, in this new feature of the *Cooking Light* Fresh Food Fast series, we focused on creating 10 meal planners that make enjoying fresh food at any meal throughout the week more practical. Each planner includes one shopping list for three dinners and a mix of breakfasts, lunches, snacks, and desserts. Cooking three nights a week? One planner's got you covered. If you're a devoted weeknight cook, you can combine two of your favorite planners for six dinners and nearly a week's worth of great meals.

The shopping lists don't include the basics: salt, pepper, oil, all-purpose flour, and cooking spray (we assume you have those) or optional ingredients. You can download printable versions of the planners at CookingLight.com/FFFShoppingLists.

Shrimp and Summer
Vegetable Sauté, page **272**

Green Spice Chicken Tenders and
Mexican-Style Grilled Corn, page **276**

Feta-Lamb Patties with
Cucumber Sauce, page **291**

Savory Cornmeal Waffles, page **261**

Mediterranean Breakfast
Sandwich, page **42**

Steak Taco Salad with Black
Bean-Corn Relish, page **185**

Turkey-Hummus Pitas, page **132**

Greek Lamb Salad, page **186**

Feta-Mint Dip, page **199**

Common ingredients in this planner are baby spinach, feta cheese, fresh basil, fresh corn, pita bread, and tomatoes.

SHOPPING LIST

produce
- [ ] English cucumber, 1
- [ ] fresh baby spinach, 1 bag
- [ ] fresh basil
- [ ] fresh cilantro
- [ ] fresh corn, 12 ears
- [ ] fresh dill
- [ ] fresh flat-leaf parsley
- [ ] fresh mint
- [ ] fresh okra, 3.5 ounces
- [ ] fresh oregano
- [ ] garlic   [ ] green onions
- [ ] large fresh tomatoes, 3
- [ ] lemons, 4   [ ] lime, 1
- [ ] onion, 1   [ ] pico de gallo, 1 cup
- [ ] plum tomatoes, ½ pound
- [ ] red bell pepper, 1
- [ ] red onion, 1
- [ ] romaine lettuce, 6 cups

meat/fish/poultry
- [ ] bacon, 8 ounces
- [ ] chicken breast tenders, 1½ pounds
- [ ] lean ground lamb, 2 pounds
- [ ] peeled and deveined large shrimp, 1¼ pounds
- [ ] skirt steak, 1 pound
- [ ] thinly sliced deli, lower-sodium turkey breast, 8 ounces

dairy
- [ ] butter
- [ ] Cotija cheese, 4 ounces
- [ ] fat-free sour cream, 6 ounces
- [ ] feta cheese, 4.5 ounces
- [ ] large eggs
- [ ] plain 2% reduced-fat Greek yogurt, 8 ounces
- [ ] reduced-fat feta cheese, 3 ounces

freezer
- [ ] frozen artichoke hearts

staples
- [ ] 10-grain whole-grain pancake and waffle mix
- [ ] black beans, 1 (15-ounce) can
- [ ] canola mayonnaise
- [ ] chickpeas, 1 (16-ounce) can
- [ ] chipotle chiles in adobo sauce, 1 (7-ounce) can
- [ ] ground cumin
- [ ] light ranch dressing
- [ ] red wine vinegar
- [ ] salt-free fiesta-lime seasoning
- [ ] smoked paprika
- [ ] toasted pine nut couscous, 1 (5.6-ounce) package
- [ ] whole-wheat pitas, 3
- [ ] yellow cornmeal

miscellaneous
- [ ] club soda
- [ ] tahini (roasted sesame seed paste)

Cut your own CORN from the cob for three recipes. (And freeze the cobs: They make great soup stock!)

We use PLUM TOMATOES in some recipes because they have a meatier texture and less juice than other tomatoes.

2

Common ingredients in this planner are asparagus, avocados, bacon, and tomatoes.

Choose center-cut BACON: It's lower in saturated fat than regular bacon, but you still get the same great taste.

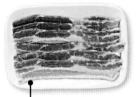

Ripen AVOCADOS in a brown paper bag on the counter. Store ripe avocados in the fridge for 2 to 3 days.

SHOPPING LIST

Why 2 kinds of GREEK YOGURT? To meet nutritional guidelines, some recipes call for fat-free Greek yogurt. You can substitute one kind for another, but the nutrition and texture of your finished dish will be different.

produce

- ❑ asparagus spears, 1¼ pounds
- ❑ avocados, 4
- ❑ baby heirloom tomatoes, 1 (12-ounce) package
- ❑ baby spinach, 1 (6-ounce) package
- ❑ Broccolini, 1 pound
- ❑ fresh basil
- ❑ fresh cilantro
- ❑ fresh corn, 2 ears ❑ garlic
- ❑ gourmet salad greens, 1⅓ cups
- ❑ grape tomatoes, 1 pint
- ❑ green onions, 1 bunch
- ❑ large tomatoes, 2
- ❑ lemons, 4 ❑ limes, 3
- ❑ peaches, 8 ❑ sweet onion, 1

meat/fish/poultry

- ❑ boneless center-cut loin pork chops, 4 (4-ounce) chops (about ½ inch thick)
- ❑ (6-ounce) salmon fillets, 4
- ❑ center-cut bacon, 1 pound
- ❑ lower-sodium bacon, 1 pound
- ❑ skinless, boneless rotisserie chicken breast, 1 whole breast

dairy

- ❑ butter ❑ large eggs
- ❑ grated fresh Parmesan cheese, 2 ounces
- ❑ herbed goat cheese, 2 ounces
- ❑ low-fat Greek yogurt, 6-ounce container
- ❑ part-skim ricotta cheese, 15-ounce container

- ❑ plain fat-free Greek yogurt, 1 (6-ounce) container
- ❑ preshredded Monterey Jack cheese with jalapeño peppers, 1 ounce
- ❑ preshredded part-skim mozzarella cheese, 6 ounces

staples

- ❑ baked tortilla chips
- ❑ canola oil
- ❑ capers
- ❑ cider vinegar
- ❑ commercial pizza dough, 1 (16-ounce) package
- ❑ corn tortillas, 9 (6-inch)
- ❑ crusty Chicago-style Italian bread
- ❑ fat-free, lower-sodium chicken broth
- ❑ ground cumin
- ❑ ground red pepper
- ❑ marinara sauce
- ❑ no-salt-added black beans, 1 (15-ounce) can
- ❑ olive oil
- ❑ stone-ground mustard
- ❑ thin-sliced 15-grain bread
- ❑ turbinado sugar

miscellaneous

- ❑ apple juice concentrate, 1 (11.5-ounce) can
- ❑ dry white wine
- ❑ whole-wheat tandoori naan, ½ (12-ounce) package (2 naan)

Shredded Chicken Tacos, page **271**

Pan-Roasted Salmon and Tomatoes and Asparagus with Lemon-Basil Yogurt Sauce, page **268**

Apple-Mustard-Glazed Pork Chops and Broccolini with Bacon, page **282**

Black Bean Omelet, page **67**

Cast-Iron Breakfast Pizza and Broiled Sweet Peaches, page **61**

Avocado BLT, page **138**

Chicken Marinara Panini, page **164**

Grilled Asparagus Pizzas, page **232**

Tomato-Avocado Dip, page **215**

3

Common ingredients in this planner are goat cheese, red bell pepper, red onions, spinach, and strawberries.

Store STRAWBERRIES in the fridge, on paper towels in a single layer. Wash them right before you use them.

Try the tasty trio of pistachios, strawberries, and SPINACH in Pistachio-Crusted Chicken and Strawberry Salad, page 307.

SHOPPING LIST

produce
- [ ] blueberries, about 5.3 ounces (1 cup)
- [ ] fresh baby spinach, 8 ounces
- [ ] fresh basil
- [ ] fresh cremini mushrooms, 3.5-ounce package
- [ ] fresh ginger
- [ ] fresh parsley
- [ ] fresh sage   [ ] fresh thyme
- [ ] garlic   [ ] lime, 1
- [ ] microwave-ready baking potatoes, 2
- [ ] prechopped onion, 4.5 ounces
- [ ] red bell peppers, 2
- [ ] red onions, 2
- [ ] strawberries, 1 quart
- [ ] sweet potatoes, 1 pound
- [ ] large tomatoes, 2
- [ ] yellow squash, 1 medium
- [ ] zucchini, 1 medium

meat/fish/poultry
- [ ] prosciutto, 4 (½-ounce) thin slices
- [ ] reduced-fat pork sausage, 8 ounces
- [ ] skinless, boneless chicken, 8 (6-ounce) breast halves

dairy
- [ ] (0.7-ounce) slices reduced-fat provolone cheese, 1 package
- [ ] goat cheese, 5 ounces
- [ ] grated fresh pecorino Romano cheese, 1 ounce
- [ ] large eggs
- [ ] paneer or queso blanco, 4 ounces
- [ ] plain low-fat Greek yogurt, about 8 ounces
- [ ] plain low-fat yogurt, 1 cup
- [ ] preshredded part-skim mozzarella cheese, 2 ounces
- [ ] shredded fresh Parmesan cheese, 2 ounces

freezer
- [ ] frozen hash browns, 2 cups

staples
- [ ] balsamic vinegar
- [ ] blush wine vinaigrette
- [ ] capers
- [ ] commercial hummus
- [ ] commercial olive tapenade
- [ ] dry Marsala wine
- [ ] garam masala
- [ ] Madras curry powder
- [ ] maple syrup
- [ ] pistachios
- [ ] red curry powder
- [ ] sourdough bread, 8 (1-ounce) slices
- [ ] sugar
- [ ] walnuts, ½ ounce
- [ ] wheat berries
- [ ] whole-wheat pitas, 4 (6-inch)

miscellaneous
- [ ] ground fresh ginger paste

Balsamic Vegetable
Pita Pizzas, page **254**

Pistachio-Crusted Chicken and
Strawberry Salad, page **307**

Chicken Saltimbocca, page **303**

Curried Paneer and Spinach-Stuffed
Potatoes, page **146**

Mediterranean Hash Brown
Cakes, page **78**

Strawberry-Ginger
Yogurt Pops, page **210**

esto Grilled Cheese Panini, page **152**

Sausage and Sweet Potato Hash, page **93**

Morning Wheat Berry Salad, page **45**

Grilled Shrimp Salad with Honey-Lime
Dressing, page **267**

Green Curry Snapper and Tropical
Jasmine Rice, page **297**

Spiced Lamb and Fruited
Couscous, page **319**

Turkey, Apricot, and Pistachio
Salad, page **131**

Lemon-Dill Chicken Salad, page **128**

Tropical Waffles with Pineapple-Orange
Syrup, page **82**

Pineapple Parfait, page **46**

Apricot-Stilton Bites, page **221**

Curried Chutney–Stuffed Celery, page **1**

Common ingredients in this planner are cilantro, coconut, dried apricots, macadamia nuts, pineapple, and pistachios.

4

SHOPPING LIST

produce
- ☐ bananas, 2
- ☐ celery
- ☐ fresh cilantro
- ☐ fresh dill or fresh tarragon
- ☐ fresh mint
- ☐ fresh pineapple, 2
- ☐ fresh thyme ☐ garlic
- ☐ gourmet salad greens, 1 (5-ounce) package
- ☐ green onions, 1 bunch
- ☐ lemons, 4
- ☐ lettuce and herb blend salad greens, 2 (4-ounce) packages
- ☐ limes, 3 ☐ onion, 2
- ☐ orange, 1

meat/fish/poultry
- ☐ cooked chicken breast, 3 breast halves
- ☐ deli smoked turkey breast, 8 ounces
- ☐ ground lamb, 1 pound
- ☐ peeled and deveined shrimp, 1 pound
- ☐ snapper fillets, 4 (6-ounce)

dairy
- ☐ ⅓-less-fat cream cheese, 4 ounces
- ☐ blue Stilton cheese, 1 ounce
- ☐ butter
- ☐ large eggs
- ☐ plain fat-free Greek yogurt, 1 (7-ounce) container
- ☐ vanilla fat-free Greek yogurt, 1 (6-ounce) container

staples
- ☐ agave syrup
- ☐ brown sugar
- ☐ canola mayonnaise
- ☐ coconut milk, 1 (13.5-ounce) can
- ☐ couscous
- ☐ Dijon mustard
- ☐ dried apricots, 1 (7-ounce) bag
- ☐ flaked sweetened coconut
- ☐ golden raisins
- ☐ ground red pepper
- ☐ honey
- ☐ honey-roasted peanuts
- ☐ jasmine rice
- ☐ macadamia nuts, about 1 ounce
- ☐ mango chutney
- ☐ pistachios, about 2 ounces shelled
- ☐ red curry powder
- ☐ rice vinegar
- ☐ self-rising flour
- ☐ slivered almonds, about 1.3 ounces

miscellaneous
- ☐ fiery 5-pepper seasoning
- ☐ garam masala
- ☐ green curry paste
- ☐ ground fresh ginger paste
- ☐ lemongrass paste
- ☐ pineapple preserves

Use PISTACHIOS in party-friendly Apricot-Stilton Bites, page 221, and serve them with Vouvray (a French white wine).

Buy PINEAPPLE with small, uniform eyes, a white core at the bottom, and a subtle pineapple fragrance.

5

Common ingredients in this planner are beef tenderloin steaks, blue cheese, fennel, goat cheese, romaine lettuce, and rotisserie chicken.

Use GOAT CHEESE three ways, including a Bagel Sandwich with Pears and Goat Cheese Spread, page 32.

If you want a mild BLUE CHEESE, choose a younger cheese. The older it is, the stronger the flavor will be.

SHOPPING LIST

FIG SUBSTITUTES: You can substitute the dried figs and figlets for one another, if you like.

produce
- ❑ Anjou pear, 1
- ❑ dried figs
- ❑ small dried Mission figs (figlets), 8
- ❑ fennel bulbs with stalks, 3
- ❑ fresh cilantro
- ❑ fresh chives
- ❑ fresh parsley
- ❑ fresh rosemary
- ❑ garlic
- ❑ green onions, 1 bunch
- ❑ lemons, 2
- ❑ lime, 1
- ❑ navel oranges, 2
- ❑ plum tomatoes, 2
- ❑ radishes, 6
- ❑ red onions, 3
- ❑ romaine lettuce, 2 heads
- ❑ shallots, 1
- ❑ sweet butter-blend salad greens, 1 (6.5-ounce) package

meat/fish/poultry
- ❑ bacon
- ❑ beef tenderloin steaks, 6 (4-ounce) steaks
- ❑ rotisserie chicken breast, about 3½ breast halves
- ❑ ground sirloin, 1 pound

dairy
- ❑ ⅓-less-fat cream cheese, 12 ounces
- ❑ blue cheese, 1 ounce
- ❑ goat cheese, 11.7 ounces
- ❑ nonfat buttermilk
- ❑ plain 2% reduced-fat Greek yogurt, 1 (7-ounce) container
- ❑ tub-style ⅓-less-fat cream cheese, 4 ounces

staples
- ❑ balsamic vinegar
- ❑ chickpeas, 1 (16-ounce) can
- ❑ canola mayonnaise
- ❑ cinnamon-raisin swirl mini-bagels, 1
- ❑ dry-roasted salted cashews
- ❑ garlic pepper
- ❑ honey
- ❑ hot sauce
- ❑ light balsamic and basil vinaigrette
- ❑ pitted kalamata olives
- ❑ sherry vinegar
- ❑ tawny port or other sweet red wine
- ❑ walnuts, 2.4 ounces
- ❑ white-wheat hamburger buns, 4 (1.8-ounce) buns

miscellaneous
- ❑ fig preserves
- ❑ mango chutney
- ❑ pimientos del piquillo peppers, 2 (9.5-ounce) jars
- ❑ steamed ready-to-eat lentils, 1 (17.63-ounce) package

Tenderloin with Peppery Fig-Port Sauce and Grilled Fennel and Red Onion, page **310**

Black and Blue Salad, page **286**

Pub Burgers, page **313**

Bagel Sandwich with Pears and Goat Cheese Spread, page **32**

Chickpea, Fennel, and Olive Chicken Salad, page **122**

Mango Chicken Salad, page **145**

Lentil Salad, page **107**

Fig-Goat Cheese Spread, page **200**

Goat Cheese-Stuffed Piquillo Peppers, page **232**

Orange-Ginger Pork Chops and
Sweet and Sour Cabbage, page **308**

Grilled Halibut with Hoisin Glaze and
Grilled Baby Bok Choy, page **298**

Ladyfingers with Mascarpone Cream and
Fresh Orange Sauce, page **355**

Grilled Chicken, Apple, and Brie
Sandwiches, page **167**

Open-Faced Chicken and Pear
Sandwiches, page **170**

Arugula-Orange Salad with Fig-Bacon
Dressing, page **135**

Citrus-Ginger Salad, page **39**

Frittata with Mascarpone and Prosciutto, page **87**

Tofu and Chinese Long Beans, page **262**

6

Common ingredients in this planner are arugula, ginger, Granny Smith apples, lower-sodium deli chicken, mascarpone cheese, and oranges.

SHOPPING LIST

produce
- ❑ arugula, 2 cups
- ❑ baby bok choy, 4 (about 1 pound)
- ❑ Chinese long beans, 1 pound
- ❑ extra-firm tofu, 1 (14-ounce) package
- ❑ fresh ginger
- ❑ Granny Smith apples, 2 medium
- ❑ grapefruit, 1
- ❑ grape tomatoes, 1 pint ❑ lime, 1
- ❑ navel oranges, 8 ❑ pear, 1
- ❑ prewashed arugula, 1 (5-ounce) package
- ❑ sweet onions, 2
- ❑ thinly sliced green cabbage, 2 cups
- ❑ thinly sliced red cabbage, 2 cups

meat/fish/poultry
- ❑ boneless center-cut loin pork chops, 4 (4-ounce) chops (about ½ inch thick)
- ❑ center-cut bacon
- ❑ halibut fillets, 4 (6-ounce) fillets
- ❑ thinly sliced deli, lower-sodium chicken, 20 ounces
- ❑ thinly sliced prosciutto, 2 ounces

dairy
- ❑ crème de Brie spreadable cheese
- ❑ fat-free cottage cheese, 1 (12-ounce) container
- ❑ goat cheese, 3 ounces
- ❑ large eggs
- ❑ mascarpone cheese
- ❑ Swiss cheese, 6 (0.5-ounce) slices

staples
- ❑ 100% whole-wheat bread, 8 (1.5-ounce) slices
- ❑ apricot preserves
- ❑ brown sugar
- ❑ cannellini beans, 1 (15-ounce) can
- ❑ cider vinegar
- ❑ country-style Dijon mustard
- ❑ crystallized ginger
- ❑ dark sesame oil
- ❑ Dijon mustard
- ❑ fig preserves
- ❑ hoisin sauce
- ❑ honey
- ❑ ladyfingers, 1 (3-ounce) package
- ❑ lower-sodium soy sauce
- ❑ microwaveable precooked whole-grain brown rice, 1 (8.8-ounce) package
- ❑ rye pumpernickel bread, 6 (1.2-ounce) slices
- ❑ seasoned rice vinegar
- ❑ sesame seeds
- ❑ sliced almonds, 1 ounce
- ❑ sugar

miscellaneous
- ❑ large-size zip-top plastic steam-cooking bag
- ❑ orange-flavored liqueur (Grand Marnier)
- ❑ Sriracha (hot chile sauce)
- ❑ vanilla bean paste

ORANGES sweeten Citrus-Ginger Salad, page 39, which you can make ahead as a quick breakfast with yogurt.

Buy GINGER that has smooth skin. You can keep it the fridge, well-wrapped, for up to three weeks.

Horseradish-Garlic Flank Steak and
Lemony Arugula Salad, page **253**

Veal Piccata and Herbed Parmesan
Capellini, page **320**

Baked Eggs with Spinach and
Goat Cheese, page **62**

Arugula, White Bean, and Sun-Dried Tomato
Cream Quesadillas, page **149**

Arugula Salad with Beets and
Pancetta Crisps, page **137**

Fried Eggs over Pancetta Grits and
Mixed Berry Cup, page **85**

Feta-Mint Dip, page **199**

Feta-Lamb Patties with Cucumber Sauce, page **291**

Mixed Berry, Flaxseed, and Yogurt Parfait, pa

7

Common ingredients in this planner are arugula, English cucumbers, feta cheese, mixed fresh berries, goat cheese, pancetta, and Parmesan cheese.

SHOPPING LIST

ARUGULA SUBSTITUTES: Substitute baby arugula for arugula, if you like.

produce
- ❏ arugula, 7 ounces
- ❏ baby arugula, 1.5 ounces
- ❏ English cucumber, 1 large
- ❏ fresh chives
- ❏ fresh dill
- ❏ fresh mint
- ❏ fresh oregano
- ❏ fresh parsley
- ❏ fresh spinach, 1 ounce
- ❏ garlic
- ❏ lemons, 4
- ❏ Meyer lemons, 2
- ❏ mixed fresh berries, 14 ounces
- ❏ prechopped green onions
- ❏ steamed peeled ready-to-eat baby red beets, 1 (8-ounce) package

meat/fish/poultry
- ❏ flank steak, 1 pound
- ❏ lean ground lamb, 1 pound
- ❏ thinly sliced pancetta, 3 ounces
- ❏ veal cutlets, 4 (4-ounce) cutlets (about ¼ inch thick)

dairy
- ❏ ⅓-less-fat cream cheese, 2 ounces
- ❏ butter
- ❏ crème fraîche
- ❏ fat-free sour cream, 7 ounces
- ❏ feta cheese, 5 ounces
- ❏ goat cheese, about 8 ounces
- ❏ half-and-half
- ❏ large eggs
- ❏ plain 2% reduced-fat Greek yogurt, 8 ounces
- ❏ plain low-fat yogurt, about 4 ounces
- ❏ shaved fresh Parmesan cheese, 2 ounces
- ❏ shredded fontina cheese, 2 ounces

staples
- ❏ cannellini beans, 1 (15-ounce) can
- ❏ capellini or angel hair pasta
- ❏ capers
- ❏ day-old French bread
- ❏ Dijon mustard
- ❏ dry white wine
- ❏ fat-free, lower-sodium chicken broth
- ❏ flaxseed meal
- ❏ honey
- ❏ light balsamic vinaigrette
- ❏ low-fat granola without raisins
- ❏ low-sugar strawberry preserves
- ❏ prepared horseradish
- ❏ quick-cooking grits
- ❏ red wine vinegar
- ❏ sliced almonds
- ❏ whole-wheat tortillas, 2 (8-inch)

miscellaneous
- ❏ oil-packed sun-dried tomato halves
- ❏ pitted dates

Use ARUGULA at least three ways with this menu, and keep it fresh by storing it unwashed in a zip-top plastic bag.

Enjoy FETA in Feta-Lamb Patties with Cucumber Sauce, page 291.

8

Common ingredients in this planner are carrots, cilantro, onions, tomatoes, and watermelon.

Refresh yourself with WATERMELON in Watermelon-Mint Sorbet, page 375, or Melon Kebabs with Lime and Chiles, page 205.

Store TOMATOES at room temperature for the best flavor. And don't miss the Red Curry Flank Steak and Thai Herb and Tomato Salad on page 315.

SHOPPING LIST

Why 2 kinds of RICE VINEGAR? We call for two kinds of rice vinegar, because seasoned rice vinegar has added sugar and salt.

produce

- ❑ cantaloupe, 1
- ❑ carrots, 5-6
- ❑ fresh basil
- ❑ fresh bean sprouts, ¾ cup
- ❑ fresh cilantro
- ❑ fresh ginger
- ❑ fresh mint
- ❑ fresh parsley
- ❑ garlic
- ❑ honeydew, 1
- ❑ hot red chiles, 2
- ❑ jalapeño pepper, 1
- ❑ large vine-ripened tomatoes, 4
- ❑ limes, 7
- ❑ mini sweet bell peppers, 1 (8-ounce) package
- ❑ napa cabbage, 1
- ❑ pickling cucumber, 1
- ❑ presliced green onions
- ❑ red bell pepper, 1
- ❑ red onion, 1
- ❑ refrigerated prechopped celery, onion, and bell pepper mix, 1 (8-ounce) container
- ❑ seedless watermelon, 1 medium
- ❑ white onions, 2

meat/fish/poultry

- ❑ boneless center-cut loin pork chop, 1 (4-ounce) chop
- ❑ flank steak, 1 pound
- ❑ large shrimp, peeled and deveined, 24 (about 1½ pounds)
- ❑ pulled skinless, boneless rotisserie chicken breast (about 2 breast halves)
- ❑ tilapia fillets, 4 (5-ounce) fillets

dairy

- ❑ goat cheese, 1 ounce
- ❑ large eggs
- ❑ plain yogurt, about 4 ounces

freezer

- ❑ frozen hash browns

staples

- ❑ agave syrup
- ❑ commercial olive tapenade
- ❑ coriander
- ❑ corn tortillas, 8 (6-inch)
- ❑ creamy peanut butter
- ❑ crushed red pepper
- ❑ crystallized ginger
- ❑ dark sesame oil
- ❑ diced tomatoes, 1 (14.5-ounce) can
- ❑ dried soba noodles
- ❑ fat-free, lower-sodium chicken broth, 1 (32-ounce) carton
- ❑ garam masala
- ❑ lightly salted peanuts
- ❑ lower-sodium soy sauce
- ❑ microwaveable precooked basmati rice, 1 (8.5-ounce) package
- ❑ rice paper, 4 (8-inch) round sheets
- ❑ rice vinegar
- ❑ seasoned rice vinegar
- ❑ sugar
- ❑ tomato paste
- ❑ whole-grain extra-wide noodles

miscellaneous

- ❑ crushed chipotle chile flakes
- ❑ orange-flavored liqueur (Cointreau)
- ❑ red curry paste
- ❑ sambal oelek (ground fresh chile paste)
- ❑ spicy peanut sauce

Red Curry Flank Steak and Thai Herb and Tomato Salad, page **315**

Sautéed Tilapia Tacos with Grilled Peppers and Onion, page **270**

Shrimp Tikka Masala, page **301**

eamy Chicken Noodle Soup, page **127**

Peanut-Sesame Noodles, page **110**

Thai Pork Roll-Ups, page **95**

iterranean Hash Brown Cakes, page **78**

Melon Kebabs with Lime and Chiles, page **205**

Watermelon-Mint Sorbet, page **375**

Schnitzel Chicken and Pan-Fried Slaw, page **304**

Chicken and Olives and Moroccan Squash, page **275**

Steak with Creamy Mushroom Gravy and Gruyère Polenta, page **288**

Chicken Marinara Panini, page **164**

Leek and Potato Soup and Mixed Greens with Hazelnut-Herb Vinaigrette, page **104**

Balsamic Peach Melba Parfaits with Spiked Mascarpone, page **326**

Blueberry-Yogurt Parfaits, page **193**

Grilled Peach and Granola Salad, page **150**

Sour Cream-Peach Tart, page **372**

9 Common ingredients in this planner are 2% milk, blueberries, chicken cutlets, mixed salad greens, peaches, and raspberries.

SHOPPING LIST

Why 2 kinds of SOUR CREAM? You can substitute one sour cream for the other; the nutritional results and the texture of your finished recipe may vary.

produce
- [ ] angel hair slaw, 2 (10-ounce) packages
- [ ] fresh basil
- [ ] fresh blueberries, 8 ounces
- [ ] fresh cilantro
- [ ] fresh ginger   [ ] fresh mint
- [ ] fresh raspberries, about 8 ounces
- [ ] fresh rosemary   [ ] garlic
- [ ] gourmet mushroom blend, 1 (4-ounce) package
- [ ] grape tomatoes, ½ pint
- [ ] lemons, 2   [ ] leeks, 2
- [ ] mixed salad greens, 13 ounces
- [ ] onions, 2   [ ] peaches, 9

meat/fish/poultry
- [ ] center-cut bacon
- [ ] chicken breast cutlets, 8
- [ ] cooked chicken breast, about 2 breast halves
- [ ] flat-iron steak, 16 ounces

dairy
- [ ] ⅓-less-fat cream cheese, 2 ounces
- [ ] 2% reduced-fat milk
- [ ] crumbled goat cheese, 4 ounces
- [ ] grated fresh Parmesan cheese, 2 ounces
- [ ] Gruyère cheese, 2 ounces   [ ] large eggs
- [ ] light sour cream   [ ] mascarpone cheese
- [ ] part-skim mozzarella cheese, 2 ounces
- [ ] plain fat-free Greek yogurt, about 8 ounces
- [ ] plain fat-free yogurt, 1 (6-ounce) container
- [ ] reduced-fat sour cream, 1 (8-ounce) container

freezer
- [ ] frozen puff pastry dough, 1 sheet

staples
- [ ] brown sugar
- [ ] canned quartered artichoke hearts
- [ ] caraway seeds
- [ ] crusty Chicago-style Italian bread, 8 (1-ounce) slices
- [ ] Dijon mustard   [ ] dry white wine
- [ ] fat-free, lower-sodium beef broth
- [ ] fat-free, lower-sodium chicken broth, 1 (32-ounce) carton
- [ ] ground cumin
- [ ] hazelnuts, 1 ounce
- [ ] honey   [ ] light raspberry vinaigrette
- [ ] low-fat granola   [ ] marinara sauce
- [ ] mixed pitted olives
- [ ] multigrain cluster cereal
- [ ] olive oil   [ ] orange marmalade
- [ ] paprika   [ ] rice vinegar
- [ ] sliced almonds, 2 ounces
- [ ] sugar
- [ ] white balsamic vinegar

miscellaneous
- [ ] instant polenta   [ ] peach brandy
- [ ] refrigerated country-style mashed potatoes, 1 (24-ounce) package
- [ ] refrigerated steam-in-bag cubed butternut squash, 1 (12-ounce) package
- [ ] toasted hazelnut oil
- [ ] whole-wheat panko (Japanese breadcrumbs)

Look at the stem end of a PEACH to judge its ripeness: Those with a green tinge aren't ready.

CHICKEN subs in for pork and veal in Schnitzel Chicken and Pan-Fried Slaw, page 304.

Common ingredients in this planner are baby spinach, canned chickpeas, cilantro, heirloom tomatoes, green onions, nectarines, and pork tenderloin.

Pair NECTARINES with tomatoes in Sausage Breakfast Braid and Heirloom Tomato and Nectarine Salad, page 88.

CILANTRO can sometimes be sandy. Dunk it in a bowl of water until it's grit-free, and then spin it dry.

Why 2 kinds of NAAN? You can swap one for another; the nutrition in your finished dish may be different.

SHOPPING LIST

produce

- ☐ baby spinach, 1 (5-ounce) package
- ☐ baby watercress or baby arugula, 2 cups
- ☐ fresh cilantro
- ☐ fresh or frozen cranberries, 1 (10-ounce) package
- ☐ fresh mint   ☐ fresh sage
- ☐ garlic   ☐ green onions, 1 bunch
- ☐ heirloom tomatoes, 2 large, 3 medium
- ☐ lemons, 5   ☐ lime, 1
- ☐ nectarines, 5
- ☐ okra pods, 1 pound
- ☐ pickling cucumbers, 6
- ☐ sweet onion, 1
- ☐ Swiss chard, 1½ pounds

meat/fish/poultry

- ☐ light smoked sausage, 4 ounces
- ☐ lump crabmeat, 1 pound
- ☐ pork tenderloins, 2 (1-pound) loins
- ☐ salmon fillets, 4 (6-ounce) fillets

dairy

- ☐ feta cheese with basil and sun-dried tomatoes, 3 ounces
- ☐ large eggs
- ☐ paneer or queso blanco, 2 ounces
- ☐ plain low-fat yogurt, 1 (6-ounce) container
- ☐ shredded reduced-fat extra-sharp cheddar cheese, 3 ounces
- ☐ unsalted butter

staples

- ☐ apple jelly   ☐ balsamic vinegar
- ☐ bottled chili sauce   ☐ brown sugar
- ☐ canola mayonnaise
- ☐ chickpeas, 2 (15-ounce) cans
- ☐ cider vinegar   ☐ crushed red pepper
- ☐ curry powder
- ☐ fat-free, lower-sodium chicken broth
- ☐ ground cumin   ☐ ground ginger
- ☐ ground red pepper
- ☐ ground turmeric   ☐ honey
- ☐ kalamata olives
- ☐ no-salt-added chickpeas, 2 (15-ounce) cans
- ☐ quartered marinated artichoke hearts, 1 (6-ounce) jar
- ☐ refrigerated pie dough, 1 (14.1-ounce) package
- ☐ refrigerated pizza crust dough, 1 (13.8-ounce) can
- ☐ smoked paprika
- ☐ sugar   ☐ turbinado sugar
- ☐ whole-grain baguette, 1 (8.5-ounce)
- ☐ whole-wheat couscous

miscellaneous

- ☐ dopiaza curry cooking sauce
- ☐ roasted garlic onion jam
- ☐ whole-grain naan, 1 (8.8-ounce) package
- ☐ whole-wheat naan, 1 (9-ounce) package (2 naan)

k Medallions with Cranberry Sauce and
Sautéed Swiss Chard, page **285**

Pizza Dopiaza, page **256**

Tandoori Salmon and Sautéed Okra, page **293**

Pork and Onion Jam
Sandwiches, page **179**

Sausage Breakfast Braid and Heirloom
Tomato and Nectarine Salad, page **88**

Curried Hummus and Spicy Cilantro
Naan Chips, page **228**

iterranean Couscous Salad, page **109**

Crab Louis Salad, page **155**

Mini Nectarine Galettes, page **323**

breakfasts
to go

Whether you're enjoying the paper or stuck in rush hour traffic, these protein-packed smoothies are sure to keep you satisfied all morning.

Banana-Blueberry Smoothies

Prep: 5 minutes

1 cup frozen blueberries
½ cup silken tofu
2 tablespoons water
1 teaspoon vanilla extract

1½ medium-sized ripe bananas, broken into pieces
1 (5.3-ounce) container plain fat-free Greek yogurt

1. Place all ingredients in a blender; process until smooth, scraping sides as necessary. Yield: 2 servings (serving size: 1½ cups).

CALORIES 198; FAT 1.7g (sat 0g, mono 0.4g, poly 0.8g); PROTEIN 11.4g; CARB 34.1g; FIBER 5g; CHOL 0mg; IRON 0.7mg; SODIUM 35mg; CALC 138mg

The sweetened cream cheese spread is also delicious on other breakfast breads, such as bagels and toast.

Cinnamon-Raisin Waffle Sandwich

Prep: 3 minutes • Cook: 10 minutes

1 (1.33-ounce) frozen multigrain waffle
2 tablespoons (1 ounce) ⅓-less-fat cream cheese, softened
2 teaspoons brown sugar

¼ teaspoon ground cinnamon
1 tablespoon raisins
1 tablespoon chopped walnuts, toasted

1. Toast waffle according to package directions.
2. Combine cream cheese, brown sugar, and cinnamon until well blended. Spread cream cheese mixture evenly over waffle. Sprinkle evenly with raisins and walnuts. Cut waffle in half. Sandwich waffle halves together with filling in center. Yield: 1 serving.

CALORIES 279; FAT 14.7g (sat 4.3g, mono 4.3g, poly 4.7g); PROTEIN 5.5g; CARB 34.8g; FIBER 4.3g; CHOL 21mg; IRON 1.4mg; SODIUM 260mg; CALC 70mg

Make this granola ahead, and store in an airtight container for a quick topping for oatmeal or yogurt, or for an on-the-go breakfast all by itself.

Almond-Apricot Granola

Prep: 6 minutes • Cook: 36 minutes

2 cups old-fashioned rolled oats
1 cup sliced almonds
¼ cup honey
2 tablespoons canola oil

¼ teaspoon ground cinnamon
⅛ teaspoon salt
Cooking spray
1 cup dried apricots, coarsely chopped

1. Preheat oven to 300°.
2. Combine oats and almonds in a large bowl. Combine honey and oil in a small saucepan. Bring to a boil, stirring occasionally. Stir in cinnamon and salt; pour honey mixture over oat mixture, tossing until oats are thoroughly coated.
3. Spread oat mixture evenly onto a 17 x 12 x 1–inch pan coated with cooking spray. Bake at 300° for 35 to 38 minutes, stirring every 10 minutes, until granola is golden brown. Let cool on baking sheet. Stir in apricots. Store in an airtight container. Yield: 8 servings (serving size: about ½ cup).

CALORIES 271; FAT 10.8g (sat 1.2g, mono 4.8g, poly 4.1g); PROTEIN 5.6g; CARB 39.8g; FIBER 4.7g; CHOL 0mg; IRON 2.5mg; SODIUM 40mg; CALC 44mg

Bagel Sandwich with Pears and Goat Cheese Spread

Prep: 6 minutes • Cook: 2 minutes

½ cup (4 ounces) goat cheese, crumbled
½ cup (4 ounces) ⅓-less-fat cream cheese, softened
2 tablespoons honey

⅓ cup chopped toasted walnuts
1 cinnamon-raisin swirl mini-bagel, halved and toasted
¼ red Anjou pear, unpeeled and thinly sliced

1. Combine first 3 ingredients in a small bowl. Stir in walnuts. Spread 1 tablespoon goat cheese spread evenly onto cut sides of bagel. Place pear slices on bottom half of bagel. Replace bagel top. Cover and chill remaining spread up to one week. Yield: 1 serving.

CALORIES 152; FAT 4.2g (sat 1.8g, mono 0.8g, poly 1.2g); PROTEIN 4.5g; CARB 25.5g; FIBER 2.5g; CHOL 7mg; IRON 1.3mg; SODIUM 128mg; CALC 24mg

Almond-Apricot Granola

Banana Bread Muffins

Prep: 8 minutes • Cook: 25 minutes

Cooking spray
9 ounces all-purpose flour (about 2 cups)
1 cup sugar
1 teaspoon baking soda
½ teaspoon salt

2 large eggs
1½ cups mashed ripe banana (3 large)
⅓ cup plain low-fat yogurt
¼ cup canola oil

1. Preheat oven to 375°.
2. Place 16 paper muffin cup liners in muffin cups; coat liners with cooking spray.
3. Weigh or lightly spoon flour into dry measuring cups; level with a knife. Combine flour, sugar, baking soda, and salt in a medium bowl; make a well in center of mixture. Place eggs in a medium bowl; beat with a whisk. Add banana, yogurt, and oil, stirring with a whisk. Add egg mixture to flour mixture, stirring just until moist. Spoon batter into liners, filling three-fourths full.
4. Bake at 375° for 25 minutes or until muffins spring back when touched lightly in center. Remove muffins from pan, and cool on a wire rack. Yield: 16 servings (serving size: 1 muffin).

CALORIES 168; FAT 4.4g (sat 0.6g, mono 2.5g, poly 1.2g); PROTEIN 2.9g; CARB 29.8g; FIBER 1g; CHOL 27mg; IRON 0.9mg; SODIUM 165mg; CALC 16mg

Cappuccino–Chocolate Chip Muffins

Prep: 8 minutes • Cook: 20 minutes

Cooking spray
1¾ cups low-fat baking mix
½ cup sugar
½ cup hot water

2 tablespoons instant espresso granules
¼ cup canola oil
1 large egg
½ cup semisweet chocolate minichips

1. Preheat oven to 400°.
2. Place 12 paper muffin cup liners in muffin cups; coat liners with cooking spray.
3. Lightly spoon baking mix into dry measuring cups; level with a knife. Combine baking mix and sugar in a medium bowl; stir with a whisk. Make a well in center of mixture. Combine ½ cup hot water and coffee granules, stirring until coffee dissolves. Combine oil and egg, stirring with a whisk; stir in coffee mixture. Add coffee mixture to baking mix mixture, stirring just until moist. Stir in chocolate minichips.
4. Spoon batter into prepared liners. Bake at 400° for 20 minutes or until muffins spring back when touched lightly in center. Remove muffins from pans immediately; place on a wire rack. Serve warm. Yield: 12 servings (serving size: 1 muffin).

CALORIES 196; FAT 8.8g (sat 2.1g, mono 4.7g, poly 1.7g); PROTEIN 2.6g; CARB 27.2g; FIBER 0.4g; CHOL 15.5mg; IRON 0.7mg; SODIUM 196mg; CALC 92mg

Wrap these muffins in plastic wrap, and freeze them in an airtight container. Take out what you need the night before, and let them thaw overnight in the refrigerator. Toast before serving.

Banana Bread Muffins

Cherry Scones

Prep: 10 minutes • Cook: 20 minutes

9 ounces all-purpose flour (about 2 cups)
¼ cup granulated sugar
1½ teaspoons baking powder
¼ teaspoon salt
¼ cup chilled unsalted butter, cut into pieces

¾ cup dried tart cherries, chopped
¾ cup low-fat buttermilk
¼ teaspoon almond extract (optional)
Cooking spray
1 tablespoon turbinado sugar (optional)

1. Preheat oven to 425°.
2. Weigh or lightly spoon flour into dry measuring cups; level with a knife. Combine flour, sugar, baking powder, and salt in a large bowl, stirring well with a whisk. Cut in butter using a pastry blender until mixture resembles coarse meal. Stir in cherries. Add buttermilk and almond extract, if desired, stirring just until moist.
3. Turn dough out onto a lightly floured surface; knead lightly 3 times with floured hands. Form dough into an 8-inch circle on a baking sheet coated with cooking spray. Cut dough into 10 wedges, cutting into but not through dough. Coat top of dough with cooking spray. Sprinkle with turbinado sugar, if desired.
4. Place baking sheet on rack in upper third of oven. Bake at 425° for 20 minutes or until golden. Yield: 10 servings (serving size: 1 scone).

CALORIES 191; FAT 5.1g (sat 3.1g, mono 1.3g, poly 0.3g); PROTEIN 3.5g; CARB 32.5g; FIBER 3.2g; CHOL 13mg; IRON 1.4mg; SODIUM 139mg; CALC 67mg

Try a combination of other fruits and nuts with the dates.

Chewy Date-Apple Bars

Prep: 5 minutes • Cook: 15 minutes

2½ cups whole pitted dates
1 cup dried apples
½ cup walnuts, toasted

½ cup old-fashioned rolled oats
¼ teaspoon ground cinnamon

1. Preheat oven to 350°.
2. Place first 3 ingredients in food processor; process until fruit and nuts are finely chopped. Add oats and cinnamon; pulse 8 to 10 times or until moist and oats are chopped. Spoon mixture into a lightly greased 9 x 5–inch loaf pan, pressing into an even layer with plastic wrap.
3. Bake at 350° for 15 minutes. Cool completely in pan on a wire rack. Cut into 12 bars. Yield: 12 servings (serving size: 1 bar).

CALORIES 194; FAT 3.6g (sat 0.4g, mono 0.6g, poly 2.5g); PROTEIN 2.5g; CARB 41.9g; FIBER 4.5g; CHOL 0mg; IRON 0.9mg; SODIUM 67mg; CALC 25mg

You can replace half the flour in this recipe with white whole-wheat pastry flour if you'd like the extra benefits of whole grains.

Cherry Scones

Cranberry-Almond Cereal Bars

A creamy, sweet mix of almond butter and honey holds these bars together. Be sure to stir the almond butter before measuring it to reincorporate any oil that has separated.

Cranberry-Almond Cereal Bars

Prep: 5 minutes • Cook: 14 minutes • Other: 1 hour and 15 minutes

½ cup almond butter
⅔ cup honey
5 cups crispy wheat cereal squares

¾ cup sweetened dried cranberries
½ cup slivered almonds, toasted
Cooking spray

1. Place almond butter and honey in a large Dutch oven. Bring to a boil over medium heat. Stir in cereal, cranberries, and almonds, tossing to coat. Spoon mixture into an 11 x 7–inch baking dish coated with cooking spray, pressing into an even layer with plastic wrap. Let stand 1 hour or until set. Cut into 12 bars. Yield: 12 servings (serving size: 1 bar).

CALORIES 268; FAT 9.2g (sat 0.9g, mono 5.6g, poly 2.1g); PROTEIN 5.3g; CARB 45g; FIBER 4.1g; CHOL 0mg; IRON 8.2mg; SODIUM 268mg; CALC 94mg

For a light, refreshing breakfast at work, pack this salad in its own container, along with a container of low-fat cottage cheese or yogurt to add protein.

Citrus-Ginger Salad

Prep: 6 minutes

2 medium navel oranges
1 medium red grapefruit
1 lime

2 tablespoons finely chopped crystallized ginger
1 tablespoon honey

1. Peel and section oranges and grapefruit over a medium bowl, reserving juice.
2. Grate 1 teaspoon rind and squeeze 1 tablespoon juice from lime. Add lime rind and lime juice to orange mixture. Add ginger and honey; toss gently. Chill until ready to serve. Yield: 3 servings (serving size: ½ cup).

CALORIES 135; FAT 0.1g (sat 0g, mono 0g, poly 0g); PROTEIN 1.6g; CARB 34.7g; FIBER 3.4g; CHOL 0mg; IRON 0.4mg; SODIUM 4mg; CALC 79mg

Maple sugar is made from the sap of maple trees—the sap is boiled until nearly all the liquid is evaporated. Using a very sharp knife or kitchen shears will make chopping the dried figs easier.

Fig-Maple Drop Biscuits

Fig-Maple Drop Biscuits

Prep: 6 minutes • Cook: 16 minutes

10.1 ounces all-purpose flour (about 2¼ cups)
¾ cup maple sugar, divided
1 tablespoon baking powder
½ teaspoon salt
6 tablespoons chilled unsalted butter, cut
  into small pieces and divided

¾ cup fat-free milk
½ cup chopped dried Calimyrna figs
  (about 4 figs)

1. Preheat oven to 400°.
2. Weigh or lightly spoon flour into dry measuring cups; level with a knife.
Combine flour, ½ cup plus 1 tablespoon maple sugar, baking powder, and salt
in a large bowl. Cut in 5 tablespoons butter with a pastry blender or two knives
until mixture resembles a coarse meal. Add milk and figs, stirring until a soft
dough forms.
3. Drop dough by heaping spoonfuls into 12 mounds 2 inches apart on a
parchment paper–lined baking sheet. Melt 1 tablespoon butter; brush evenly
over biscuits. Sprinkle biscuits evenly with 3 tablespoons maple sugar.
4. Bake at 400° for 16 minutes or until biscuits are golden. Yield: 12 servings
(serving size: 1 biscuit).

CALORIES 189; FAT 6.1g (sat 3.7g, mono 1.5g, poly 0.3g); PROTEIN 3.2g; CARB 30.8g; FIBER 1.2g; CHOL 16mg; IRON 1.4mg; SODIUM 206mg; CALC 103mg

Loaded with fruit and packed with an extra
boost of iron from spinach, this smoothie is a
nutritious and sweet start to a busy day. Be sure to try it in
the summer when ripe, sweet honeydew melon is available.

Go-Getter Green Smoothie

Prep: 5 minutes

1 cup (½-inch) cubes honeydew melon
1 cup bagged baby spinach
1 cup sliced ripe banana, frozen (about 1
  large)

½ cup vanilla light soy milk
1 (5.3-ounce) container fat-free Greek yogurt
  with honey
1 cubed peeled kiwifruit

1. Place all ingredients in a blender. Process until smooth. Serve immediately.
Yield: 2 servings (serving size: 1½ cups).

CALORIES 224; FAT 1.1g (sat 0.2g, mono 0.2g, poly 0.5g); PROTEIN 9.4g; CARB 47.9g; FIBER 4.3g; CHOL 0mg; IRON 1mg; SODIUM 91mg; CALC 180mg

Huevos Rancheros Soft Tacos

Prep: 6 minutes • Cook: 2 minutes

2   large eggs
2   large egg whites
⅛   teaspoon freshly ground black pepper
Cooking spray
½   cup fat-free refried black beans, warmed

2   (6-inch) flour tortillas, warmed
½   cup (2 ounces) shredded Oaxaca cheese
¼   cup fresh salsa
¼   cup diced peeled avocado

1. Combine first 3 ingredients in a small bowl, stirring with a whisk. Heat a medium skillet over medium heat. Coat pan with cooking spray. Add egg mixture; cook 1 minute or until soft-scrambled, stirring often.
2. Spread ¼ cup beans over each tortilla; top evenly with scrambled egg mixture, and sprinkle evenly with cheese. Spoon salsa and avocado evenly over eggs. Fold tortillas over filling. Yield: 2 servings (serving size: 1 taco).

CALORIES 371; FAT 16.6g (sat 6.6g, mono 4.9g, poly 1.5g); PROTEIN 24.4g; CARB 30.7g; FIBER 5.7g; CHOL 227mg; IRON 3.4mg; SODIUM 819mg; CALC 303mg

Mediterranean Breakfast Sandwich

Prep: 6 minutes • Cook: 6 minutes

Cooking spray
¼   cup chopped red bell pepper
2   tablespoons chopped frozen
      artichoke hearts, thawed
1   large egg

1   large egg white
½   teaspoon chopped fresh oregano
2   tablespoons crumbled feta cheese
½   cup fresh baby spinach leaves
1   whole-wheat pita half

1. Heat a medium nonstick skillet over medium-high heat. Coat pan with cooking spray. Add bell pepper; sauté 3 minutes. Add artichokes; sauté 1 minute or until thoroughly heated. Remove pepper mixture from pan. Wipe pan with paper towels. Coat pan with cooking spray.
2. Combine egg, egg white, and oregano in a small bowl, stirring with a whisk. Add egg mixture to pan; cook over medium heat 1 minute. Do not stir until mixture begins to set on bottom. Add pepper mixture and cheese. Draw a heat-resistant spatula through egg mixture to form large curds. Do not stir constantly. Cook just until egg mixture is thickened, but still moist.
3. Stuff spinach into pita half; add egg mixture. Yield: 1 serving.

CALORIES 253; FAT 10.7g (sat 4.6g, mono 3.4g, poly 1.2g); PROTEIN 16.7g; CARB 24.1g; FIBER 3.6g; CHOL 228mg; IRON 2.4mg; SODIUM 784mg; CALC 138mg

Baleadas, a street food in Honduras, inspired these handheld, filled tortillas. Authentic baleadas use quesillo cheese, which can be hard to find; use Oaxaca cheese as a substitute.

Huevos Rancheros Soft Tacos

Layer this parfait in an insulated coffee mug before you head to work, and it will stay cold until you arrive.

Mixed Berry, Flaxseed, and Yogurt Parfait

Mixed Berry, Flaxseed, and Yogurt Parfait

Prep: 5 minutes

½ cup plain low-fat yogurt
2 tablespoons low-sugar strawberry preserves
¼ teaspoon grated lemon rind
¼ cup low-fat granola without raisins

1 tablespoon sliced almonds, toasted
1 tablespoon flaxseed meal
⅔ cup mixed fresh berries

1. Combine first 3 ingredients in a small bowl. Combine granola, almonds, and flaxseed meal in a separate small bowl. Spoon half of yogurt mixture into bottom of 1 (10-ounce) glass; top with half of granola mixture and ⅓ cup berries. Repeat layers with remaining yogurt mixture, granola mixture, and berries. Yield: 1 serving.

CALORIES 321; FAT 9.1g (sat 1.7g, mono 3.3g, poly 2.2g); PROTEIN 11.2g; CARB 52.1g; FIBER 9.6g; CHOL 13mg; IRON 2.8mg; SODIUM 123mg; CALC 256mg

Cook the wheat berries for this whole-grain breakfast salad over the weekend so you can enjoy this dish throughout the week without much prep work.

Morning Wheat Berry Salad

Prep: 4 minutes • Cook: 1 hour • Other: 8 hours

1 cup uncooked wheat berries
1 cup plain low-fat yogurt
¼ cup maple syrup

1 cup blueberries
1 cup sliced strawberries
½ cup sliced almonds, toasted (optional)

1. Place wheat berries in a bowl; cover with water to 2 inches above berries. Cover and let stand 8 hours. Drain.
2. Place wheat berries in a medium saucepan; cover with water to 2 inches above berries. Bring to a boil; reduce heat, and cook, uncovered, 1 hour or until wheat berries are tender. Drain.
3. Combine yogurt and syrup in a large bowl, stirring with a whisk. Add wheat berries, blueberries, and strawberries; toss well. Sprinkle with almonds, if desired. Yield: 6 servings (serving size: ¾ cup).

CALORIES 188; FAT 1.2g (sat 0.5g, mono 0.1g, poly 0.3g); PROTEIN 6.2g; CARB 40.5g; FIBER 5.1g; CHOL 3mg; IRON 0.3mg; SODIUM 31mg; CALC 82mg

Peanutty Granola Bars

Prep: 8 minutes • Cook: 25 minutes • Other: 1 hour

Cooking spray
2 cups old-fashioned rolled oats
1 cup unsalted, dry-roasted peanuts
1 cup flaked sweetened coconut

⅔ cup honey
¼ cup creamy peanut butter
3 tablespoons canola oil

1. Preheat oven to 325°.
2. Coat an 11 x 7–inch baking dish with cooking spray.
3. Combine oats, peanuts, and coconut on a 17½ x 12½ x 1–inch pan. Bake at 325° for 15 minutes or until lightly toasted. Transfer oat mixture to a large bowl.
4. Combine honey, peanut butter, and oil in a small saucepan. Bring to a boil over medium heat, stirring occasionally; pour over oat mixture, stirring to coat. Pour mixture into prepared dish; place heavy-duty plastic wrap on surface of mixture, and press firmly to an even thickness.
5. Bake at 325° for 10 minutes or until golden brown. Cool 1 hour or until completely cool; cut into 16 bars. (Mixture will become firm when completely cool.) Yield: 16 bars (serving size: 1 bar).

CALORIES 211; FAT 12g (sat 3.2g, mono 5g, poly 2.9g); PROTEIN 4.6g; CARB 23.6g; FIBER 2.2g; CHOL 0mg; IRON 0.9mg; SODIUM 35mg; CALC 6mg

Let the pineapple cool slightly before layering this tropical-inspired parfait.

Pineapple Parfait

Prep: 4 minutes • Cook: 3 minutes

1 teaspoon butter
⅔ cup cubed fresh pineapple
1 tablespoon brown sugar
1 (6-ounce) carton vanilla fat-free Greek yogurt

1 tablespoon chopped macadamia nuts, toasted
1 tablespoon flaked sweetened coconut, toasted

1. Melt butter in a small nonstick skillet over medium-high heat. Add pineapple and brown sugar; cook 2 minutes or until pineapple is golden brown.
2. Layer half of yogurt in a small glass. Top with half of pineapple mixture. Repeat layers once. Sprinkle with nuts and coconut. Yield: 1 serving.

CALORIES 346; FAT 11.8g (sat 4.8g, mono 6.1g, poly 0.3g); PROTEIN 17.5g; CARB 44.8g; FIBER 2.7g; CHOL 10mg; IRON 0.7mg; SODIUM 145mg; CALC 33mg

Peanutty Granola Bars

Protein-Packed Oatmeal

Protein-Packed Oatmeal

Prep: 1 minute • Cook: 5 minutes

½ cup old-fashioned rolled oats
½ cup water
½ cup fat-free milk
⅛ teaspoon salt
2 teaspoons natural-style peanut butter

2 teaspoons honey
¼ cup sliced banana
2 teaspoons chopped honey-roasted peanuts

1. Combine first 4 ingredients in a medium microwave-safe bowl. Microwave, uncovered, at MEDIUM 5 to 6 minutes or until liquid is absorbed. Stir in peanut butter and honey. Top with banana, and sprinkle with peanuts. Yield: 1 serving.

CALORIES 372; FAT 11.4g (sat 1.8g, mono 5g, poly 3.4g); PROTEIN 13.5g; CARB 56.9g; FIBER 6.1g; CHOL 2mg; IRON 2.2mg; SODIUM 406mg; CALC 156mg

Prepare this batter ahead, and keep it in your refrigerator for up to three days. Add six minutes of baking time if you're putting cold batter in the oven.

Raisin Bran Muffins

Prep: 7 minutes • Cook: 17 minutes • Other: 15 minutes

4.5 ounces all-purpose flour (about 1 cup)
1½ teaspoons baking soda
¼ teaspoon salt
1¼ cups fat-free milk
½ cup honey
2 tablespoons canola oil

1 large egg
2 cups wheat bran flakes cereal with raisins, crushed
½ cup golden raisins (optional)
Cooking spray

1. Preheat oven to 400°.
2. Weigh or lightly spoon flour into a dry measuring cup; level with a knife. Combine flour, baking soda, and salt in a large bowl, stirring with a whisk. Combine milk and next 3 ingredients in a medium bowl, stirring with a whisk. Stir in cereal. Add cereal mixture to flour mixture; stir just until moist. Fold in raisins, if desired. Let batter stand 15 minutes.
3. Spoon batter into 16 muffin cups coated with cooking spray. Bake at 400° for 17 minutes or until a wooden pick inserted in center comes out clean. Cool slightly on a wire rack. Serve warm. Yield: 16 servings (serving size: 1 muffin).

CALORIES 111; FAT 2.4g (sat 0.4g, mono 1g, poly 0.9g); PROTEIN 2.6g; CARB 21.2g; FIBER 1.1g; CHOL 14mg; IRON 2.2mg; SODIUM 204mg; CALC 31mg

Make this muesli just before bedtime, and then top it with fruit on your way out the door the next morning.

Tropical Muesli
Prep: 8 minutes • Other: 8 hours

⅔ cup light coconut milk
3 tablespoons honey
1¼ cups unsweetened muesli
1 (6-ounce) container plain fat-free yogurt

1 cup chopped fresh pineapple
1 cup chopped peeled kiwifruit
1 cup chopped banana

1. Combine first 4 ingredients in a medium bowl, stirring well with a spoon. Cover and chill up to 8 hours. Stir in fruit just before serving. Yield: 4 servings (serving size: 1 cup).

CALORIES 288; FAT 4.6g (sat 0.5g, mono 2.1g, poly 1.4g); PROTEIN 8.2g; CARB 62.7g; FIBER 7.8g; CHOL 1mg; IRON 1.7mg; SODIUM 29mg; CALC 103mg

Use a 6-ounce container of vanilla low-fat yogurt if you want a sweeter smoothie.

Vanilla-Berry Smoothie
Prep: 3 minutes

1 (5.3-ounce) carton vanilla fat-free Greek yogurt
1 cup frozen mixed berries

½ cup fat-free milk
2 teaspoons honey
3 ice cubes

1. Place first 4 ingredients in a blender; process until smooth. Remove center cap from blender lid; with blender on, add ice cubes, 1 at a time, processing until smooth. Yield: 1 serving.

CALORIES 250; FAT 0.6g (sat 0.1g, mono 0.1g, poly 0.4g); PROTEIN 19.4g; CARB 45.9g; FIBER 4g; CHOL 2mg; IRON 0.4mg; SODIUM 118mg; CALC 174mg

Tropical Muesli

When fresh figs aren't in season, stir ¼ cup chopped dried figs into the yogurt with the orange marmalade. If you prefer a tangy taste to sweetness, use plain 2% reduced-fat Greek yogurt instead of vanilla.

Yogurt with Orange-Honey Figs
Prep: 5 minutes

1 (6-ounce) container vanilla fat-free Greek yogurt
1 tablespoon orange marmalade

2 fresh figs, quartered
2 teaspoons chopped pistachios
2 teaspoons orange blossom honey

1. Combine yogurt and orange marmalade in a small bowl. Top with figs; sprinkle with pistachios, and drizzle with honey. Yield: 1 serving.

CALORIES 315; FAT 2.7g (sat 0.3g, mono 1.3g, poly 0.9g); PROTEIN 18g; CARB 58.2g; FIBER 3.6g; CHOL 0mg; IRON 0.7mg; SODIUM 88mg; CALC 49mg

If you enjoy the taste of bagels and lox, this sandwich will become a favorite. Smoked trout can stand in for the salmon.

Smoked Salmon Breakfast Sandwiches
Prep: 5 minutes • Cook: 2 minutes

2 tablespoons (1 ounce) light tub-style cream cheese with chives and onion
2 (1.5-ounce) bagel thins, toasted
1 (4-ounce) package cold-smoked salmon slices, halved

¼ small red onion, cut vertically into thin slices
1 tablespoon chopped fresh dill
2 teaspoons drained capers
¼ teaspoon freshly ground black pepper

1. Spread 1½ teaspoons cream cheese over cut side of each bagel half. Layer salmon, onion, dill, and capers evenly on bottoms of bagel thins. Sprinkle evenly with pepper. Cover with bagel thin tops. Yield: 2 servings (serving size: 1 sandwich).

CALORIES 201; FAT 5.5g (sat 1.9g, mono 1.8g, poly 0.7g); PROTEIN 15.6g; CARB 25.2g; FIBER 4g; CHOL 19.9mg; IRON 1.9mg; SODIUM 802mg; CALC 94mg

Yogurt with Orange-Honey Figs

To shave time, purchase preboiled eggs. You can make this egg salad in advance for the week ahead.

Breakfast Egg Salad Sandwiches

Breakfast Egg Salad Sandwiches

Prep: 12 minutes

6 hard-cooked large eggs, chopped
6 hard-cooked large egg whites, chopped
¼ cup canola mayonnaise
½ cup (2 ounces) shredded reduced-fat
   extra-sharp cheddar cheese
6 center-cut bacon slices, cooked and crumbled
½ teaspoon salt
¼ teaspoon freshly ground black pepper
16 (0.7-ounce) slices whole-wheat bread

1. Combine all ingredients except bread. Spoon mixture evenly onto 8 bread slices. Top with remaining bread slices. Yield: 8 servings (serving size: 1 sandwich).

CALORIES 238; FAT 12.6g (sat 3.2g, mono 6g, poly 2.6g); PROTEIN 15.7g; CARB 21g; FIBER 6g; CHOL 152.7mg; IRON 5.2mg; SODIUM 609mg; CALC 154mg

Bake these small biscuits, and freeze them in an airtight container. Each morning, pull some out, reheat, and add ham.

Cornmeal Biscuit and Ham Sandwiches

Prep: 8 minutes • Cook: 12 minutes • Other: 5 minutes

8.5 ounces self-rising flour (about 2 cups)
½ cup yellow cornmeal
5 tablespoons chilled unsalted butter, cut into
   small pieces
¾ cup fat-free buttermilk
Cooking spray
6 ounces lower-sodium deli ham
3 tablespoons honey (optional)

1. Preheat oven to 450°.
2. Weigh or lightly spoon flour into dry measuring cups; level with a knife. Combine flour and cornmeal in a medium bowl; cut in butter with a pastry blender or two knives until mixture resembles coarse meal. Add buttermilk, stirring just until moist.
3. Turn dough out onto a lightly floured surface; knead lightly 5 or 6 times. Roll dough to a ½-inch thickness; cut with a 2-inch biscuit cutter into 18 biscuits. Place on a baking sheet coated with cooking spray. Coat tops of biscuits with cooking spray.
4. Bake at 450° for 12 minutes or until golden. Cool on pan 5 minutes. Cut biscuits in half horizontally. Top bottom halves of biscuits evenly with ham, and drizzle each with ½ teaspoon honey, if desired. Top with biscuit tops. Yield: 6 servings (serving size: 3 biscuits).

CALORIES 318; FAT 10.5g (sat 6.1g, mono 2.5g, poly 0.5g); PROTEIN 11.1g; CARB 43.2g; FIBER 1.4g; CHOL 38mg; IRON 2.4mg; SODIUM 774mg; CALC 139mg

One-bowl breakfasts are a popular freezer item. Here is a homemade mixture of hash browns, grits, eggs, ham, and cheese that's sure to give you energy for the day ahead.

Hearty Breakfast Bowl

Hearty Breakfast Bowl
Prep: 1 minute • Cook: 11 minutes

1½ teaspoons canola oil
½ cup frozen Southern-style hash browns
½ cup water
2½ tablespoons quick-cooking grits
Dash of salt
1 large egg

1 large egg white
⅛ teaspoon freshly ground black pepper
¼ cup chopped lean ham
2 tablespoons shredded reduced-fat extra-sharp cheddar cheese

1. Heat oil in a small skillet over medium-high heat. Add hash browns; cook 6 to 8 minutes or until browned. Reduce heat to low.
2. While hash browns cook, combine water, grits, and salt in a 4-cup glass measure. Microwave at HIGH 2 to 3 minutes or until thick, stirring after 2 minutes.
3. Combine egg, egg white, and pepper; stir well with a whisk until foamy. Add egg mixture and ham to potatoes in pan. Cook 3 minutes or just until eggs are set, stirring occasionally. Spoon grits into a bowl; top with egg mixture, and sprinkle with cheese. Yield: 1 serving.

CALORIES 368; FAT 15.8g (sat 4.4g, mono 6.0g, poly 4.1g); PROTEIN 22g; CARB 33.7g; FIBER 1.8g; CHOL 234mg; IRON 2.2mg; SODIUM 664mg; CALC 132mg

Mexican Egg Sandwiches
Prep: 8 minutes • Cook: 7 minutes

¼ pound Mexican chorizo
4 large egg whites, lightly beaten
2 large eggs, lightly beaten
2 tablespoons chopped fresh cilantro

4 whole-wheat English muffins, split and toasted
¼ cup salsa verde
¼ cup queso fresco, crumbled

1. Remove casing from chorizo. Cook chorizo in a large nonstick skillet over medium-high heat 5 minutes or until browned; stir to crumble. Drain well; return chorizo to pan.
2. Combine egg whites, eggs, and cilantro in a medium bowl, stirring with a whisk.
3. Add egg mixture to chorizo; cook over medium heat 2 minutes. Do not stir until mixture begins to set on bottom. Draw a heat-resistant spatula through egg mixture to form large curds. Do not stir constantly. Egg mixture is done when thickened, but still moist.
4. Spoon egg mixture evenly onto bottom half of each English muffin; top each with 1 tablespoon salsa verde and 1 tablespoon queso fresco. Top sandwiches with remaining 4 muffin halves. Yield: 4 servings (serving size: 1 sandwich).

CALORIES 330; FAT 15.9g (sat 5.7g, mono 6.5g, poly 1.4g); PROTEIN 21.4g; CARB 25.8g; FIBER 3g; CHOL 136mg; IRON 2.5mg; SODIUM 795mg; CALC 122mg

Precooked sausage is a time-saver in this recipe; simply chop the sausage, and add it to the dough along with the cheese. You can also use veggie sausage patties.

Sausage Drop Scones

Prep: 10 minutes • Cook: 15 minutes

3 cups low-fat baking mix
1½ teaspoons freshly ground black pepper
2 tablespoons chilled butter, cut into small pieces
¾ cup low-fat evaporated milk

4 fully cooked turkey sausage patties, chopped
½ cup (2 ounces) reduced-fat cheddar cheese with jalapeño peppers, shredded
Cooking spray

1. Preheat oven to 425°.

2. Combine baking mix and pepper in a large bowl. Cut in butter with a pastry blender or 2 knives until mixture resembles coarse meal. Add milk, sausage, and cheese; stir until just moist. Drop dough by ¼ cupfuls onto a baking sheet lined with parchment paper. Coat dough with cooking spray.

3. Bake at 425° for 15 minutes or until scones are golden. Yield: 15 servings (serving size: 1 scone).

CALORIES 135; FAT 4.8g (sat 1.6g, mono 1.9g, poly 0.6g); PROTEIN 5.5g; CARB 18g; FIBER 0.7g; CHOL 15mg; IRON 1mg; SODIUM 376mg; CALC 186mg

Savory Loaded Oatmeal

Prep: 2 minutes • Cook: 5 minutes

½ cup old-fashioned rolled oats
½ cup water
½ cup fat-free milk
⅛ teaspoon salt
2 tablespoons reduced-fat shredded sharp cheddar cheese

1 teaspoon butter
1 center-cut bacon slice, cooked and crumbled
1 tablespoon chopped green onions (optional)

1. Combine first 4 ingredients in a medium microwave-safe bowl. Microwave at MEDIUM 5 to 6 minutes or until liquid is absorbed.

2. Add cheese, butter, and bacon, stirring until cheese and butter melt. Sprinkle with green onions, if desired. Yield: 1 serving.

CALORIES 291; FAT 11.3g (sat 5.5g, mono 3.5g, poly 1.4g); PROTEIN 14.7g; CARB 33.6g; FIBER 4g; CHOL 28mg; IRON 1.8mg; SODIUM 582mg; CALC 256mg

Sausage Drop Scones

weekend
breakfasts & brunches

Use a well-seasoned cast-iron skillet—it eliminates the need for extra oil to grease the pan. For a crisp pizza crust, heat the skillet on the cooktop before transferring it to the oven.

Cast-Iron Breakfast Pizza
Prep: 12 minutes • Cook: 23 minutes

1 (16-ounce) package commercial pizza dough
1 cup part-skim ricotta cheese
5 lower-sodium bacon slices, cooked and crumbled
1 cup (4 ounces) shredded part-skim mozzarella cheese
¼ teaspoon freshly ground black pepper
Cooking spray
1 (6-ounce) package fresh baby spinach

1. Preheat oven to 450°.
2. Roll out dough to a 12-inch circle. Press dough into bottom and 1 inch up sides of a well-seasoned 10-inch cast-iron skillet. Fold edges under and crimp.
3. Spread ricotta cheese in bottom of crust; top with bacon, mozzarella cheese, and pepper. Place skillet over high heat; cook 3 minutes. Transfer skillet to oven.
4. Bake at 450° for 18 minutes or until crust is lightly browned and cheese melts.
5. While pizza cooks, heat a large skillet over medium-high heat. Coat pan with cooking spray. Add spinach. Cook 1 minute or until spinach wilts, turning often with tongs. Remove spinach from pan; drain and squeeze out excess liquid. Top pizza with wilted spinach. Cut pizza into 8 wedges. Yield: 8 servings (serving size: 1 wedge).

CALORIES 260; FAT 8.2g (sat 3.7g, mono 1.4g, poly 1.1g); PROTEIN 13.7g; CARB 34.1g; FIBER 2g; CHOL 22mg; IRON 2.6mg; SODIUM 562mg; CALC 210mg

serve with
Broiled Sweet Peaches
Prep: 3 minutes • Cook: 8 minutes

8 peaches, halved and pitted
2 tablespoons butter, melted
¼ cup turbinado sugar
⅓ cup plain fat-free Greek yogurt

1. Preheat broiler. Place a rack 6 inches from the heat.
2. Place peach halves on a baking sheet lined with foil; brush with butter, and sprinkle with turbinado sugar. Broil 8 minutes or until sugar melts and is lightly browned. Spoon 1 teaspoon yogurt over each peach half. Yield: 8 servings (serving size: 2 peach halves).

CALORIES 104; FAT 3.3g (sat 1.9g, mono 0.9g, poly 0.2g); PROTEIN 2.2g; CARB 19.2g; FIBER 2.2g; CHOL 7.6mg; IRON 0.4mg; SODIUM 24mg; CALC 16mg

These light, airy eggs are ideal for brunch. Serve with sliced tomatoes or fruit salad and toast.

Baked Eggs with Spinach and Goat Cheese

Prep: 20 minutes • Cook: 10 minutes

Cooking spray
4 large egg whites
¼ teaspoon salt
¼ teaspoon freshly ground black pepper
¼ cup (2 ounces) goat cheese, crumbled

1 cup chopped fresh spinach
4 large egg yolks
2 tablespoons crème fraîche
1 tablespoon chopped fresh chives

1. Preheat oven to 350°.
2. Coat 4 (6-ounce) custard cups with cooking spray. Place egg whites, salt, and pepper in a medium bowl; beat with a mixer at high speed 1 minute or until stiff peaks form. Gently fold in cheese and spinach. Divide mixture evenly among prepared custard cups.
3. Make an indentation in the center of egg white mixture in each custard cup. Place 1 egg yolk into each indentation. Spoon 1½ teaspoons crème fraîche on top of each egg yolk. Place custard cups on a baking sheet.
4. Bake at 350° for 10 to 12 minutes or until egg white mixture is puffed and pale. (Yolks will not be set in center.) Sprinkle with chives, and serve immediately. Yield: 4 servings.

CALORIES 140; FAT 10.8g (sat 5.2g, mono 2.6g, poly 0.8g); PROTEIN 9.3g; CARB 1.3g; FIBER 0.3g; CHOL 225mg; IRON 1.4mg; SODIUM 280mg; CALC 52mg

use extra spinach in

Pizza Dopiaza, page **256**

Go-Getter Green Smoothie, page **41**

Turkey-Hummus Pitas, page **132**

The caramelized bananas are reminiscent of bananas Foster and would be good served over frozen yogurt.

Buttermilk Pancakes with Caramelized Bananas
Prep: 9 minutes • Cook: 4 minutes

4.5 ounces self-rising flour (about 1 cup)
⅛ teaspoon baking soda
1 cup nonfat buttermilk

2 tablespoons canola oil
1 large egg
Caramelized Bananas

1. Weigh or lightly spoon flour into a dry measuring cup; level with a knife. Combine flour and baking soda in a large bowl, stirring with a whisk. Combine buttermilk, oil, and egg in a medium bowl, stirring with a whisk; add to flour mixture, stirring until smooth.
2. Pour about ¼ cup batter per pancake onto a hot nonstick griddle. Cook 1 minute or until tops are covered with bubbles and edges look cooked. Carefully turn pancakes over; cook 1 minute or until bottoms are lightly browned.
3. While pancakes cook, prepare Caramelized Bananas. Serve pancakes with bananas. Yield: 4 servings (serving size: 2 pancakes and ¼ cup bananas).

CALORIES 349; FAT 14.5g (sat 4.9g, mono 5g, poly 3.6g); PROTEIN 7.6g; CARB 49.3g; FIBER 2.5g; CHOL 69mg; IRON 1.9mg; SODIUM 518mg; CALC 201mg

Caramelized Bananas
Prep: 1 minute • Cook: 2 minutes

2 tablespoons unsalted butter
¼ cup light brown sugar
¼ teaspoon ground cinnamon

2 tablespoons dark rum (optional)
2 firm, ripe bananas, sliced diagonally into
   ½-inch slices (1⅓ cups)

1. Melt butter in a 10-inch nonstick skillet over medium heat. Add sugar, cinnamon, and rum, if desired. Add banana; cook 1½ minutes or until banana is caramelized, stirring occasionally. Yield: 4 servings (serving size: ¼ cup).

CALORIES 138; FAT 6g (sat 3.7g, mono 1.5g, poly 0.3g); PROTEIN 0.7g; CARB 22.5g; FIBER 1.6g; CHOL 15mg; IRON 0.2mg; SODIUM 4mg; CALC 14mg

This omelet is stuffed with salsa, Monterey Jack cheese with jalapeño peppers, and black beans. Continue the theme by serving Southwestern-style potatoes on the side.

Black Bean Omelet

Prep: 7 minutes • Cook: 6 minutes

2 large eggs
4 large egg whites
⅛ teaspoon salt
¼ teaspoon freshly ground black pepper
Cooking spray
½ cup no-salt-added black beans, rinsed and drained

¼ cup (1 ounce) preshredded Monterey Jack cheese with jalapeño peppers
2 tablespoons sliced green onions
Tomato-Avocado Salsa

1. Combine first 4 ingredients in a medium bowl; stir with a whisk until blended.
2. Heat an 8-inch pan over medium heat. Coat pan with cooking spray. Add egg mixture, and cook 3 minutes or until set (do not stir). Sprinkle with beans, cheese, and green onions. Loosen omelet with a spatula; fold in half. Cook 1 to 2 minutes or until cheese melts. Slide omelet onto a plate. Cut in half. Top each half with Tomato-Avocado Salsa. Yield: 2 servings (serving size: ½ omelet and ¼ cup salsa).

CALORIES 252; FAT 12.9g (sat 4.6g, mono 5.3g, poly 1.2g); PROTEIN 20.7g; CARB 14.2g; FIBER 4.9g; CHOL 227mg; IRON 2.2mg; SODIUM 571mg; CALC 149mg

Tomato-Avocado Salsa

Prep: 3 minutes

¼ cup chopped tomato
¼ cup chopped peeled avocado
1 tablespoon fresh lemon juice

⅛ teaspoon salt
⅛ teaspoon ground cumin

1. Combine all ingredients in a small bowl. Yield: 2 servings (serving size: ¼ cup).

CALORIES 37; FAT 2.8g (sat 0.4g, mono 1.8g, poly 0.4g); PROTEIN 0.6g; CARB 3.2g; FIBER 1.6g; CHOL 0mg; IRON 0.2mg; SODIUM 150mg; CALC 6mg

Breakfast Bakers

Prep: 5 minutes • Cook: 10 minutes

4 (8-ounce) ready-to-microwave baking potatoes
4 large eggs, lightly beaten
¼ teaspoon salt
¼ teaspoon freshly ground black pepper
2 teaspoons butter

4 tablespoons ⅓-less-fat tub-style chive and onion cream cheese
½ cup (2 ounces) preshredded reduced-fat sharp cheddar cheese
2 center-cut bacon slices, cooked and crumbled

1. Microwave potatoes according to label directions.
2. While potatoes cook, combine eggs, salt, and pepper in a medium bowl, stirring with a whisk. Melt butter in a large nonstick skillet over medium-high heat. Pour egg mixture into pan. Cook 4 minutes or until soft-scrambled, stirring frequently. Remove from heat.
3. Cut potatoes in half. Scoop out pulp, leaving a ⅛-inch shell. Place pulp in a bowl; add cream cheese, and mash with a potato masher until cream cheese melts. Spoon potato mixture evenly into potato shells. Top evenly with scrambled eggs; sprinkle evenly with cheddar cheese and bacon. Yield: 4 servings (serving size: 1 stuffed potato, 2 tablespoons cheddar cheese, and 2 teaspoons bacon).

CALORIES 337; FAT 13g (sat 6.6g, mono 4.2g, poly 1.1g); PROTEIN 15.8g; CARB 39.6g; FIBER 2.7g; CHOL 237mg; IRON 1.6mg; SODIUM 488mg; CALC 158mg

use extra ingredients

Potatoes	Cheddar Cheese	Bacon

Curried Paneer and Spinach-Stuffed Potatoes, page **146**	Savory Loaded Oatmeal, page **58**	Arugula-Orange Salad with Fig-Bacon Dressing, page **135**

Pesto Hollandaise replaces the basil that's in a traditional Caprese salad. You will have extra hollandaise sauce left over; spoon it over grilled fish.

Caprese Eggs Benedict
Prep: 8 minutes • Cook: 5 minutes

Cooking spray
4 large eggs
2 English muffins, split and toasted
4 (¼-inch-thick) slices tomato
4 (1-ounce) slices fresh mozzarella cheese
¼ cup Pesto Hollandaise
4 large fresh basil leaves (optional)

1. Coat 4 (6-ounce) custard cups with cooking spray. Break 1 egg into each cup. Pierce yolk of each egg once with a wooden pick. Microwave at MEDIUM 1 minute and 15 seconds or to desired doneness.
2. Place 1 muffin half, cut side up, on each of 4 plates. Top each with 1 tomato slice, 1 mozzarella slice, 1 egg, and 1 tablespoon Pesto Hollandaise. Top each with 1 basil leaf, if desired. Yield: 4 servings.

CALORIES 248; FAT 17.6g (sat 6.2g, mono 4.3g, poly 1.9g); PROTEIN 13.6g; CARB 9.8g; FIBER 1.3g; CHOL 238mg; IRON 1.4mg; SODIUM 188mg; CALC 91mg

Pesto Hollandaise
Prep: 2 minutes • Cook: 45 seconds

⅓ cup nonfat buttermilk
⅓ cup canola mayonnaise
1 tablespoon fresh lemon juice
2 tablespoons refrigerated pesto
1 teaspoon butter

1. Combine first 4 ingredients in a 1-cup glass measure, stirring with a whisk until blended. Microwave at MEDIUM 45 seconds or until warm. Add butter, stirring until melted. Keep warm. Yield: 14 servings (serving size: 1 tablespoon).

CALORIES 54; FAT 5.5g (sat 0.7g, mono 2.4g, poly 1.2g); PROTEIN 0.5g; CARB 0.6g; FIBER 0.1g; CHOL 3mg; IRON 0.1mg; SODIUM 65mg; CALC 13mg

Make the Mixed Berry Topping while the filled crepes bake in the oven; you don't have to thaw the berries first, so you can make the sauce quickly with any berries you have on hand, straight from the freezer.

Cheese Blintzes
Prep: 5 minutes • Cook: 6 minutes

¼ cup (2 ounces) ⅓-less-fat cream cheese, softened
¼ cup part-skim ricotta cheese
1 tablespoon brown sugar

2 (½-ounce) commercial crepes
Cooking spray
Mixed Berry Topping

1. Preheat oven to 450°.
2. Place first 3 ingredients in a food processor; process until smooth. Spoon ¼ cup cheese mixture down center of each crepe; fold sides and ends over filling. Place crepes, seam sides down, in an 11 x 7–inch glass or ceramic baking dish coated with cooking spray. Coat crepes with cooking spray. Bake at 450° for 5 minutes or until lightly browned.
3. While blintzes bake, prepare Mixed Berry Topping. Spoon topping evenly over blintzes. Yield: 2 servings (serving size: 1 blintz and 6 tablespoons topping).

CALORIES 217; FAT 9.7g (sat 5.6g, mono 2.6g, poly 0.6g); PROTEIN 7.1g; CARB 27.4g; FIBER 2.1g; CHOL 35mg; IRON 0.4mg; SODIUM 202mg; CALC 121mg

Mixed Berry Topping
Prep: 2 minutes • Cook: 2 minutes

1 cup frozen mixed berries
2 teaspoons honey

½ teaspoon grated lemon rind
2 teaspoons chopped fresh mint

1. Combine first 3 ingredients in small saucepan. Cook, stirring constantly, over medium-high heat 2 minutes or until thoroughly heated. Remove from heat. Stir in mint. Yield: 2 servings (serving size: 6 tablespoons).

CALORIES 52; FAT 0.3g (sat 0g, mono 0g, poly 0g); PROTEIN 0.6g; CARB 14.3g; FIBER 2.1g; CHOL 0mg; IRON 0.2mg; SODIUM 0mg; CALC 12mg

The butter and brown sugar cook with the apples to create a delicious syrup for drizzling over the French toast.

Cinnamon-Apple–Stuffed French Toast

Prep: 7 minutes • Cook: 8 minutes

Cinnamon-Apple Filling
 4 (1-ounce) slices diagonally cut French bread (about 1 inch thick)
 ½ cup fat-free milk

 1 teaspoon vanilla extract
 1 large egg
Cooking spray
 1 tablespoon powdered sugar (optional)

1. Prepare Cinnamon-Apple Filling.
2. Cut a horizontal slit through the side of each bread slice to form a pocket. Stuff 3 tablespoons Cinnamon-Apple Filling into each pocket.
3. Place milk, vanilla, and egg in a shallow dish; stir with a whisk until blended. Heat a large skillet over medium-high heat. Coat pan with cooking spray.
4. Dip each side of stuffed bread in egg mixture to coat. Add stuffed bread to pan; cook 2 minutes on each side or until golden brown. Sprinkle with powdered sugar, if desired; top evenly with remaining filling. Yield: 4 servings (serving size: 1 toast slice and 5 tablespoons apple filling).

CALORIES 230; FAT 7.9g (sat 4.2g, mono 2.2g, poly 0.7g); PROTEIN 6.2g; CARB 34.6g; FIBER 2.2g; CHOL 69mg; IRON 1.4mg; SODIUM 259mg; CALC 73mg

Cinnamon-Apple Filling

Prep: 2 minutes • Cook: 4 minutes

 2 tablespoons butter
 2 cups chopped unpeeled Gala apple (about 1 large)

 ¼ cup brown sugar
 ½ teaspoon ground cinnamon

1. Melt butter in a large nonstick skillet over medium-high heat. Add remaining ingredients; sauté 3 minutes or until apples are golden. Yield: 4 servings (serving size: 5 tablespoons).

CALORIES 115; FAT 5.9g (sat 3.7g, mono 1.5g, poly 0.2g); PROTEIN 0.2g; CARB 16.9g; FIBER 1.5g; CHOL 15mg; IRON 0.2mg; SODIUM 44mg; CALC 16mg

Use your favorite waffle toppings; these are dressed up with blueberries, maple syrup, and powdered sugar.

Cornmeal-Yogurt Waffles

Prep: 14 minutes • Cook: 21 minutes

4.5 ounces self-rising flour (about 1 cup)
¾ cup yellow cornmeal
4 large eggs
1 cup water
1 (5.3-ounce) container vanilla organic Greek yogurt

2 tablespoons unsalted butter, melted
¼ cup powdered sugar (optional)
6 tablespoons maple syrup (optional)
2 cups blueberries (optional)

1. Preheat a waffle iron.
2. Weigh or lightly spoon flour into a dry measuring cup; level with a knife. Combine flour and cornmeal in a large mixing bowl, stirring with a whisk.
3. Separate eggs. Place egg whites in a large bowl. Combine 1 egg yolk, 1 cup water, yogurt, and butter in a medium bowl, stirring well with a whisk. (Discard or reserve remaining egg yolks for another use.) Add yogurt mixture to flour mixture, stirring until smooth.
4. Beat egg whites with a mixer at high speed until stiff peaks form. Gently fold one-quarter of egg whites into cornmeal mixture; fold in remaining egg whites.
5. Spoon about ⅓ cup batter per 4-inch waffle onto hot waffle iron, spreading batter to edges. Cook 4 to 5 minutes or until steaming stops; repeat procedure with remaining batter. Sift 1 teaspoon powdered sugar over each waffle, if desired; top with 1 tablespoon maple syrup and about ⅓ cup blueberries, if desired. Serve immediately. Yield: 6 servings (serving size: 2 waffles).

CALORIES 346; FAT 7.4g (sat 3.5g, mono 2.3g, poly 0.9g); PROTEIN 10.4g; CARB 58.6g; FIBER 2.3g; CHOL 134.2mg; IRON 2.2mg; SODIUM 395mg; CALC 124mg

use extra blueberries in

Blueberry-Yogurt Parfait, page **193**

Grilled Peach and Granola Salad, page **150**

Morning Wheat Berry Salad, page **45**

Prepare the Olive-Tomato Topping while the hash brown cakes cook, so you are ready to top the cakes right when they come out of the skillet.

Mediterranean Hash Brown Cakes
Prep: 9 minutes • Cook: 5 minutes

1 large egg
1 large egg white
2 cups frozen hash browns, thawed
¼ cup chopped red bell pepper
1 tablespoon chopped fresh parsley
¼ teaspoon salt
¼ teaspoon freshly ground black pepper
Cooking spray
Olive-Tomato Topping

1. Place egg and egg white in a large bowl; beat with a whisk until foamy. Stir in hash browns and next 4 ingredients.
2. Heat a large skillet over medium-high heat. Coat pan with cooking spray. Pour ⅓ cup potato mixture per potato cake onto hot pan; cook 2 minutes on each side or until browned. Serve with Olive-Tomato Topping. Yield: 2 servings (serving size: 2 cakes and ¼ cup topping).

CALORIES 183; FAT 9.1g (sat 2.9g, mono 4.9g, poly 0.9g); PROTEIN 9.8g; CARB 17.8g; FIBER 2.8g; CHOL 109mg; IRON 2.5mg; SODIUM 543mg; CALC 54mg

Olive-Tomato Topping
Prep: 4 minutes

¼ cup chopped seeded tomato
2 tablespoons crumbled goat cheese
2 tablespoons commercial olive tapenade
1 tablespoon chopped fresh parsley

1. Combine all ingredients in a small bowl. Yield: 2 servings (serving size: ¼ cup).

CALORIES 69; FAT 6.2g (sat 2g, mono 3.7g, poly 0.5g); PROTEIN 2.6g; CARB 2.1g; FIBER 1.3g; CHOL 3mg; IRON 1mg; SODIUM 178mg; CALC 35mg

Chopped meatless sausage-style patties are a lower-fat alternative in this traditionally rich breakfast favorite. The gravy is also tasty spooned into a baked potato for the same flavor as hash browns.

"Sausage" Gravy on Grilled Toast Slabs

Prep: 11 minutes • Cook: 12 minutes

4 frozen hot and spicy meatless sausage patties
2 tablespoons all-purpose flour
¼ teaspoon salt
⅛ teaspoon freshly ground black pepper
1½ cups 1% low-fat milk
8 teaspoons butter, softened
4 (1-ounce) diagonally cut French bread slices

1. Microwave sausage patties according to package directions; chop.
2. Combine flour, salt, and pepper in a medium saucepan; gradually add milk, stirring with a whisk until smooth. Bring to a boil over medium-high heat, stirring occasionally. Stir in sausage. Cover, reduce heat, and simmer 2 minutes or until thick, stirring occasionally.
3. While gravy cooks, spread 1 teaspoon butter over each side of bread slices. Heat a large nonstick skillet over medium-high heat. Add bread slices; cook 2 minutes on each side or until golden brown. Spoon gravy over toast slices. Serve immediately. Yield: 4 servings (serving size: 1 toast slice and about ½ cup gravy).

CALORIES 273; FAT 12.1g (sat 5.6g, mono 2.9g, poly 2.1g); PROTEIN 14.9g; CARB 26.6g; FIBER 1.8g; CHOL 25mg; IRON 2.7mg; SODIUM 654mg; CALC 125mg

Coconut milk and banana replace the milk and sugar normally found in waffle batter, giving these waffles the flavor of the tropics.

Tropical Waffles

Prep: 4 minutes • Cook: 6 minutes per batch

4.5 ounces self-rising flour (about 1 cup)
1 cup light coconut milk
⅓ cup mashed ripe banana

1 large egg
Pineapple-Orange Syrup

1. Weigh or lightly spoon flour into a dry measuring cup; level with a knife. Place flour in a large bowl.
2. Combine coconut milk, banana, and egg in a medium bowl, stirring with a whisk until blended. Add to flour, stirring until smooth.
3. Preheat a nonstick Belgian waffle iron.
4. Spoon about ½ cup batter per 4-inch waffle onto hot waffle iron, spreading batter to edges. Cook 5 to 6 minutes or until steaming stops. Spoon Pineapple-Orange Syrup over waffles. Yield: 4 servings (serving size: 1 waffle and about 3 tablespoons syrup).

CALORIES 252; FAT 6.2g (sat 2.3g, mono 3g, poly 0.4g); PROTEIN 5.5g; CARB 44.4g; FIBER 2g; CHOL 53mg; IRON 1.9mg; SODIUM 436mg; CALC 118mg

Pineapple-Orange Syrup

Prep: 2 minutes • Cook: 30 seconds

¼ cup pineapple preserves
¼ cup fresh orange juice

2 tablespoons chopped macadamia nuts
2 tablespoons flaked sweetened coconut

1. Combine preserves and juice in a 1-cup glass measure. Microwave at HIGH 30 seconds or until preserves melt. Stir in macadamia nuts and coconut. Yield: 4 servings (serving size: about 3 tablespoons).

CALORIES 99; FAT 4g (sat 1.2g, mono 2.5g, poly 0.1g); PROTEIN 0.5g; CARB 16.5g; FIBER 0.6g; CHOL 0mg; IRON 0.2mg; SODIUM 19mg; CALC 5mg

Fontina and pancetta form a dynamic duo in this breakfast dish, but in a pinch, cheddar and bacon are fine substitutes. For the berries, we used a combo of raspberries, blueberries, and strawberries; use whatever fresh, ripe berries you have available.

Fried Eggs over Pancetta Grits
Prep: 1 minute • Cook: 14 minutes

1½ cups water
½ cup half-and-half
¼ teaspoon salt
½ cup quick-cooking grits
⅓ cup (1¼ ounces) shredded fontina cheese

1 ounce thinly sliced pancetta
4 large eggs
Freshly ground black pepper (optional)
Chopped fresh chives (optional)

1. Bring first 3 ingredients to a boil in a medium saucepan. Gradually add grits, stirring constantly with a whisk. Reduce heat to medium-low; cover and cook 4 minutes or until thick, stirring occasionally. Remove from heat; stir in cheese.
2. While grits cook, heat a large nonstick skillet over medium-high heat; add pancetta. Cook 4 minutes or until lightly browned, stirring occasionally; drain on paper towels. Reduce heat to low. Crack eggs into pan; cover and cook 2 to 5 minutes or until whites are set. Remove from heat.
3. Crumble pancetta; stir into grits. Spoon grits evenly into 4 serving bowls. Top each serving with 1 egg, sprinkle with freshly ground pepper and chives, if desired. Yield: 4 servings (serving size: about ½ cup grits and 1 egg).

CALORIES 243; FAT 13.7g (sat 6.5g, mono 4.7g, poly 1.4g); PROTEIN 12.2g; CARB 17.3g; FIBER 0.3g; CHOL 238mg; IRON 1.7mg; SODIUM 416mg; CALC 108mg

serve with
Mixed Berry Cup
Prep: 12 minutes

2 cups mixed fresh berries
¼ cup coarsely chopped Meyer lemon
    sections (2 lemons)

2 tablespoons chopped fresh mint
2 tablespoons honey

1. Combine all ingredients in a small bowl, tossing gently. Yield: 4 servings (serving size: ½ cup).

CALORIES 74; FAT 0.4g (sat 0g, mono 0g, poly 0.2g); PROTEIN 0.9g; CARB 19.2g; FIBER 4.4g; CHOL 0mg; IRON 0.4mg; SODIUM 1mg; CALC 26.5mg

While the onion sautés, prepare the frittata ingredients. You'll have time to toss the salad topping as the frittata cooks.

Frittata with Mascarpone and Prosciutto
Prep: 4 minutes • Cook: 10 minutes

Cooking spray
½ cup chopped onion
8 large eggs
⅛ teaspoon salt

¼ teaspoon freshly ground black pepper
2 ounces thinly sliced prosciutto, chopped
8 teaspoons mascarpone cheese
Arugula-Tomato Topping

1. Preheat broiler.
2. Heat a 10-inch oven-proof skillet over medium heat. Coat pan with cooking spray. Add onion; sauté 3 minutes or until onion is tender.
3. Combine eggs, salt, and pepper in a medium bowl; stir with a whisk until foamy. Stir in prosciutto. Pour egg mixture over onion in pan. Dollop 1 teaspoon mascarpone over egg mixture at each of 8 equal intervals around edge of eggs. (Each of 8 wedges, when cut, will contain a small dollop.) Cook 3 minutes or until almost set, gently lifting edges of frittata with a spatula and tilting pan so uncooked portion flows underneath.
4. Broil frittata 2 minutes or until completely set in center.
5. While frittata cooks, prepare Arugula-Tomato Topping. Spoon topping over frittata, and cut into 8 wedges just before serving. Yield: 8 servings (serving size: 1 wedge frittata and about ⅓ cup topping).

CALORIES 147; FAT 11.3g (sat 4.3g, mono 2.7g, poly 0.8g); PROTEIN 9.4g; CARB 2.6g; FIBER 0.5g; CHOL 229mg; IRON 1.1mg; SODIUM 340mg; CALC 54mg

Arugula-Tomato Topping
Prep: 2 minutes

2 cups arugula
1 cup grape tomatoes, halved
2 teaspoons olive oil

⅛ teaspoon salt
¼ teaspoon freshly ground black pepper

1. Combine all ingredients in a medium bowl, tossing gently. Serve immediately. Yield: 8 servings (serving size: about ⅓ cup).

CALORIES 15; FAT 1.2g (sat 0.2g, mono 0.8g, poly 0.1g); PROTEIN 0.3g; CARB 1g; FIBER 0.4g; CHOL 0mg; IRON 0.1mg; SODIUM 39mg; CALC 11mg

Sausage Breakfast Braid

Prep: 6 minutes • Cook: 19 minutes • Other: 5 minutes

1 (13.8-ounce) can refrigerated pizza crust dough
Cooking spray
4 ounces light smoked sausage, chopped
3 large eggs, lightly beaten
¼ teaspoon freshly ground black pepper
¾ cup (3 ounces) shredded reduced-fat extra-sharp cheddar cheese
1 large egg white, lightly beaten

1. Preheat oven to 425°.

2. Unroll dough onto a baking sheet coated with cooking spray; pat dough into a 15 x 10–inch rectangle.

3. Heat a large skillet over medium heat. Coat pan with cooking spray. Add sausage; cook 2 minutes or until lightly browned, stirring occasionally. Stir in eggs and pepper; cook 1 minute or until set, stirring occasionally. Remove from heat.

4. Sprinkle ½ cup cheese lengthwise down center of dough, leaving a 2-inch border on each side. Spoon egg mixture evenly over cheese, and sprinkle with ¼ cup cheese.

5. Make 2-inch-long diagonal cuts about 1 inch apart on both sides of dough to within ½ inch of filling using a sharp knife or kitchen shears. Arrange dough strips over filling, alternating strips diagonally over filling. Press ends under to seal. Brush with egg white. Bake at 425° for 15 minutes or until golden brown. Let stand 5 minutes. Cut crosswise into slices. Yield: 8 servings (serving size: 1 slice).

CALORIES 212; FAT 7.8g (sat 3.4g, mono 2.3g, poly 1g); PROTEIN 11.5g; CARB 24g; FIBER 0.8g; CHOL 95mg; IRON 1.9mg; SODIUM 602mg; CALC 87mg

serve with
Heirloom Tomato and Nectarine Salad

Prep: 6 minutes

2 large heirloom tomatoes, each cut into 8 slices
2 tablespoons fresh lemon juice
4 teaspoons extra-virgin olive oil
2 teaspoons honey
2 ripe nectarines, coarsely chopped
¼ cup vertically sliced sweet onion
1 tablespoon chopped fresh mint

1. Arrange tomato slices on a serving platter. Combine lemon juice, oil, and honey in a medium bowl; add nectarines and onion, tossing well. Spoon nectarine mixture over tomatoes; drizzle with any remaining juices. Sprinkle with fresh mint. Yield: 8 servings (serving size: 2 tomato slices and ¼ cup nectarine mixture).

CALORIES 53; FAT 2.6g (sat 0.3g, mono 1.8g, poly 0.2g); PROTEIN 0.6g; CARB 7.6g; FIBER 0.8g; CHOL 0mg; IRON 0.2mg; SODIUM 2mg; CALC 8mg

Peaches or cubed watermelon sub nicely for the nectarines in the side salad.

Sure to become a family favorite, these hash browns are delicious with eggs, but you can also substitute cheddar cheese.

Sausage Hash Browns with Eggs
Prep: 2 minutes • Cook: 12 minutes

4 ounces reduced-fat pork sausage
2 teaspoons olive oil
1 (20-ounce) package refrigerated diced potatoes with onions
1 cup refrigerated prechopped tricolor bell pepper mix

2 teaspoons chopped fresh thyme
¼ teaspoon salt
¼ teaspoon freshly ground black pepper
4 large eggs
Freshly ground black pepper (optional)

1. Cook sausage in a small nonstick skillet over medium-high heat 4 to 5 minutes or until lightly browned, stirring to crumble. Remove sausage from pan.
2. While sausage cooks, heat a large nonstick skillet over medium heat. Add oil to pan; swirl to coat. Add potatoes and bell pepper mix, spreading into a single layer. Cook 7 minutes or until vegetables are lightly browned, stirring occasionally. Stir in sausage, thyme, salt, and pepper.
3. Crack eggs into potato mixture, spacing an even distance apart near edge of pan. Cover and cook over medium heat 3 minutes or until egg whites are firm and yolks barely move when pan is touched. Sprinkle with additional pepper, if desired. Yield: 4 servings (serving size: 1 egg and ¼ of potato mixture).

CALORIES 300; FAT 12.5g (sat 3.7g, mono 5.8g, poly 1.6g); PROTEIN 14.7g; CARB 32.4g; FIBER 3.9g; CHOL 231mg; IRON 2.2mg; SODIUM 673mg; CALC 32mg

serve with
Lemon Balm–Citrus Salad
Prep: 15 minutes

2 navel oranges
1 red grapefruit
½ cup seedless red grapes, halved

2 tablespoons chopped fresh lemon balm or mint
2 tablespoons agave nectar

1. Peel and section oranges and grapefruit over a bowl; squeeze membranes to extract juice. Add grapes, lemon balm, and agave nectar; toss well. Chill until ready to serve. Yield: 4 servings (serving size: about ½ cup).

CALORIES 101; FAT 0.2g (sat 0g, mono 0g, poly 0.1g); PROTEIN 1.1g; CARB 26.3g; FIBER 2.6g; CHOL 0mg; IRON 0.3mg; SODIUM 2mg; CALC 41mg

Use the shredder blade on your food processor to quickly grate the sweet potatoes.

Sausage and Sweet Potato Hash
Prep: 2 minutes • Cook: 13 minutes

8 ounces reduced-fat pork sausage
1 pound sweet potatoes
2 teaspoons canola oil
¾ cup prechopped onion
1¼ cups sliced cremini mushrooms

1 teaspoon chopped fresh thyme
½ teaspoon freshly ground black pepper
½ cup water
½ cup (2 ounces) preshredded fresh
   Parmesan cheese

1. Cook sausage in a small nonstick skillet over medium-high heat 5 minutes or until browned; stir to crumble. Remove from skillet and keep warm.
2. While sausage cooks, peel sweet potatoes. Place potatoes in a food processor; using coarse-shredding disc, shred to measure 4 cups.
3. Heat a large nonstick skillet over medium-high heat; add oil. Cook sweet potato, onion, and next 3 ingredients in hot oil 7 minutes, stirring frequently and adding ½ cup water, 1 tablespoon at a time, as necessary to prevent sticking. Add sausage; cook, stirring constantly, 1 minute. Remove from heat; sprinkle with cheese. Serve immediately. Yield: 6 servings (serving size: 1 cup).

CALORIES 234; FAT 11.3g (sat 4.6g, mono 1.7g, poly 0.8g); PROTEIN 12.1g; CARB 21.5g; FIBER 3.2g; CHOL 33mg; IRON 1.4mg; SODIUM 451mg; CALC 154mg

use extra ingredients

Pork Sausage

Cremini Mushrooms

Thyme

Sausage Hash Browns with Eggs, page **90**

Balsamic Vegetable Pita Pizzas, page **254**

Crostini with Sun-Dried Tomato-Olive Tapenade, page **195**

portable
lunches

Look for rice paper at Asian markets or in the Asian ingredients section of the supermarket. If you can't find it, substitute two whole-grain tortillas.

Thai Pork Roll-Ups
Prep: 10 minutes • Cook: 4 minutes

Cooking spray
1 (4-ounce) boneless center-cut loin pork chop, cut into 8 thin strips
½ cup shredded napa (Chinese) cabbage
½ cup matchstick-cut carrots

2 tablespoons spicy peanut sauce
4 (8-inch) round sheets rice paper
2 tablespoons fresh cilantro leaves
2 tablespoons lightly salted peanuts

1. Heat a small nonstick skillet over medium-high heat. Coat pan with cooking spray. Add pork; sauté 3 minutes or until lightly browned. Remove from pan.
2. Combine cabbage, carrots, and peanut sauce in a medium bowl.
3. Pour hot water to a depth of 1 inch into a large shallow dish. Place 1 rice paper sheet in hot water; let stand 30 seconds or until softened. Remove rice paper from water; place on work surface. Arrange 2 pieces pork on one-half of rice paper sheet; top with one-fourth of cabbage mixture, 1½ teaspoons cilantro, and 1½ teaspoons peanuts. Fold sides over filling and roll up. Place roll in an airtight container. Repeat procedure with remaining rice paper sheets, pork, cabbage mixture, cilantro, and peanuts, placing rolls in a single layer in container. Cover and store in refrigerator until ready to serve. Yield: 2 servings (serving size: 2 roll-ups).

CALORIES 241; FAT 9.4g (sat 1.9g, mono 4g, poly 2.2g); PROTEIN 16.5g; CARB 22.3g; FIBER 1.7g; CHOL 33mg; IRON 0.7mg; SODIUM 339mg; CALC 30mg

to-go tip

Wrap the rolls individually in damp paper towels to keep them moist.

Make this soup the night before, and pack it in a microwaveable container to heat up at work.

Black Bean Soup

Prep: 5 minutes • Cook: 10 minutes

2 (15-ounce) cans lower-sodium black beans, rinsed and drained
1½ cups organic vegetable broth
½ cup fresh salsa
1 tablespoon fresh lime juice
1 teaspoon chopped chipotle chile, canned in adobo sauce
½ teaspoon ground cumin
2 tablespoons chopped fresh cilantro
⅓ cup queso fresco, crumbled
4 lime wedges

1. Place beans in a medium saucepan. Mash beans slightly with a potato masher. Stir in broth and next 4 ingredients. Bring to a boil; reduce heat, and simmer, uncovered, 5 minutes or until thoroughly heated. Remove from heat; stir in cilantro. Ladle soup into bowls; sprinkle evenly with cheese. Serve with lime wedges. Yield: 4 servings (serving size: 1 cup soup, about 1 tablespoon cheese, and 1 lime wedge).

CALORIES 167; FAT 2.4g (sat 1.1g, mono 0.6g, poly 0.8g); PROTEIN 10.4g; CARB 29.8g; FIBER 7g; CHOL 7mg; IRON 3.3mg; SODIUM 492mg; CALC 143mg

to-go tip Carry the cheese and lime wedges in a small separate container. Top your soup after it's heated.

The longer this salad sits, the longer the flavors have to develop and the rice has to soak up the dressing. The lentils are a refrigerated item located in the produce section of most supermarkets.

Curried Lentil and Rice Salad
Prep: 5 minutes • Cook: 5 minutes

1 (8.5-ounce) package microwaveable precooked basmati rice
1 (17.63-ounce) package dried petite green lentils
½ cup golden raisins
½ cup thinly sliced red onion
¼ cup pine nuts, toasted
2 tablespoons roasted-garlic rice vinegar
1 tablespoon curry powder
⅛ teaspoon salt
2 tablespoons extra-virgin olive oil

1. Microwave rice according to package directions; place in a large bowl. Add lentils and next 3 ingredients; toss gently.
2. Combine vinegar, curry powder, and salt in a small bowl. Slowly add oil, stirring with a whisk.
3. Pour dressing over rice mixture; toss gently. Serve immediately or cover and refrigerate 2 hours. Yield: 6 servings (serving size: 1 cup).

CALORIES 484; FAT 10.6g (sat 1.4g, mono 5.7g, poly 3.2g); PROTEIN 22.2g; CARB 78.9g; FIBER 15.2g; CHOL 0mg; IRON 6.6mg; SODIUM 150mg; CALC 59mg

If you'd like less heat, omit the Sriracha. You'll still get a bit of devilish kick from the mustard and jalapeño peppers.

Deviled Egg Salad with Pickled Jalapeños

Prep: 8 minutes

¼ cup canola mayonnaise
2 tablespoons finely chopped pickled jalapeño pepper rings
1 tablespoon Creole mustard
1 teaspoon Sriracha (hot chile sauce)

¼ teaspoon freshly ground black pepper
4 hard-cooked large eggs, peeled
4 Boston lettuce leaves
2 tablespoons chopped green onion tops

1. Combine first 5 ingredients in a medium bowl.
2. Slice eggs in half lengthwise; remove yolk. Finely chop egg white; press yolk through a sieve using the back of a spoon. Gently fold egg into mayonnaise mixture. Top each lettuce leaf with about ¼ cup egg salad and 1½ teaspoons green onion tops. Yield: 2 servings (serving size: 2 filled lettuce leaves).

CALORIES 259; FAT 19.7g (sat 3.3g, mono 9.1g, poly 4.4g); PROTEIN 12.9g; CARB 3.9g; FIBER 0.7g; CHOL 424mg; IRON 1.6mg; SODIUM 601mg; CALC 60mg

switch it up

SALAD to OPEN-FACED SANDWICH:
Prepare egg salad as above. Top each of 2 slices country bread with a lettuce leaf; top each lettuce leaf with ¼ cup egg salad and 1½ teaspoons green onion tops. Yield: 2 open-faced sandwiches.

CALORIES 250; FAT 18.3g (sat 3.1g, mono 8.2, poly 5.1g); PROTEIN 13g; CARB 3.1g; FIBER 0.9g; CHOL 372mg; IRON 2.2mg; SODIUM 746mg; CALC 73mg

Fresh herbs and lemon brighten canned chickpeas, a perfect protein-packed base for a meatless lunch. This salad is equally delicious chilled or at room temperature.

Feta-Chickpea Salad

Prep: 7 minutes

½ cup chopped sun-dried tomatoes, packed without oil
1½ tablespoons chopped fresh basil
1½ tablespoons chopped fresh parsley
2 (16-ounce) cans chickpeas (garbanzo beans), rinsed and drained
2 ounces feta cheese, crumbled (½ cup)
1 small shallot, minced
2 tablespoons fresh lemon juice
1½ tablespoons extra-virgin olive oil
¼ teaspoon freshly ground black pepper

1. Combine first 6 ingredients in a medium bowl. Combine lemon juice, oil, and pepper in a small bowl; pour over chickpea mixture, tossing to coat. Serve immediately or refrigerate until ready to serve. Yield: 4 servings (serving size: 1 cup).

CALORIES 278; FAT 10g (sat 2.6g, mono 5g, poly 1.4g); PROTEIN 11.2g; CARB 38.6g; FIBER 7.5g; CHOL 10.4mg; IRON 3mg; SODIUM 559mg; CALC 99mg

use extra ingredients

Sun-Dried Tomatoes

Arugula, White Bean, and Sun-Dried Tomato Cream Quesadillas, page **149**

Feta Cheese

Mediterranean Couscous Salad, page **109**

Shallots

Beef Tenderloin with Peppery Fig-Port Sauce, page **310**

Leek and Potato Soup

Prep: 6 minutes • Cook: 26 minutes

2 leeks
1 (24-ounce) package refrigerated country-style mashed potatoes
2 center-cut bacon slices
1 cup fat-free, lower-sodium chicken broth, divided

¼ teaspoon salt
2 cups 2% low-fat milk
¼ teaspoon freshly ground black pepper

1. Remove roots, outer leaves, and tops from leeks, leaving only white part of leeks. Cut white part of leeks in half lengthwise. Cut crosswise into ½-inch-thick slices to measure 1 cup. Rinse with cold water; drain.
2. Microwave potatoes according to package directions.
3. While potatoes heat, cook bacon in a large saucepan over medium heat until crisp. Remove bacon from pan; crumble. Add leek to drippings in pan; sauté 3 minutes, adding 2 tablespoons broth to prevent sticking. Sauté 4 minutes or until tender.
4. Stir in remaining broth, scraping pan to loosen browned bits. Stir in potatoes and salt. Gradually add milk, stirring until smooth. Cook, uncovered, over medium heat 10 minutes or until thoroughly heated, stirring occasionally. Stir in pepper. Ladle soup into 4 bowls; sprinkle with crumbled bacon. Yield: 4 servings (serving size: 1½ cups soup and 1 tablespoon bacon).

CALORIES 242; FAT 6.3g (sat 3.4g, mono 1.7g, poly 0.4g); PROTEIN 9.2g; CARB 37.2g; FIBER 3.6g; CHOL 20.4mg; IRON 1.5mg; SODIUM 554mg; CALC 173mg

serve with

Mixed Greens with Hazelnut-Herb Vinaigrette

Prep: 9 minutes • Cook: 5 minutes

1 (5-ounce) package mixed salad greens
¾ cup grape tomatoes, halved
½ cup drained canned quartered artichoke hearts
¼ cup torn fresh mint leaves (optional)
2 tablespoons white balsamic vinegar

1 tablespoon toasted hazelnut oil
1 teaspoon Dijon mustard
1 teaspoon honey
⅛ teaspoon salt
⅛ teaspoon freshly ground black pepper
2 tablespoons chopped hazelnuts, toasted

1. Combine first 3 ingredients and mint, if desired, in a large bowl. Combine balsamic vinegar and next 5 ingredients in a small bowl, stirring with a whisk.
2. Drizzle greens mixture with dressing, and sprinkle with toasted nuts. Yield: 4 servings (serving size: 1½ cups).

CALORIES 87; FAT 5.7g (sat 0.4g, mono 4.4g, poly 0.8g); PROTEIN 1.9g; CARB 8g; FIBER 1.5g; CHOL 0mg; IRON 0.9mg; SODIUM 182mg; CALC 9mg

For the best results, use just the white portion of leeks; it has the mildest flavor. Avoid slicing too far into the green part, which can make the soup bitter.

This salad gets better as it marinates, so lunch will be twice as good the second day. Purchase romaine hearts and precrumbled cheese to reduce the prep time.

Lentil Salad

Prep: 9 minutes

1 (17.63-ounce) package steamed ready-to-eat lentils
1 (9.5-ounce) jar pimientos del piquillo peppers, drained and chopped
⅓ cup light balsamic and basil vinaigrette
¼ cup sliced green onions
2 tablespoons chopped fresh parsley
¼ teaspoon freshly ground black pepper
1 small garlic clove, minced
4 romaine lettuce leaves
¼ cup (1 ounce) crumbled goat cheese

1. Combine lentils, peppers, and next 5 ingredients in a medium bowl; toss gently to coat. Serve at room temperature or cover and chill. Serve on lettuce-lined plates; sprinkle with cheese. Yield: 4 servings (serving size: 1 lettuce leaf, 1 cup lentil mixture, and 1 tablespoon cheese).

CALORIES 228; FAT 5.6g (sat 1.4g, mono 1.4g, poly 2g); PROTEIN 12.9g; CARB 32g; FIBER 10.6g; CHOL 3mg; IRON 4.6mg; SODIUM 636mg; CALC 48mg

to-go tip To keep the lettuce leaves crisp, wrap them in plastic wrap and package them separately from the lentil salad.

use extra romaine in

Black and Blue Salad, page **286**

Cranberry-Orange Turkey Salad Sandwiches, page **124**

Steak Taco Salad with Black Bean–Corn Relish, page **185**

Perfect for a picnic or lunch at your desk, this flavorful salad needs nothing more than a few crunchy crackers on the side and a piece of fruit.

Mediterranean Couscous Salad

Prep: 4 minutes • Cook: 3 minutes • Other: 5 minutes

- 1 cup uncooked whole-wheat couscous
- 1 (6-ounce) jar quartered marinated artichoke hearts, undrained
- 1 cup coarsely chopped fresh baby spinach
- ¼ cup prechopped green onions
- 3 tablespoons sliced kalamata olives
- ½ teaspoon freshly ground black pepper
- ¾ cup (3 ounces) crumbled feta cheese with basil and sun-dried tomatoes, divided
- 4 lemon wedges

1. Prepare couscous according to package directions, omitting salt and fat.
2. Drain artichokes, reserving marinade. Coarsely chop artichokes. Combine chopped artichokes and reserved marinade in a medium bowl. Add hot couscous, spinach, and next 3 ingredients, tossing gently to slightly wilt spinach. Add ½ cup cheese; toss well. Sprinkle servings with remaining feta cheese, and garnish with lemon wedges. Yield: 4 servings (serving size: about 1¼ cups salad, about 1 tablespoon cheese, and 1 lemon wedge).

CALORIES 228; FAT 7.9g (sat 2.2g, mono 3.7g, poly 0.8g); PROTEIN 9.4g; CARB 35.3g; FIBER 7.1g; CHOL 12.5mg; IRON 1.5mg; SODIUM 390mg; CALC 78mg

use extra spinach in

Turkey-Hummus Pitas, page **132**

Baked Eggs with Spinach and Goat Cheese, page **62**

Go-Getter Green Smoothie, page **41**

While the noodles cook, make the sauce and put the veggies in a bowl. Once the noodles are done, toss everything together, and you're ready to serve lunch. This dish is typically served chilled, but it's just as tasty at room temperature. You can substitute spaghetti or linguine for the soba noodles.

Peanut-Sesame Noodles

Prep: 4 minutes • Cook: 13 minutes

¼ pound dried soba noodles
Peanut-Sesame Sauce
⅓ cup julienne-cut pickling cucumber

¼ cup matchstick-cut carrots
2 tablespoons presliced green onions
1 teaspoon sesame seeds (optional)

1. Cook soba noodles according to package directions.
2. While noodles cook, prepare Peanut-Sesame Sauce.
3. Drain noodles, and rinse under cold, running water. Drain. Combine noodles, cucumber, carrots, and green onions in a medium bowl. Drizzle with Peanut-Sesame Sauce; toss gently to coat. Serve at room temperature, or cover and chill. Garnish with sesame seeds, if desired. Yield: 2 servings (serving size: 1¼ cups).

CALORIES 306; FAT 9.6g (sat 1.5g, mono 4.2g, poly 3.5g); PROTEIN 8.8g; CARB 48.3g; FIBER 4.1g; CHOL 0mg; IRON 1.6mg; SODIUM 339mg; CALC 27mg

Peanut-Sesame Sauce

Prep: 3 minutes

1 tablespoon creamy peanut butter
1 tablespoon lower-sodium soy sauce
2 teaspoons dark sesame oil

2 teaspoons seasoned rice vinegar
⅛ teaspoon crushed red pepper
½ small garlic clove, minced

1. Combine all ingredients in a small bowl, stirring with a whisk until smooth. Yield: 2 servings (serving size: about 1½ tablespoons).

CALORIES 98; FAT 8.6g (sat 1.5g, mono 3.7g, poly 3g); PROTEIN 2.6g; CARB 3.4g; FIBER 0.5g; CHOL 0mg; IRON 0.2mg; SODIUM 331mg; CALC 6mg

Here's the perfect meatless main-dish salad; it's simple, quick, and nutritious, thanks to a vacuum-packed medley of beans. Add chopped cooked chicken for a heartier salad, if you like.

Six Bean Salad
Prep: 7 minutes

2 tablespoons extra-virgin olive oil
2 tablespoons fresh lemon juice
¼ teaspoon salt
¼ teaspoon freshly ground black pepper
1 (12.3-ounce) package six bean medley
½ cup refrigerated prechopped celery, onion, and bell pepper mix

2 tablespoons finely chopped fresh parsley
2 teaspoons finely chopped fresh rosemary
3 tablespoons crumbled goat cheese with herbs

1. Combine first 4 ingredients in a medium bowl, stirring with a whisk. Add bean medley and next 3 ingredients, tossing to coat. Top servings evenly with cheese. Yield: 3 servings (serving size: ¾ cup salad and 1 tablespoon cheese).

CALORIES 275; FAT 14.3g (sat 4g, mono 8.1g, poly 1.3g); PROTEIN 10.5g; CARB 32.4g; FIBER 6.4g; CHOL 7mg; IRON 2.5mg; SODIUM 388mg; CALC 45mg

use extra fresh parsley in

Mediterranean Hash Brown Cakes with Olive-Tomato Topping, page **78**

Lemon-Artichoke Spread with Spicy Pita Crisps, page **235**

Grilled Spiced Lamb Chops with Chickpea Relish, page **316**

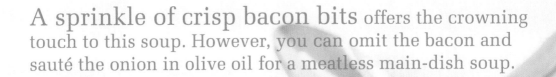

A sprinkle of crisp bacon bits offers the crowning touch to this soup. However, you can omit the bacon and sauté the onion in olive oil for a meatless main-dish soup.

White Bean–Tomato Soup

Prep: 2 minutes • Cook: 13 minutes

4 lower-sodium bacon slices, each cut into 4 pieces
1 cup chopped onion
2 cups lower-sodium vegetable juice
¼ teaspoon freshly ground black pepper

1 (14-ounce) can diced tomatoes with basil, garlic, and oregano, undrained
2 (15-ounce) cans no-salt-added cannellini beans, rinsed, drained, and divided

1. Cook bacon in a large saucepan over medium heat until crisp. Remove bacon from pan, reserving 1 tablespoon drippings in pan; crumble bacon and set aside. Add onion to drippings in pan; sauté 3 minutes or until lightly browned. Add vegetable juice, pepper, tomatoes, and 1 can of beans. Bring to a simmer; cook 5 minutes or until thoroughly heated, stirring occasionally.
2. Place half of tomato mixture in a blender. Remove center piece of blender lid (to allow steam to escape); secure blender lid on blender. Place a clean towel over opening in blender lid (to avoid splatters). Blend until smooth; pour into a bowl. Repeat procedure with remaining half of tomato mixture. Stir remaining can of beans into puréed soup. Ladle soup into bowls; top with crumbled bacon. Yield: 4 servings (serving size: 1½ cups soup and 2 teaspoons bacon).

CALORIES 226; FAT 4.1g (sat 1.5g, mono 1.4g, poly 0.8g); PROTEIN 11.6g; CARB 35.3g; FIBER 8g; CHOL 5mg; IRON 3.2mg; SODIUM 610mg; CALC 79mg

serve with
Goat Cheese Toast

Prep: 5 minutes • Cook: 1 minute

¼ cup (2 ounces) goat cheese
2 teaspoons butter, softened
4 (1-ounce) slices diagonally cut French bread baguette

¼ teaspoon freshly ground black pepper
2 tablespoons chopped fresh basil

1. Preheat broiler.
2. Combine cheese and butter in a small bowl, stirring until smooth. Spread cheese mixture evenly over bread slices. Place bread slices on a baking sheet.
3. Broil 1 minute or just until bubbly. Sprinkle toast with pepper and basil. Serve immediately. Yield: 4 servings (serving size: 1 slice).

CALORIES 138; FAT 5.4g (sat 3.4g, mono 1.3g, poly 0.4g); PROTEIN 6g; CARB 16.3g; FIBER 0.7g; CHOL 11.6mg; IRON 1.4mg; SODIUM 215mg; CALC 36mg

Alongside this salad, fill your lunchbox
with rice crackers, fresh fruit, and sparkling water for a
truly enjoyable meal. For the best flavor, pack the radishes
separately and serve them on the side.

Asian Fresh Tuna Salad
Prep: 5 minutes • Cook: 6 minutes

1 pound tuna steak (1 inch thick)
Cooking spray
¼ cup light sesame-ginger dressing
1 tablespoon fresh lime juice
2 teaspoons wasabi paste
¼ teaspoon freshly ground black pepper
⅛ teaspoon salt

¾ cup refrigerated shelled edamame
   (green soybeans)
⅓ cup finely chopped red onion
3 radishes, sliced
12 rice crackers
3 lime wedges

1. Heat a medium well-seasoned cast-iron skillet over medium-high heat until very hot. Coat tuna with cooking spray. Add tuna to pan. Cook 2 minutes on each side or to desired degree of doneness.
2. While tuna cooks, combine dressing, lime juice, and wasabi paste in a large bowl, stirring with a whisk. Break tuna into chunks in a bowl; sprinkle with pepper and salt.
3. Add tuna, edamame, and onion to dressing in bowl; toss gently to coat. Serve immediately, or cover and chill. Serve with radishes, rice crackers, and lime wedges. Yield: 3 servings (serving size: 1⅓ cups salad, 1 sliced radish, 4 rice crackers, and 1 lime wedge).

CALORIES 250; FAT 3.6g (sat 0.4g, mono 1g, poly 1.1g); PROTEIN 30.2g; CARB 20.7g; FIBER 3.4g; CHOL 51mg; IRON 1.5mg; SODIUM 394mg; CALC 43mg

switch it up

SALAD to SANDWICH: Spoon the tuna mixture into a lettuce-lined pita half just before serving to prevent soggy bread.

CALORIES 388; FAT 11g (sat 2.1g, mono 3.2, poly 3.2g); PROTEIN 41.7g; CARB 27g; FIBER 3.9g; CHOL 57.5mg; IRON 3.7mg; SODIUM 603mg; CALC 60mg

Here, *banh mi,* the popular Vietnamese street food, becomes a flavor-packed lunch.

Barbecue Chicken Banh Mi
Prep: 5 minutes • Cook: 5 minutes

½ cup rice vinegar
1 tablespoon sugar
⅛ teaspoon kosher salt
1½ cups thinly sliced English cucumber (about 1 medium)
1 (8.5-ounce) soft French bread baguette

2 cups shredded skinless, boneless rotisserie chicken
⅓ cup Asian barbecue sauce
¼ cup jalapeño pepper slices (about 2 peppers)
16 fresh cilantro leaves

1. Preheat oven to 400°.
2. Combine first 3 ingredients in a medium bowl, stirring to dissolve. Add cucumber; toss gently.
3. Place baguette directly on oven rack. Bake at 400° for 5 minutes or until crusty. Cut 1 inch off each end of baguette, reserving ends for another use. Cut baguette in half lengthwise. Hollow out top and bottom halves of bread, leaving a ½-inch-thick shell; reserve torn bread for another use. Brush top half of bread with 2 tablespoons vinegar mixture. Top bottom half of bread with cucumber slices.
4. Combine chicken and barbecue sauce; spread chicken mixture over cucumber slices on bottom half of bread. Top with jalapeño slices, cilantro leaves, and top half of bread. Cut sandwich crosswise into 4 pieces. Yield: 4 servings (serving size: 1 piece).

CALORIES 341; FAT 5.9g (sat 1.5g, mono 2.5g, poly 0.9g); PROTEIN 24.9g; CARB 48.1g; FIBER 1.4g; CHOL 68mg; IRON 3.1mg; SODIUM 870mg; CALC 38mg

Chicken cooked at home is a healthier, lower-sodium option over rotisserie chicken.
This soup puts leftover cooked chicken to good use.

Chicken Tortilla Soup
Prep: 3 minutes • Cook: 10 minutes

1 teaspoon olive oil
½ cup chopped onion
1 garlic clove, minced
1 cup fat-free, lower-sodium chicken broth
1 cup water

2 cups shredded cooked chicken
2 tablespoons fresh lime juice
¼ teaspoon chipotle chile powder
1 (10-ounce) can diced tomatoes and green chiles, undrained
¼ cup tortilla strips

1. Heat oil in medium saucepan over medium-high heat. Add onion and garlic; sauté 3 minutes or until tender. Add broth and next 5 ingredients. Bring to a boil; reduce heat, and simmer, uncovered, 5 minutes. Ladle soup into 3 bowls, and sprinkle with tortilla strips. Yield: 3 servings (serving size: about 1⅓ cups soup and about 1 tablespoon tortilla strips).

CALORIES 280; FAT 8.4g (sat 1.4g, mono 3.6g, poly 2.3g); PROTEIN 31.4g; CARB 17.7g; FIBER 2.3g; CHOL 79.3mg; IRON 1.5mg; SODIUM 665mg; CALC 44mg

to-go tip Pack the soup in an airtight container. Keep the tortilla strips in a separate container, and top your soup after it's heated.

This Mediterranean-inspired salad showcases fresh fennel, olives, and protein-packed chickpeas tossed with a simple vinaigrette of lemon juice and olive oil.

Chickpea, Fennel, and Olive Chicken Salad

Prep: 15 minutes

1 tablespoon lemon juice
1 tablespoon olive oil
½ teaspoon freshly ground black pepper
¼ teaspoon salt
2¼ cups finely chopped fennel bulb (1 medium)
1½ cups chopped rotisserie chicken breast

½ cup chopped radishes (6 radishes)
⅓ cup chopped pitted kalamata olives
¼ cup chopped fresh parsley
2 navel oranges, peeled and chopped
1 (16-ounce) can chickpeas (garbanzo beans), rinsed and drained

1. Combine first 4 ingredients in a medium bowl, stirring with a whisk. Add fennel and remaining ingredients; toss well. Yield: 5 servings (serving size: about 1⅓ cups).

CALORIES 194; FAT 7.6g (sat 1g, mono 4.6g, poly 0.8g); PROTEIN 15.2g; CARB 18g; FIBER 4.7g; CHOL 35mg; IRON 1.5mg; SODIUM 576mg; CALC 69mg

use extra ingredients

Radishes

Asian Fresh Tuna Salad, page **116**

Kalamata Olives

Goat Cheese-Stuffed Piquillo Peppers, page **232**

Navel Oranges

Ladyfingers with Mascarpone Cream and Fresh Orange Sauce, page **355**

Leftover turkey gets a makeover with grated orange rind, cranberries, almonds, and ginger.

Cranberry-Orange Turkey Salad Sandwiches

Prep: 7 minutes • Cook: 5 minutes

½ cup plain fat-free Greek yogurt
1 teaspoon grated orange rind
1 teaspoon grated peeled fresh ginger
½ teaspoon salt
2 cups chopped cooked turkey breast

⅓ cup dried cranberries
¼ cup sliced almonds, toasted
8 (1-ounce) slices 100% whole-wheat bread
4 romaine lettuce leaves

1. Combine first 4 ingredients in a medium bowl. Add turkey, cranberries, and almonds, tossing to coat.

2. Top each of 4 bread slices with 1 lettuce leaf and ½ cup turkey salad. Cover with remaining bread slices. Cut sandwiches in half diagonally. Yield: 4 servings (serving size: 1 sandwich).

CALORIES 320; FAT 5.4g (sat 0.8g, mono 2.8g, poly 1.2g); PROTEIN 32.8g; CARB 35.4g; FIBER 5.7g; CHOL 59mg; IRON 3mg; SODIUM 608mg; CALC 114mg

switch it up

SANDWICH TO SALAD: Prepare the turkey salad through step 1. Increase romaine lettuce leaves to 8, and arrange 2 lettuce leaves on each of four plates. Top each plate with ½ cup turkey salad. Yield: 4 salads.

CALORIES 331; FAT 5.5g (sat 0.4g, mono 2.4g, poly 1.8g); PROTEIN 33.2g; CARB 37.7g; FIBER 5.5g; CHOL 64.1mg; IRON 3mg; SODIUM 619mg; CALC 169mg

A bit of flour mixed with broth replaces cream
to give this comforting soup its luscious texture.

Creamy Chicken Noodle Soup
Prep: 4 minutes • Cook: 24 minutes

1 tablespoon olive oil
½ cup chopped carrot
1 (8-ounce) container refrigerated prechopped celery, onion, and bell pepper mix
2 tablespoons all-purpose flour
1 (32-ounce) carton fat-free, lower-sodium chicken broth, divided

1 cup water
2 cups pulled skinless, boneless rotisserie chicken breast
2 cups uncooked whole-grain extra-wide noodles
½ teaspoon freshly ground black pepper
Chopped fresh parsley (optional)

1. Heat oil in a Dutch oven over medium-high heat. Add carrot and celery mix; cook 8 minutes, stirring frequently, until tender.
2. While vegetables cook, combine flour and 3 tablespoons broth in a small bowl, stirring with a whisk until smooth.
3. Add remaining broth, water, and chicken to vegetables. Bring to a boil; add noodles, and boil 7 minutes or until noodles are tender.
4. Stir flour mixture with a whisk until smooth; add to soup. Cook, stirring constantly, 3 minutes or until soup is slightly thickened. Stir in pepper. Garnish with chopped fresh parsley, if desired. Yield: 6 servings (serving size: 1 cup).

CALORIES 163; FAT 4.2g (sat 0.7g, mono 2.4g, poly 0.6g); PROTEIN 18.2g; CARB 14.5g; FIBER 2.3g; CHOL 42mg; IRON 0.9mg; SODIUM 619mg; CALC 25mg

Serve this salad as a sandwich or on top of mixed greens for a great lunch.

Lemon-Dill Chicken Salad
Prep: 15 minutes

2 lemons
½ cup canola mayonnaise
1 tablespoon chopped fresh dill or fresh tarragon
¼ teaspoon salt

¼ teaspoon freshly ground black pepper
3 cups finely chopped cooked chicken breast
½ cup chopped celery
½ cup finely chopped onion
2 tablespoons slivered almonds, toasted

1. Grate 2 teaspoons rind and squeeze 3 tablespoons juice from lemons. Combine rind, juice, mayonnaise, and next 3 ingredients in a large bowl. Add chicken and remaining ingredients; toss gently. Cover and chill until ready to serve. Yield: 7 servings (serving size: ½ cup).

CALORIES 232; FAT 15.7g (sat 1.8g, mono 8.2g, poly 4.1g); PROTEIN 19.2g; CARB 2.4g; FIBER 0.6g; CHOL 57mg; IRON 0.8mg; SODIUM 249mg; CALC 21mg

switch
it up

SALAD to SANDWICH: Prepare the chicken salad as instructed. Split one whole-wheat sandwich thin. Top the bottom half of the sandwich thin with ½ cup of chicken salad (cover and chill remaining chicken salad for later use). Cover with top of sandwich thin. Yield: 1 sandwich.

CALORIES 332; FAT 16.7g (sat 1.3g, mono 9.3g, poly 4.7g); PROTEIN 24.2g; CARB 23.3g; FIBER 5.6g; CHOL 56.7mg; IRON 1.8mg; SODIUM 468mg; CALC 61mg

Smoked turkey, sweet dried apricots, and meaty pistachios provide the backbone to this light yet filling salad. Fresh thyme, citrus, and naturally sweet rice vinegar marry beautifully as a light vinaigrette to add subtle flavor without overpowering the star ingredients.

Turkey, Apricot, and Pistachio Salad

Prep: 9 minutes

Lemon-Thyme Vinaigrette
- 1 (5-ounce) package gourmet salad greens (7 cups)
- 1½ cups coarsely chopped deli smoked turkey breast (8 ounces)
- ⅓ cup chopped dried apricots
- ¼ cup chopped pistachios

1. Prepare Lemon-Thyme Vinaigrette.
2. Place greens and remaining 3 ingredients in a large bowl; drizzle with vinaigrette, and toss well. Yield: 4 servings (serving size: 2 cups).

CALORIES 242; FAT 13.4g (sat 1.9g, mono 6.9g, poly 3.9g); PROTEIN 19.1g; CARB 12.7g; FIBER 2.5g; CHOL 43mg; IRON 2mg; SODIUM 595mg; CALC 30mg

Lemon-Thyme Vinaigrette

Prep: 4 minutes

- 3 tablespoons rice vinegar
- 2 tablespoons canola oil
- 1 tablespoon fresh lemon juice
- 1 teaspoon honey
- ½ teaspoon Dijon mustard
- ½ teaspoon chopped fresh thyme
- ¼ teaspoon freshly ground black pepper

1. Combine all ingredients, stirring with a whisk. Yield: 4 servings (serving size: 4 teaspoons).

CALORIES 70; FAT 7g (sat 0.5g, mono 4.4g, poly 2g); PROTEIN 0.1g; CARB 2.1g; FIBER 0.1g; CHOL 0mg; IRON 0.1mg; SODIUM 16mg; CALC 2mg

Extra hummus can become an afternoon snack with whole-wheat crackers, carrot sticks, or other fresh vegetables. Store the hummus in the refrigerator in an airtight container for up to a week.

Turkey-Hummus Pitas
Prep: 12 minutes

½ cup Herbed Hummus
2 (6-inch) whole-wheat pitas, cut in half
8 ounces thinly sliced deli, lower-sodium turkey breast
4 (¼-inch-thick) slices tomato, halved
¼ cup crumbled feta cheese
1 cup bagged baby spinach leaves (optional)

1. Prepare Herbed Hummus.
2. Spread 2 tablespoons Herbed Hummus in each pita half. Fill each pita with 2 ounces turkey, 1 tomato slice, 1 tablespoona feta cheese, and ¼ cup spinach, if desired. Yield: 4 servings (serving size: 1 pita half).

CALORIES 220; FAT 6.8g (sat 2.1g, mono 3g, poly 1.1g); PROTEIN 17.7g; CARB 21.9g; FIBER 3.4g; CHOL 29mg; IRON 1.8mg; SODIUM 668mg; CALC 64mg

Herbed Hummus
Prep: 7 minutes

1 garlic clove, peeled
1 (16-ounce) can chickpeas (garbanzo beans), rinsed and drained
2 tablespoons olive oil
2 tablespoons fresh lemon juice
2 tablespoons water
2 tablespoons fresh flat-leaf parsley leaves
2 teaspoons tahini (roasted sesame seed paste)
¼ teaspoon smoked paprika

1. Drop garlic through food chute with food processor on; process until minced. Add chickpeas and remaining ingredients; process until smooth, scraping sides of bowl once. Yield: 10 servings (serving size: 2 tablespoons).

CALORIES 65; FAT 3.6g (sat 0.5g, mono 2.3g, poly 0.7g); PROTEIN 1.6g; CARB 7.1g; FIBER 1.4g; CHOL 0mg; IRON 0.5mg; SODIUM 86mg; CALC 12mg

Sweet fig preserves, salty bacon, and peppery arugula are a delicious trio that gives this salad plenty of flavor.

Arugula-Orange Salad with Fig-Bacon Dressing

Prep: 13 minutes • Cook: 30 seconds

Fig-Bacon Dressing
1 (5-ounce) package prewashed arugula
1 (15-ounce) can cannellini beans, rinsed and drained

1 cup navel orange slices, peeled and quartered (2 oranges)
⅓ cup (1.3 ounces) crumbled goat cheese
½ teaspoon freshly ground black pepper

1. Prepare Fig-Bacon Dressing.
2. Place Fig-Bacon Dressing, arugula, beans, and orange in a large bowl; toss well.
3. Divide salad evenly among 4 salad plates. Sprinkle salads evenly with goat cheese and pepper. Yield: 4 servings (serving size: 2 cups salad, about 4 teaspoons cheese, and dash of pepper).

CALORIES 238; FAT 8.9g (sat 3.9g, mono 3.8g, poly 0.7g); PROTEIN 10.9g; CARB 29.8g; FIBER 5.5g; CHOL 12.3mg; IRON 2.1mg; SODIUM 318mg; CALC 152mg

Fig-Bacon Dressing

Prep: 3 minutes • Cook: 30 seconds

3 tablespoons fig preserves
¼ cup cider vinegar
1 tablespoon olive oil

½ teaspoon grated orange rind
2 center-cut bacon slices, cooked and crumbled

1. Spoon fig preserves into a large microwave-safe bowl. Cover and microwave at HIGH 30 seconds or until preserves melt. Add vinegar, olive oil, rind, and bacon; stir with a whisk until blended. Yield: 4 servings (serving size: 2 tablespoons).

CALORIES 77; FAT 4g (sat 0.7g, mono 2.5g, poly 0.4g); PROTEIN 1g; CARB 8.5g; FIBER 0g; CHOL 2.5mg; IRON 0.1mg; SODIUM 44mg; CALC 2mg

to-go tip

Pack the orange slices and the Fig-Bacon Dressing separately from the rest of the salad; the acid in the oranges and the dressing will wilt the arugula.

The best time to make this salad is when there's a leftover end of French bread hanging around on the counter. Once the bread is dry and hard, it's the perfect addition to this salad.

Arugula Salad with Beets and Pancetta Crisps

Prep: 5 minutes • Cook: 5 minutes

8 very thin slices pancetta (1½ ounces)
4 cups arugula
1½ cups (1-inch) cubes day-old French bread, toasted
¼ cup chopped pitted dates
3 tablespoons prechopped green onions
3 tablespoons light balsamic vinaigrette
1 (8-ounce) package steamed peeled ready-to-eat baby red beets, quartered
½ cup (4 ounces) crumbled goat cheese

1. Cook pancetta in a large nonstick skillet over medium heat 5 minutes or until crisp, turning occasionally. Remove pancetta from skillet; drain on paper towels.
2. Combine arugula and next 3 ingredients in a large bowl. Drizzle with vinaigrette; toss gently to coat. Divide greens mixture evenly among 4 bowls. Top salads evenly with beets and pancetta; sprinkle evenly with cheese. Yield: 4 servings (serving size: 1¼ cups greens mixture, about 7 beet wedges, 1 pancetta slice, and about 1 ounce cheese).

CALORIES 220; FAT 10g (sat 5.4g, mono 2.8g, poly 0.8g); PROTEIN 10.8g; CARB 24.4g; FIBER 2.7g; CHOL 20.6mg; IRON 2.2mg; SODIUM 567mg; CALC 96mg

to-go tip

If you're packing this salad to travel, store the bread, dressing, pancetta, and cheese separately to preserve the crisp texture of the arugula and pancetta and the color of the cheese. Toss the salad in your container just before you plan to have lunch.

A creamy, healthful avocado spread replaces the traditional mayonnaise in this sandwich loaded with bacon, gourmet greens, and juicy, ripe tomatoes.

Avocado BLT

Prep: 9 minutes • Cook: 5 minutes

½ cup Creamy Avocado Spread
8 (1-ounce) slices thin-sliced 15-grain bread, toasted

2 cups gourmet salad greens
4 (¼-inch-thick) slices tomato
8 center-cut bacon slices, cooked

1. Spread 2 tablespoons Creamy Avocado Spread over 4 bread slices. Top each of the 4 bread slices with ½ cup greens, 1 tomato slice, and 2 bacon slices. Top with remaining bread slices. Yield: 4 servings (serving size: 1 sandwich).

CALORIES 272; FAT 12.7g (sat 2.7g, mono 6.7g, poly 1.9g); PROTEIN 12.1g; CARB 31.5g; FIBER 8.5g; CHOL 15mg; IRON 1.7mg; SODIUM 680mg; CALC 45mg

Creamy Avocado Spread

Prep: 4 minutes

1 peeled ripe avocado, coarsely mashed
1 tablespoon fresh lemon juice
1 garlic clove, minced

¼ teaspoon salt
⅛ teaspoon ground red pepper

1. Combine all ingredients in a small bowl, stirring with a fork until blended. Yield: 4 servings (serving size: 2 tablespoons).

CALORIES 59; FAT 5.3g (sat 0.7g, mono 3.3g, poly 0.6g); PROTEIN 0.7g; CARB 3.5g; FIBER 2.4g; CHOL 0mg; IRON 0.2mg; SODIUM 150mg; CALC 6mg

During the summer months, use fresh lima beans and corn for a real treat. Add additional water or broth if the consistency becomes too thick.

Brunswick Stew
Prep: 3 minutes • Cook: 12 minutes

1 cup pulled smoked pork
1 cup pulled skinless smoked chicken
1 cup fat-free, lower-sodium chicken broth
1 (14.5-ounce) can fire-roasted diced tomatoes, undrained

½ cup frozen baby lima beans
½ cup frozen whole-kernel corn
¼ cup Carolina sweet barbecue sauce
¼ teaspoon freshly ground black pepper

1. Combine all ingredients in a Dutch oven. Bring to boil. Cover, reduce heat, and simmer 12 minutes or until vegetables are tender. Yield: 4 servings (serving size: 1¼ cups).

CALORIES 293; FAT 11.4g (sat 4.1g, mono 4.6g, poly 1.7g); PROTEIN 28.1g; CARB 18.3g; FIBER 2.4g; CHOL 76mg; IRON 2.4mg; SODIUM 569mg; CALC 42mg

Substitute dried Calimyrna figs when fresh figs are no longer in season.

Prosciutto-Fig Salad
Prep: 10 minutes

¼ cup sherry vinegar
2 tablespoons olive oil
¼ teaspoon freshly ground black pepper
2 (6-ounce) packages fresh baby spinach

¼ cup chopped walnuts, toasted
8 fresh figs, quartered
3 ounces thinly sliced prosciutto, torn
¼ cup (1 ounce) crumbled Gorgonzola cheese

1. Combine first 3 ingredients in a large bowl, stirring with a whisk. Add spinach and next 3 ingredients; toss gently to coat. Divide spinach mixture evenly among 4 bowls. Sprinkle each serving with cheese. Yield: 4 servings (serving size: about 2½ cups spinach mixture and 1 tablespoon cheese).

CALORIES 292; FAT 16.1g (sat 3.7g, mono 7.2g, poly 4.6g); PROTEIN 11.5g; CARB 30.3g; FIBER 7.7g; CHOL 18mg; IRON 3.6mg; SODIUM 611mg; CALC 140mg

use extra ingredients

Baby Spinach

Cast-Iron Breakfast Pizza, page **61**

Figs

Yogurt with Orange-Honey Figs, page **52**

Prosciutto

Frittata with Mascarpone and Prosciutto, page **87**

at home
lunches

This tropical chicken salad derives its flavor from mango chutney, fresh cilantro, and lime juice. Greek yogurt, which imparts a rich creaminess, replaces the usual mayonnaise and sour cream. Try Mango Chicken Salad as a filling for sandwiches; see our suggestion below.

Mango Chicken Salad

Prep: 8 minutes

½ cup plain 2% reduced-fat Greek yogurt
¼ cup chopped red onion
¼ cup mango chutney
3 tablespoons chopped fresh cilantro
1 tablespoon fresh lime juice

2 cups shredded rotisserie chicken breast
1 (6.5-ounce) package sweet butter-blend salad greens
¼ cup chopped dry-roasted cashews, salted

1. Combine first 5 ingredients in a medium bowl. Add chicken, and toss well.
2. Place 1¼ cups salad greens on each of 4 salad plates. Top each serving with about ½ cup chicken mixture and 1 tablespoon chopped cashews. Yield: 4 servings (serving size: 1 salad).

CALORIES 244; FAT 7g (sat 1.8g, mono 3.3g, poly 1g); PROTEIN 25.1g; CARB 21.2g; FIBER 1.1g; CHOL 65mg; IRON 0.9mg; SODIUM 430mg; CALC 35mg

SALAD to SANDWICH: Prepare Mango Chicken Salad through step 1 above. Place about ½ cup chicken mixture on bottom half of each of 4 (1.5-ounce) whole-grain white sandwich thins. Top each with 1 tablespoon chopped dry-roasted cashews and ¾ cup salad greens. Cover with sandwich thin tops. Yield: 4 servings (serving size: 1 sandwich).

CALORIES 343; FAT 8g (sat 2g, mono 3.7g, poly 1.2g); PROTEIN 29g; CARB 42.9g; FIBER 6.1g; CHOL 65mg; IRON 2mg; SODIUM 657mg; CALC 83mg

Curried Paneer and Spinach–Stuffed Potatoes

Prep: 2 minutes • Cook: 12 minutes

2 microwave-ready baking potatoes
Cooking spray
1 teaspoon olive oil
½ cup prechopped onion
1 cup chopped tomato
1 teaspoon red curry powder
1 teaspoon ground fresh ginger paste
¼ teaspoon salt
1 cup chopped bagged baby spinach leaves
1 cup (4 ounces) diced paneer or queso blanco
¼ teaspoon garam masala
1 tablespoon chopped fresh cilantro (optional)

1. Microwave potatoes according to package directions for cooking 2 potatoes at one time.
2. While potatoes cook, heat a large nonstick skillet over medium-high heat. Coat pan with cooking spray. Add oil to pan; swirl to coat. Add onion; sauté onion in hot oil 2 minutes. Add tomato, red curry powder, ginger, and salt; cook 2 minutes, stirring occasionally. Remove from heat. Add spinach; stirring until spinach wilts. Stir in cheese and garam masala.
3. Unwrap potatoes. Cut a slit down top of each potato; push ends toward center to open potatoes. Spoon about ¾ cup tomato mixture into center of each potato. Garnish with cilantro, if desired. Yield: 2 servings (serving size: 1 stuffed potato).

CALORIES 293; FAT 7.9g (sat 3.4g, mono 3.4g, poly 0.6g); PROTEIN 11.5g; CARB 46.1g; FIBER 5g; CHOL 18mg; IRON 1.8mg; SODIUM 399mg; CALC 202mg

use extra ingredients

Tomato	Baby Spinach	Cilantro

Tomato-Avocado Dip, page **215**	Cast-Iron Breakfast Pizza, page **61**	Shrimp Tikka Masala, page **301**

Queso blanco, a Mexican cheese made almost exactly the same way as paneer, has a very similar flavor. It is available in most large supermarkets.

A combo of tangy goat cheese and reduced-fat cream cheese adds a creamy texture to these lightened vegetarian quesadillas. They also get a considerable amount of flavor from the sun-dried tomatoes and peppery arugula.

Arugula, White Bean, and Sun-Dried Tomato Cream Quesadillas

Prep: 6 minutes • Cook: 4 minutes

2 ounces ⅓-less-fat cream cheese, softened
¼ cup chopped drained oil-packed sun-dried tomato halves
2 (8-inch) whole-wheat tortillas
½ cup rinsed and drained cannellini beans
¼ cup crumbled goat cheese
2 cups baby arugula
Cooking spray

1. Combine cream cheese and sun-dried tomato in a small bowl; spread evenly over tortillas. Mash beans with a fork. Spread beans evenly over cream cheese mixture. Top evenly with goat cheese and arugula. Fold tortillas in half.
2. Heat a large skillet over medium heat. Coat pan with cooking spray. Place quesadillas in pan; cook 2 to 3 minutes on each side or until golden and cheese melts. Cut each quesadilla into 3 wedges. Serve immediately. Yield: 2 servings (serving size: 3 wedges).

CALORIES 299; FAT 12.4g (sat 6.5g, mono 4.1g, poly 0.9g); PROTEIN 13.1g; CARB 34.5g; FIBER 4.9g; CHOL 27mg; IRON 2.4mg; SODIUM 536mg; CALC 157mg

use extra arugula in

Frittata with Mascarpone and Prosciutto, page **87**

Horseradish-Garlic Flank Steak and Lemony Arugula Salad, page **253**

Arugula Salad with Beets and Pancetta Crisps, page **137**

If you prefer, remove the skins from the peaches after they're grilled.

Grilled Peach and Granola Salad
Prep: 6 minutes • Cook: 6 minutes

4 large peaches, halved and pitted
Cooking spray
8 cups mixed salad greens
⅓ cup light raspberry vinaigrette
1 cup fresh raspberries

1 cup blueberries
½ cup sliced almonds, toasted
¾ cup low-fat granola
1 cup (4 ounces) crumbled goat cheese

1. Preheat grill to medium-high heat.
2. Coat peach halves with cooking spray. Place peaches, cut sides down, on grill rack coated with cooking spray. Grill 3 minutes on each side or until grill marks appear on peach halves. Cut each peach half into 4 wedges.
3. Place salad greens in a large bowl; drizzle with vinaigrette, tossing to coat. Add berries, almonds, and granola; toss gently. Place 2½ cups salad mixture on each of 4 salad plates. Sprinkle each serving with 2 tablespoons cheese; top each with 8 peach wedges. Yield: 4 servings (serving size: 1 salad).

CALORIES 356; FAT 13.5g (sat 4.6g, mono 5.2g, poly 2.2g); PROTEIN 13.4g; CARB 52.3g; FIBER 10.7g; CHOL 13mg; IRON 3.3mg; SODIUM 420mg; CALC 97mg

use extra ingredients

Peaches

White Cranberry-Peach
Spritzers, page **250**

Raspberries

Balsamic Peach Melba Parfaits
with Spiked Mascarpone,
page **326**

Goat Cheese

Goat Cheese-Stuffed Piquillo
Peppers, page **232**

Pesto Grilled Cheese Panini

Prep: 2 minutes • Cook: 11 minutes

1 red bell pepper, cut into 4 wedges
Olive oil-flavored cooking spray
¼ cup Basil-Walnut Pesto
8 (1-ounce) slices sourdough bread
4 (0.7-ounce) slices reduced-fat provolone
  cheese

½ cup (2 ounces) shredded part-skim
  mozzarella cheese
Cooking spray

1. Preheat panini grill.
2. Coat both sides of bell pepper wedges with cooking spray. Place on panini grill; cook 8 minutes or until tender and lightly charred.
3. While bell pepper cooks, prepare Basil-Walnut Pesto. Spread 1½ teaspoons pesto on each bread slice. Top each of 4 bread slices with 1 provolone slice, 2 tablespoons mozzarella, and 1 bell pepper wedge; top with remaining bread slices. Coat both sides of sandwiches with cooking spray.
4. Place sandwiches on panini grill. Grill 3 minutes or until bread is browned and cheese melts. Cut panini in half before serving, if desired. Yield: 4 servings (serving size: 1 panino).

CALORIES 293; FAT 15.2g (sat 6.1g, mono 5.2g, poly 2.8g); PROTEIN 12.2g; CARB 24.5g; FIBER 1.9g; CHOL 56mg; IRON 0.6mg; SODIUM 560mg; CALC 317mg

Basil-Walnut Pesto

Prep: 4 minutes

2 tablespoons coarsely chopped walnuts
1 garlic clove, peeled
2 cups fresh basil leaves

¼ cup grated fresh pecorino Romano cheese
⅛ teaspoon salt
2 tablespoons extra-virgin olive oil

1. Drop nuts and garlic through food chute with food processor on; process until minced. Add basil, cheese, and salt; process until finely minced. With processor on, slowly pour oil through food chute; process until blended. Yield: 8 servings (serving size: 1 tablespoon).

CALORIES 59; FAT 5.6g (sat 1.3g, mono 3.1g, poly 1.2g); PROTEIN 1.5g; CARB 0.6g; FIBER 0.3g; CHOL 2mg; IRON 0.4mg; SODIUM 94mg; CALC 64mg

Bursting with flavor, this grown-up grilled cheese makes a perfect warm lunch with simply dressed greens. Save leftover pesto to use as a sandwich spread, a pizza topping, or a sauce for pasta or fish.

This version of a Crab Louis Salad features a healthier dressing with all the traditional flavors. Use pickling cucumbers to avoid the bitter seeds in larger varieties.

Crab Louis Salad
Prep: 11 minutes

Louis Dressing
- 3 medium heirloom tomatoes, each cut into 6 wedges
- 1 pound lump crabmeat, drained and shell pieces removed
- 6 pickling cucumbers (about 1½ pounds), each cut lengthwise into 6 wedges
- 6 hard-cooked large eggs, quartered
- ¼ teaspoon freshly ground black pepper

1. Prepare Louis Dressing.
2. Arrange 3 tomato wedges on each of 6 plates. Spoon ½ cup crabmeat into center of each serving of tomato wedges. Arrange 6 cucumber wedges and 4 egg quarters around crabmeat. Drizzle 2½ tablespoons Louis Dressing over crabmeat. Sprinkle each salad evenly with pepper. Yield: 6 servings (serving size: 1 salad).

CALORIES 294; FAT 18.1g (sat 2.3g, mono 10.1g, poly 5.2g); PROTEIN 21g; CARB 10g; FIBER 1.8g; CHOL 263mg; IRON 2.1mg; SODIUM 630mg; CALC 130mg

Louis Dressing
Prep: 4 minutes

- 7 tablespoons canola mayonnaise
- ¼ cup bottled chili sauce
- 2 tablespoons minced green onions
- 2 teaspoons fresh lemon juice
- ⅛ teaspoon ground red pepper

1. Combine all ingredients in a medium bowl, stirring well. Yield: 6 servings (serving size: 2½ tablespoons).

CALORIES 132; FAT 12.8g (sat 0.6g, mono 8.2g, poly 4.1g); PROTEIN 0g; CARB 3.7g; FIBER 0.1g; CHOL 6mg; IRON 0mg; SODIUM 259mg; CALC 2mg

switch it up

SALAD to SANDWICH: Decrease tomato to 1; slice. Decrease hard-cooked eggs to 2; chop. Decrease cucumber to 1; slice. Cut 2 (8-ounce) baguettes into 4 equal pieces each, reserving 2 pieces for a later use. Cut a slice in center of each of 6 baguette pieces. Arrange tomato and cucumber slices in each baguette piece. Top each sandwich with ½ cup crabmeat. Sprinkle each evenly with chopped egg; drizzle each with 2½ tablespoons Louis Dressing. Yield: 6 sandwiches.

CALORIES 410; FAT 15g (sat 1.3g, mono 8.9g, poly 4.6g); PROTEIN 24g; CARB 44.7g; FIBER 2.8g; CHOL 138.9mg; IRON 3.2mg; SODIUM 1001mg; CALC 92mg

Don't be afraid of the anchovy paste in the vinaigrette; the small amount isn't enough to add fishiness, but it does add a savory, rich note. If you prefer, you can omit it.

Mediterranean Tuna with Greens

Prep: 7 minutes • Cook: 5 minutes

 1 pound small fingerling or baby potatoes
Cooking spray
 4 (4-ounce) tuna steaks (¾ inch thick)
 ½ teaspoon freshly ground black pepper, divided
1½ tablespoons olive oil
 1 tablespoon fresh lemon juice
 1 teaspoon Dijon mustard
 ½ teaspoon anchovy paste
 ¼ teaspoon salt
 1 (6-ounce) package Italian blend salad greens (about 6 cups)
 1 (12-ounce) jar artichoke salad, drained and coarsely chopped
 1 tablespoon drained capers

1. Scrub potatoes; pierce with a fork. Place potatoes in a single layer on a microwave-safe plate; cover with wax paper. Microwave at HIGH 5 minutes or until tender. Cut potatoes in half.

2. While potatoes cook, heat a grill pan over medium-high heat. Coat pan with cooking spray. Sprinkle tuna with ¼ teaspoon pepper. Add tuna to pan. Cook 2 to 3 minutes on each side or to desired degree of doneness. Cut tuna into ¼-inch-thick slices.

3. Combine ¼ teaspoon pepper, olive oil, and next 4 ingredients in a medium bowl, stirring with a whisk. Place 1½ cups salad greens on each of 4 salad plates. Top each with 1 tuna steak, about ½ cup artichoke salad, and ¾ teaspoon capers. Divide potatoes evenly among each plate, and drizzle each salad with 1 tablespoon dressing. Yield: 4 servings (serving size: 1 salad).

CALORIES 439; FAT 22.4g (sat 3.8g, mono 12.2g, poly 5.5g); PROTEIN 30.6g; CARB 28.6g; FIBER 2.5g; CHOL 45.4mg; IRON 3.2mg; SODIUM 572mg; CALC 28mg

switch it up

SALAD to OPEN-FACED SANDWICH: Omit potatoes. Prepare tuna and dressing as above. Toss 1 (6-ounce) package mixed salad greens with dressing. Top 4 (1-inch-thick) toasted peasant bread slices evenly with tuna, artichoke salad, dressed greens, and capers. Yield: 4 servings (serving size: 1 open-faced sandwich).

CALORIES 548; FAT 23.4g (sat 3.8g, mono 12.4g, poly 6g); PROTEIN 34.6g; CARB 48.5g; FIBER 4.5g; CHOL 45.4mg; IRON 4.6mg; SODIUM 770mg; CALC 68mg

Sardine skeptics, take note: This tasty, highly nutritious open-faced sandwich is filled with omega-3 fatty acids and calcium. Mustardy sardines, capers, and citrus pair perfectly with slightly bitter Italian greens and toasted peasant bread for a mouthful of flavor.

Sardine, Caper, and Radicchio Sandwiches

Prep: 5 minutes • Cook: 2 minutes

4 (1½-ounce) slices peasant bread
1 tablespoon stone-ground mustard
2 teaspoons fresh lemon juice
2 teaspoons olive oil
¼ teaspoon freshly ground black pepper

4 cups torn romaine lettuce
2¼ cups radicchio, shredded
2 (4.375-ounce) cans low-sodium skinless, boneless sardines, drained
4 teaspoons drained capers

1. Preheat broiler.
2. Place bread slices on a baking sheet. Broil 1 minute on each side or until lightly toasted.
3. While bread cooks, combine mustard and next 3 ingredients in a medium bowl. Add lettuce and radicchio; toss gently.
4. Break sardines into chunks and place evenly on bread slices; sprinkle with capers. Top evenly with lettuce mixture. Yield: 4 servings (serving size: 1 open-faced sandwich).

CALORIES 234; FAT 8.4g (sat 1.1g, mono 3.7g, poly 3g); PROTEIN 17.7g; CARB 22g; FIBER 1.3g; CHOL 75mg; IRON 3.3mg; SODIUM 626mg; CALC 221mg

Other fresh herbs, such as chives or tarragon, would work well in the Creamy Horseradish Dressing.

Smoked Trout Salad with Creamy Horseradish Dressing

Prep: 8 minutes • Cook: 5 minutes

1 pound fingerling or baby potatoes (about 22 potatoes)
Creamy Horseradish Dressing
6 cups gourmet salad greens

1 (8-ounce) package smoked trout, skinned and broken into pieces
1 tablespoon drained capers

1. Scrub potatoes; pierce with a fork. Place potatoes in a single layer on a microwave-safe plate; cover with wax paper. Microwave at HIGH 5 minutes or until tender. Cut potatoes in half, if desired.
2. While potatoes cook, prepare Creamy Horseradish Dressing.
3. Place 1½ cups salad greens on each of 4 salad plates. Top greens evenly with smoked trout and potatoes. Drizzle 2½ tablespoons dressing evenly over salads; sprinkle each with ¾ teaspoon capers. Yield: 4 servings (serving size: 1 salad).

CALORIES 281; FAT 9.4g (sat 1.7g, mono 3.9g, poly 3g); PROTEIN 22.3g; CARB 27.1g; FIBER 3.8g; CHOL 47mg; IRON 2mg; SODIUM 242mg; CALC 49mg

Creamy Horseradish Dressing

Prep: 4 minutes

¼ cup plain 2% reduced-fat Greek yogurt
¼ cup canola mayonnaise
3 tablespoons water
2 teaspoons chopped fresh dill
1 tablespoon prepared horseradish

1 teaspoon grated lemon rind
1 tablespoon fresh lemon juice
1 teaspoon country-style Dijon mustard
⅛ teaspoon freshly ground black pepper

1. Combine all ingredients in a small bowl, stirring well. Yield: 4 servings (serving size: 2½ tablespoons).

CALORIES 71; FAT 5.2g (sat 0.5g, mono 2.5g, poly 1.5g); PROTEIN 2.9g; CARB 2.5g; FIBER 0.2g; CHOL 2mg; IRON 0mg; SODIUM 143mg; CALC 34mg

Serve these fun pizzas that deliver the same flavor as Buffalo wings at your next game-day party.

Buffalo Chicken Pizzas

Prep: 2 minutes • Cook: 13 minutes

1 (6-inch) pita, split
¾ teaspoon hot pepper sauce
6 tablespoons commercial hummus
½ cup shredded rotisserie chicken breast (about 3 ounces)

¼ cup (1 ounce) crumbled blue cheese
¼ cup thinly sliced celery with leaves

1. Preheat oven to 400°.
2. Place pita halves on a baking sheet. Bake at 400° for 10 minutes or until crisp, turning after 5 minutes.
3. Stir hot sauce into hummus. Spread 3 tablespoons hummus mixture over each pita half. Top each pizza with ¼ cup shredded chicken breast and 2 table-spoons crumbled blue cheese.
4. Bake at 400° for 3 minutes or until cheese begins to melt and pizzas are thoroughly heated. Remove from oven; sprinkle each pizza with 2 tablespoons celery. Serve immediately. Yield: 2 servings (serving size: 1 pizza).

CALORIES 268; FAT 10.1g (sat 3.6g, mono 3.6g, poly 2.2g); PROTEIN 18.2g; CARB 25.1g; FIBER 2.3g; CHOL 42mg; IRON 1.7mg; SODIUM 777mg; CALC 111mg

use extra celery in

Crab Salad in Wonton Cups,
page **219**

Lemon-Dill Chicken Salad,
page **128**

Curried Chutney-Stuffed Celery,
page **196**

Serve this Italian-flavored sandwich with a bowl of fruit or a light side salad. Use home-cooked chicken breast if you're keeping an eye on sodium.

Chicken Marinara Panini
Prep: 9 minutes • Cook: 6 minutes

⅓ cup marinara sauce
8 (1-ounce) slices crusty Chicago-style Italian bread
16 fresh basil leaves
2 cups shredded cooked chicken breast (about 8½ ounces)

½ cup (2 ounces) preshredded part-skim mozzarella cheese
½ cup (2 ounces) grated fresh Parmesan cheese
Olive oil-flavored cooking spray

1. Preheat panini grill.
2. Spread marinara sauce evenly over 4 bread slices. Top evenly with basil leaves, shredded chicken, cheeses, and remaining bread slices. Coat outsides of sandwiches with cooking spray.
3. Place sandwiches on panini grill; cook 3 minutes or until golden and cheese melts. Cut panini in half before serving. Yield: 4 servings (serving size: 1 panino).

CALORIES 365; FAT 10.6g (sat 4.6g, mono 3.1g, poly 1.9g); PROTEIN 34.4g; CARB 30.9g; FIBER 2.1g; CHOL 77mg; IRON 2.7mg; SODIUM 715mg; CALC 287mg

use extra ingredients

Basil

Shrimp and Summer Vegetable Sauté, page **272**

Cooked Chicken

Chicken Tortilla Soup, page **121**

Mozzarella Cheese

Pesto Grilled Cheese Panini, page **152**

Spreadable Brie cheese makes this sandwich quick and easy. Find it in the deli section of your supermarket. Make these sandwiches in a panini press or in a skillet.

Grilled Chicken, Apple, and Brie Sandwiches

Prep: 7 minutes • Cook: 5 minutes

¼ cup apricot preserves
2 teaspoons country-style Dijon mustard
8 (1.5-ounce) slices 100% whole-wheat bread
8 ounces thinly sliced deli, lower-sodium chicken breast

1 small Granny Smith apple, thinly sliced
½ cup crème de Brie spreadable cheese
Olive oil-flavored cooking spray

1. Combine apricot preserves and mustard in a small bowl; spread evenly over 4 bread slices. Layer chicken and apple slices evenly over apricot mixture. Spread cheese evenly over remaining bread slices; place on top of sandwiches.
2. Heat a large nonstick skillet over medium-high heat. Coat sandwiches with cooking spray. Place sandwiches in pan. Cook 1 to 2 minutes on each side or until toasted and cheese begins to melt. Yield: 4 servings (serving size: 1 sandwich).

CALORIES 402; FAT 11.1g (sat 4.9g, mono 2.3g, poly 0.2g); PROTEIN 27g; CARB 49g; FIBER 4.4g; CHOL 63mg; IRON 2.7mg; SODIUM 858mg; CALC 134mg

use extra apples in

Cinnamon-Apple-Stuffed French Toast, page **75**

Cheddar-Apple Cracker Bites, page **193**

Orange-Ginger Pork Chops with Sweet and Sour Cabbage, page **308**

Chicken cutlets or thinly sliced chicken breasts speed up the recipe; they take less time to grill.

Grilled Chicken Salad with Dried Cherries and Goat Cheese
Prep: 7 minutes • Cook: 6 minutes • Other: 2 minutes

1 pound thinly sliced skinless, boneless chicken breast halves	Cooking spray
½ cup Herbed Balsamic Dressing, divided	1 (5-ounce) package baby spring mix salad greens
¼ teaspoon salt	½ cup dried cherries
¼ teaspoon freshly ground black pepper	½ cup (2 ounces) crumbled goat cheese

1. Preheat grill to medium-high heat.

2. Brush chicken with ¼ cup Herbed Balsamic Dressing; sprinkle with salt and pepper. Place chicken on grill rack coated with cooking spray; grill 3 to 4 minutes on each side or until chicken is done. Let chicken stand 2 minutes; cut crosswise into thin slices.

3. Combine salad greens, cherries, and ¼ cup Herbed Balsamic Dressing, tossing gently to coat. Place 1¼ cups salad mixture on each of 4 salad plates. Arrange one-fourth of chicken over each salad. Sprinkle each serving with 2 tablespoons goat cheese. Yield: 4 servings (serving size: 1 salad).

CALORIES 334; FAT 11g (sat 3.4g, mono 5.2g, poly 1.1g); PROTEIN 28.3g; CARB 27.7g; FIBER 2.4g; CHOL 79.1mg; IRON 1.4mg; SODIUM 382mg; CALC 45mg

Herbed Balsamic Dressing
Prep: 5 minutes

⅓ cup balsamic vinegar	1 teaspoon Dijon mustard
1½ tablespoons olive oil	1 tablespoon minced shallots
2 tablespoons honey	2 tablespoons chopped fresh basil

1. Combine first 4 ingredients, stirring with a whisk. Stir in shallots and basil. Yield: 5 servings (serving size: about 2 tablespoons).

CALORIES 81; FAT 4.1g (sat 0.6g, mono 3g, poly 0.4g); PROTEIN 0.2g; CARB 10.2g; FIBER 0g; CHOL 0mg; IRON 0.2mg; SODIUM 28mg; CALC 7mg

Apple would be a good substitute for the pear, as would cheddar cheese instead of Swiss.

Open-Faced Chicken and Pear Sandwiches

Prep: 5 minutes • Cook: 2 minutes

2 tablespoons Dijon mustard
6 (1.2-ounce) slices rye pumpernickel bread
12 ounces shaved deli, lower-sodium chicken breast
1 ripe pear, sliced
6 (0.5-ounce) slices Swiss cheese

1. Preheat broiler.
2. Spread 1 teaspoon mustard on each bread slice. Top each with 2 ounces chicken. Top evenly with pear and cheese.
3. Broil 2 minutes or until cheese melts. Serve immediately. Yield: 6 servings (serving size: 1 sandwich).

CALORIES 192; FAT 5.3g (sat 2.6g, mono 1.3g, poly 0.5g); PROTEIN 19.4g; CARB 19.7g; FIBER 2.6g; CHOL 43mg; IRON 1.2mg; SODIUM 767mg; CALC 132mg

use extra ingredients

Deli, Lower-Sodium Chicken Breast

Grilled Chicken, Apple, and Brie Sandwiches, page **167**

Pears

Bagel Sandwich with Pears and Goat Cheese, page **32**

Pears

Roasted Pears with Amaretto and Crème Fraîche, page **371**

To add a tangy bite to the sandwiches, use Dijonnaise rather than canola mayonnaise.

Fried Green Tomato Sandwiches
Prep: 8 minutes • Cook: 7 minutes

Fried Green Tomatoes
- 8 teaspoons canola mayonnaise
- 4 (1.5-ounce) whole-grain white sandwich thins
- 4 green leaf lettuce leaves
- 4 bacon slices, cooked and halved

1. Prepare Fried Green Tomatoes.
2. Spread 1 teaspoon mayonnaise on cut side of each sandwich thin half. Place 1 lettuce leaf and 2 Fried Green Tomato slices on bottom half of each sandwich thin; top each with 2 bacon slice halves. Cover with tops of sandwich thins. Yield: 4 servings (serving size: 1 sandwich).

CALORIES 292; FAT 11.2g (sat 1.4g, mono 5.7g, poly 2.8g); PROTEIN 10.5g; CARB 39.5g; FIBER 6.2g; CHOL 9mg; IRON 2.2mg; SODIUM 516mg; CALC 83mg

Fried Green Tomatoes
Prep: 5 minutes • Cook: 7 minutes

- ¼ cup nonfat buttermilk
- 1 large egg white
- ⅓ cup yellow cornmeal
- 2 tablespoons all-purpose flour
- ¼ teaspoon freshly ground black pepper
- 8 (¼-inch-thick) slices green tomato (about 2 medium tomatoes)
- 1 tablespoon canola oil
- Cooking spray

1. Combine buttermilk and egg white in shallow dish, stirring with a whisk. Combine cornmeal, flour, and pepper in another shallow dish.
2. Dip tomato slices in buttermilk mixture; dredge in cornmeal mixture.
3. Heat oil in a large nonstick skillet over medium-high heat. Add tomato slices; cook 3 minutes. Coat slices with cooking spray. Turn slices over; cook 3 minutes or until golden. Yield: 4 servings (serving size: 2 tomato slices).

CALORIES 115; FAT 3.9g (sat 0.3g, mono 2.2g, poly 1g); PROTEIN 3.3g; CARB 16.7g; FIBER 0.9g; CHOL 0mg; IRON 0.8mg; SODIUM 34mg; CALC 26mg

These grilled sandwiches balance sweet pineapple preserves against the subtle heat of Dijon mustard. Top with the lettuce after pressing them to keep the green leaves crisp.

Hawaiian Ham and Pineapple Panini
Prep: 6 minutes • Cook: 2 minutes

¼ cup (2 ounces) ⅓-less-fat cream cheese, softened
1 tablespoon country-style Dijon mustard
4 (2.2-ounce) mini sub rolls

¼ cup pineapple preserves
8 ounces thinly sliced lower-sodium deli ham
4 green leaf lettuce leaves

1. Preheat panini grill.
2. Combine cream cheese and mustard. Spread cream cheese mixture evenly over bottom half of each roll. Spread preserves evenly over top halves of rolls. Top each portion of cheese mixture with 2 ounces ham. Replace roll tops. Grill panini 2 minutes or until toasted. Immediately lift top of each panino and insert 1 lettuce leaf. Serve immediately. Yield: 4 servings (serving size: 1 panino).

CALORIES 351; FAT 9.1g (sat 5g, mono 2.8g, poly 0.6g); PROTEIN 17.2g; CARB 50.9g; FIBER 1.1g; CHOL 70mg; IRON 1.9mg; SODIUM 793mg; CALC 52mg

use extra lettuce in

Pub Burgers with Blue Cheese-Bacon Spread, page **313**

Fried Green Tomato Sandwiches, page **173**

Cranberry-Orange Turkey Salad Sandwiches, page **124**

Find the pillowy-soft steamed Mandarin buns at an Asian grocery store. For the salad, blond sesame seeds will work if you don't have black.

Mini Pork Buns
Prep: 8 minutes • Cook: 4 minutes

1½ cups thin English cucumber slices
½ cup rice vinegar, divided
8 steamed Mandarin buns

1 cup pulled smoked pork
2 tablespoons hoisin sauce

1. Combine cucumber slices and ¼ cup vinegar in a medium bowl.
2. Microwave buns according to package directions. Split buns, and brush cut sides evenly with 3 tablespoons vinegar from cucumber mixture. Evenly divide and arrange cucumber slices on bottom halves of buns.
3. Combine pork, remaining ¼ cup vinegar, and hoisin sauce in a medium bowl. Spoon 2 tablespoons pork mixture over cucumber slices on each bun; top each with 4 additional cucumber slices. Cover with bun tops. Yield: 4 servings (serving size: 2 sandwiches).

CALORIES 382; FAT 9.5g (sat 2.8g, mono 4.1g, poly 1.8g); PROTEIN 22.8g; CARB 50.7g; FIBER 0.8g; CHOL 34mg; IRON 2.7mg; SODIUM 750mg; CALC 32mg

serve with
Asian Pear Salad
Prep: 4 minutes

2 cups sliced Asian pears
4 cups mixed baby greens
⅓ cup chopped green onions

⅓ cup light sesame-ginger dressing
1 tablespoon black sesame seeds

1. Combine all ingredients in a large bowl; toss well. Serve immediately, or cover and refrigerate until thoroughly chilled. Yield: 4 servings (serving size: 1 cup).

CALORIES 107; FAT 2.4g (sat 0.2g, mono 0.9g, poly 1g); PROTEIN 1.8g; CARB 21.8g; FIBER 6.9g; CHOL 0mg; IRON 1.2mg; SODIUM 244mg; CALC 34mg

Sweet onion jam, pork tenderloin, and peppery watercress combine for a flavor explosion of pure goodness. You can prepare these hearty and healthy sandwiches open-faced on peasant bread or other European-style bread.

Pork and Onion Jam Sandwiches
Prep: 5 minutes • Cook: 20 minutes • Other: 5 minutes

1 (1-pound) pork tenderloin, trimmed
¼ teaspoon salt
½ teaspoon coarsely ground black pepper
Cooking spray
½ cup roasted garlic onion jam

1 tablespoon balsamic vinegar
1 (8.5-ounce) whole-grain baguette, halved lengthwise
2 cups baby watercress or baby arugula

1. Preheat broiler.
2. Sprinkle pork evenly with salt and pepper. Coat pork with cooking spray. Heat a large nonstick skillet over medium-high heat. Coat pan with cooking spray. Add pork; cook 3 minutes or until browned on 1 side.
3. Reduce heat to medium-low; turn pork over. Cover and cook 17 minutes or until a thermometer registers 145°, turning pork after 10 minutes. Remove pork from pan. Cover and let stand 5 minutes. Cut pork into ⅓-inch-thick slices.
4. While pork stands, combine onion jam and balsamic vinegar in a small bowl. Place baguette halves, cut sides up, on a baking sheet. Broil 2 minutes or until lightly toasted.
5. Spread onion jam mixture on cut sides of both baguette halves. Arrange pork slices evenly in a single layer on bottom half of baguette. Top pork with watercress. Cover watercress with top half of baguette. Cut sandwich crosswise into 4 equal portions. Yield: 4 servings (serving size: 1 sandwich).

CALORIES 371; FAT 3.2g (sat 0.8g, mono 0.9g, poly 0.4g); PROTEIN 29.2g; CARB 54.1g; FIBER 1.2g; CHOL 74mg; IRON 2.7mg; SODIUM 525mg; CALC 28mg

Corn bread croutons lend a unique twist to this traditional Southern barbecue salad. To add your personal touch, make your favorite corn bread recipe for the croutons rather than buying premade corn bread from the local grocery store deli.

Smoked Pork Salad
Prep: 2 minutes • Cook: 10 minutes

1½ cups (¾-inch) cubes prepared corn bread (4 ounces)
Cooking spray
¼ cup barbecue sauce
¼ cup light ranch dressing
8 cups chopped romaine lettuce (3 romaine hearts)

2 cups pulled smoked pork (8 ounces)
1 cup grape tomatoes, halved
½ cup vertically sliced red onion
2 ounces reduced-fat extra-sharp cheddar cheese, shredded

1. Preheat oven to 450°.
2. Place corn bread on a baking sheet. Coat corn bread cubes on all sides with cooking spray. Bake at 450° for 10 minutes or until toasted.
3. While corn bread bakes, combine barbecue sauce and ranch dressing in small bowl. Combine lettuce and next 4 ingredients in a large bowl. Add dressing mixture to lettuce mixture; toss well. Place 2½ cups salad mixture on each of 4 plates. Top each serving with 6 tablespoons corn bread croutons. Yield: 4 servings (serving size: 1 salad).

CALORIES 299; FAT 12.4g (sat 4g, mono 3.8g, poly 2.8g); PROTEIN 22g; CARB 23.9g; FIBER 2.7g; CHOL 81mg; IRON 1.6mg; SODIUM 641mg; CALC 152mg

use extra ingredients

Pulled Smoked Pork

Grape Tomatoes

Red Onion

Brunswick Stew, page **140**

Pan-Roasted Salmon and Tomatoes, page **268**

Crab Salad in Wonton Cups, page **219**

A number of different cheeses, from processed cheese sauce in a can to sharp provolone, typically crown this Philly favorite. We chose shredded reduced-fat extra-sharp cheddar to make it both tasty and fast to prepare.

Philly Cheese Steak Sandwiches
Prep: 6 minutes • Cook: 6 minutes

Cheddar Cheese Sauce
¾ pound boneless sirloin steak
Cooking spray
2 cups refrigerated presliced green, yellow, and red bell pepper strips

½ cup refrigerated chopped onion
¼ teaspoon freshly ground black pepper
4 (2½-ounce) whole-wheat hoagie rolls

1. Prepare Cheddar Cheese Sauce.
2. While sauce cooks, cut steak diagonally across the grain into ⅛-inch-thick slices.
3. Heat a large cast-iron skillet 2 minutes over high heat. Coat pan with cooking spray. Add steak, bell pepper, and onion to pan. Sprinkle steak and vegetables with black pepper; sauté 6 minutes or until meat is browned and vegetables are tender. Drain.
4. Stand rolls on uncut edge; fill each roll with about ¾ cup steak mixture. Spoon about 3 tablespoons Cheddar Cheese Sauce over each sandwich. Serve immediately. Yield: 4 servings (serving size: 1 sandwich).

CALORIES 342; FAT 7.9g (sat 3.1g, mono 2.5g, poly 1.7g); PROTEIN 29g; CARB 40.9g; FIBER 5.3g; CHOL 52.3mg; IRON 2.9mg; SODIUM 442mg; CALC 189mg

Cheddar Cheese Sauce
Prep: 3 minutes • Cook: 4 minutes

1½ tablespoons all-purpose flour
¾ cup 1% low-fat milk
¼ cup (1 ounce) shredded reduced-fat extra-sharp cheddar cheese

⅛ teaspoon salt
⅛ teaspoon ground red pepper
⅛ teaspoon onion powder

1. Place flour in a small saucepan. Gradually add milk, stirring with a whisk until smooth. Cook over medium-high heat until thick (about 3 minutes), stirring frequently. Remove from heat; add cheese, stirring until cheese melts. Stir in salt, pepper, and onion powder. Yield: 4 servings (serving size: about 3 tablespoons).

CALORIES 53; FAT 2g (sat 1.3g, mono 0.1g, poly 0g); PROTEIN 3.6g; CARB 4.9g; FIBER 0.1g; CHOL 7.3mg; IRON 0.2mg; SODIUM 155mg; CALC 109mg

Skirt steak is a lean cut with a lot of flavor. Be sure to let it stand, and then cut across the grain for a more tender texture.

Steak Taco Salad with Black Bean–Corn Relish

Prep: 6 minutes • Cook: 9 minutes • Other: 5 minutes

Cooking spray
1 pound skirt steak, trimmed
2 teaspoons salt-free fiesta-lime seasoning
¼ teaspoon salt

Black Bean-Corn Relish
6 cups chopped romaine lettuce
⅓ cup light ranch dressing
4 lime wedges (optional)

1. Heat a grill pan over medium-high heat. Coat pan with cooking spray. Sprinkle steak evenly with fiesta-lime seasoning and salt. Cook steak 3 minutes on each side or to desired degree of doneness. Remove from heat; let stand 5 minutes.
2. While steak stands, prepare Black Bean–Corn Relish.
3. Place 1½ cups lettuce on each of 4 serving plates; top each serving with ⅔ cup Black Bean–Corn Relish and 3 ounces steak. Drizzle each with about 1½ table-spoons dressing. Garnish with lime wedges, if desired. Yield: 4 servings (serving size: 1 salad).

CALORIES 359; FAT 14.4g (sat 4.4g, mono 5.9g, poly 2.2g); PROTEIN 29.4g; CARB 29.4g; FIBER 5.1g; CHOL 80.4mg; IRON 4.3mg; SODIUM 1054mg; CALC 57mg

Black Bean–Corn Relish

Prep: 3 minutes • Cook: 3 minutes

Cooking spray
1 cup fresh corn kernels (about 2 ears)
1 (15-ounce) can black beans, rinsed and drained

1 cup pico de gallo
1 tablespoon chopped fresh cilantro
¼ teaspoon ground cumin

1. Heat a medium nonstick skillet over medium-high heat. Coat pan with cooking spray. Add corn to pan. Sauté 3 minutes or until corn begins to brown. Transfer corn to a medium bowl; stir in remaining ingredients. Yield: 4 servings (serving size: ⅔ cup).

CALORIES 108; FAT 0.8g (sat 0.1g, mono 0.2g, poly 0.2g); PROTEIN 4.6g; CARB 22.4g; FIBER 3.6g; CHOL 0mg; IRON 1mg; SODIUM 532mg; CALC 24mg

Pack leftovers of this salad for lunch. If you cannot find ground lamb, substitute lean ground beef.

Greek Lamb Salad

Prep: 8 minutes • Cook: 6 minutes • Other: 5 minutes

1 pound ground lamb
1¼ cups water
1 (5.6-ounce) package toasted pine nut couscous (such as Near East)
2 lemons, divided
1 tablespoon chopped fresh oregano
1 tablespoon olive oil

¼ teaspoon salt
½ teaspoon freshly ground black pepper
⅔ cup (2.6 ounces) crumbled reduced-fat feta cheese
1 cup chopped English cucumber
½ cup chopped red onion
2 cups chopped tomato (1 large)

1. Cook lamb in a large nonstick skillet over medium-high heat 6 minutes or until browned; stir to crumble. Drain.
2. Bring 1¼ cups water to a boil in a medium saucepan; gradually stir in couscous and seasoning packet. Remove from heat; cover, and let stand 5 minutes.
3. While couscous stands, grate rind and squeeze juice from 1 lemon to measure 2 teaspoons rind and 2 tablespoons juice. Cut remaining lemon into 6 wedges. Combine lemon rind, lemon juice, oregano, olive oil, salt, and pepper in a small bowl, stirring with a whisk.
4. Fluff couscous with a fork. Combine lamb, couscous, cheese, and next 3 ingredients in a large bowl. Drizzle lamb mixture with dressing, and toss gently to coat. Serve with lemon wedges. Yield: 6 servings (serving size: about 1⅓ cups couscous mixture and 1 lemon wedge).

CALORIES 316; FAT 16.1g (sat 6.1g, mono 6.8g, poly 1.8g); PROTEIN 20.8g; CARB 23.6g; FIBER 2.7g; CHOL 55mg; IRON 1.7mg; SODIUM 592mg; CALC 81mg

use extra cucumber in

Cucumber-Gin Sipper, page **243**

Feta-Lamb Patties with Cucumber Sauce, page **291**

Mini Pork Buns, page **177**

snacks

Sugared Spicy Nuts, Mini Pesto Pretzels,
Pecan Biscotti (page 209)

Store nuts in your freezer to keep them fresh longer. For this recipe, let them come to room temperature first, or toast them a minute longer.

Sugared Spicy Nuts

Prep: 2 minutes • Cook: 9 minutes

1 cup whole natural almonds	1 tablespoon water
½ cup walnut halves	¼ teaspoon ground red pepper
½ cup cashews	¼ teaspoon salt
2 tablespoons butter	2 teaspoons chopped fresh thyme
½ cup packed light brown sugar	Cooking spray

1. Place nuts in a large skillet. Cook over medium heat 8 minutes or until toasted, stirring often. Transfer to a small bowl.

2. Add butter and next 4 ingredients to pan. Cook over medium heat 1 minute, stirring until sugar dissolves. Add nuts and thyme, stirring to coat. Cook an additional 2 minutes or until nuts are glazed and golden brown.

3. Spread mixture in a single layer on a foil-lined baking sheet coated with cooking spray. Cool completely. Yield: 26 servings (serving size: 2 tablespoons).

CALORIES 83; FAT 6.1g (sat 1.1g, mono 2.8g, poly 1.8g); PROTEIN 1.9g; CARB 6.5g; FIBER 0.9g; CHOL 2mg; IRON 0.5mg; SODIUM 32mg; CALC 22mg

Mini Pesto Pretzels

Prep: 30 minutes • Cook: 12 minutes

1 (11-ounce) can refrigerated breadstick dough	3 tablespoons commercial pesto
⅓ cup grated fresh Parmesan cheese	Cooking spray

1. Preheat oven to 425°.

2. Unroll dough; separate into 12 breadsticks. Cut each breadstick in half lengthwise. Roll each breadstick half into a 16-inch rope. Cross one end of rope over the other to form a circle. Twist rope once at base of the circle. Fold ends over circle and into traditional pretzel shape, pinching gently to seal.

3. Place cheese in a shallow dish. Brush top side of pretzels evenly with pesto. Press pesto side of pretzels into cheese. Place pretzels, cheese side up, on a baking sheet coated with cooking spray.

4. Bake at 425° for 12 minutes or until golden brown. Yield: 24 servings (serving size: 1 pretzel).

CALORIES 51; FAT 1.9g (sat 0.8g, mono 0.8g, poly 0.2g); PROTEIN 1.9g; CARB 6.4g; FIBER 0.3g; CHOL 2mg; IRON 0.4mg; SODIUM 137mg; CALC 27mg

Avocado adds creaminess and a very mild flavor to this healthy, refreshing smoothie.

Apple-Avocado Smoothie

Prep: 6 minutes

1 Hass avocado
2 cups crushed ice
1 cup almond milk
2 tablespoons honey
2 teaspoons fresh lime juice

1 (6-ounce) carton vanilla low-fat yogurt
1 (3.9-ounce) container Granny Smith applesauce (about ½ cup)
2½ teaspoons sliced almonds, toasted (optional)

1. Cut avocado in half lengthwise; discard pit. Scoop pulp from avocado halves, and place in a blender. Add ice and next 5 ingredients; process until smooth. Garnish with almonds, if desired. Serve immediately. Yield: 5 servings (serving size: about ¾ cup).

CALORIES 143; FAT 6.8g (sat 1.1g, mono 4.3g, poly 0.8g); PROTEIN 2.2g; CARB 19.5g; FIBER 3.1g; CHOL 2mg; IRON 0.3mg; SODIUM 53mg; CALC 83mg

You can prepare the eggs a day before; cover with plastic wrap, and refrigerate.

Bacon-Horseradish–Stuffed Eggs

Prep: 9 minutes

4 hard-cooked large eggs
2 tablespoons potato flakes
2 tablespoons canola mayonnaise
1½ tablespoons minced green onions (about 1 onion)
1½ tablespoons fat-free sour cream

1 teaspoon prepared horseradish
½ teaspoon prepared mustard
¼ teaspoon freshly ground black pepper
Dash of salt
2 center-cut bacon slices, cooked and crumbled

1. Cut eggs in half lengthwise; remove yolks. Place 2 yolks in a small bowl; reserve remaining yolks for another use. Add potato flakes and next 7 ingredients; stir until blended. Spoon 1 tablespoon egg yolk mixture into each egg white half. Sprinkle evenly with bacon. Yield: 4 servings (serving size: 2 stuffed egg halves and 1½ teaspoons bacon).

CALORIES 121; FAT 8.9g (sat 1.5g, mono 4.8g, poly 2.3g); PROTEIN 6.5g; CARB 2.9g; FIBER 0.3g; CHOL 100mg; IRON 0.6mg; SODIUM 231mg; CALC 30mg

Bacon-Horseradish-Stuffed Eggs

Blueberry-Yogurt Parfaits

Layer the berries and yogurt ahead, and store in the refrigerator. Top with cereal just before serving for a satisfying afternoon snack or light breakfast.

Blueberry-Yogurt Parfaits
Prep: 5 minutes

1 cup plain fat-free Greek yogurt
¼ teaspoon grated lemon rind
2 teaspoons honey

½ cup blueberries
2 tablespoons multigrain cluster cereal (such as Kashi Go Lean Crunch!)

1. Combine first 3 ingredients in a small bowl. Spoon 2 tablespoons yogurt mixture into each of 2 parfait glasses. Top with 2 tablespoons blueberries. Repeat layers. Top each serving with 1 tablespoon cereal. Serve immediately. Yield: 2 servings (serving size: 1 parfait).

CALORIES 115; FAT 0.3g (sat 0g, mono 0.1g, poly 0.1g); PROTEIN 10.9g; CARB 17.8g; FIBER 1.4g; CHOL 0mg; IRON 0.2mg; SODIUM 56mg; CALC 81mg

Using different cheeses or mustards, or even pears instead of apples, gives you more options for snack time or a buffet table.

Cheddar-Apple Cracker Bites
Prep: 5 minutes

2 (0.7-ounce) slices reduced-fat cheddar cheese, cut into quarters
8 (0.1-ounce, 3 x 1½-inch) flatbread crackers

16 thin vertical Fuji apple slices (1 medium)
1 tablespoon honey
2 teaspoons stone-ground mustard

1. Place 1 cheese quarter on top of each cracker. Top each with 2 apple slices.
2. Combine honey and mustard in small bowl. Drizzle evenly over apples. Yield: 8 servings (serving size: 1 topped cracker).

CALORIES 45; FAT 1.2g (sat 0.6g, mono 0.3g, poly 0g); PROTEIN 1.7g; CARB 7.3g; FIBER 0.6g; CHOL 4mg; IRON 0.2mg; SODIUM 78mg; CALC 72mg

Chocolate-Hazelnut Popcorn

This popcorn is a healthier alternative to a candy bar.

Chocolate-Hazelnut Popcorn
Prep: 6 minutes • Cook: 23 minutes

Cooking spray
8 cups popcorn (popped without salt and fat)
½ cup chopped toasted hazelnuts

6 tablespoons chocolate-hazelnut spread
⅓ cup honey

1. Preheat oven to 300°.
2. Coat a large jelly-roll pan with cooking spray.
3. Place popcorn and hazelnuts on prepared pan. Combine chocolate-hazelnut spread and honey in a medium saucepan. Cook, stirring constantly, over medium-low heat 3 minutes or until melted and smooth. Drizzle hazelnut mixture over popcorn mixture, tossing gently to coat.
4. Bake at 300° for 20 minutes, stirring twice. Transfer mixture to a sheet of parchment paper; cool completely. Yield: 16 servings (serving size: ½ cup).

CALORIES 97; FAT 4.5g (sat 2.2g, mono 1.7g, poly 0.4g); PROTEIN 1.5g; CARB 13.7g; FIBER 1.3g; CHOL 0mg; IRON 0.6mg; SODIUM 3mg; CALC 12mg

For a fast entrée option, spoon the tapenade over grilled tuna or chicken, or toss with pasta.

Crostini with Sun-Dried Tomato–Olive Tapenade
Prep: 12 minutes • Cook: 5 minutes

1 garlic clove, halved
⅔ cup pitted kalamata olives (24 olives)
1 tablespoon oil from sun-dried tomatoes
⅓ cup drained oil-packed sun-dried tomato halves (about 8)

1 teaspoon fresh thyme leaves
½ teaspoon grated lemon rind
¼ teaspoon freshly ground black pepper
18 (¼-inch-thick) slices diagonally cut French bread baguette, toasted

1. Drop garlic clove through food chute with food processor on, and process until minced. Add olives and next 5 ingredients; pulse 10 times or until minced. Spread 2 teaspoons tapenade on each baguette slice. Yield: 6 servings (serving size: 3 topped crostini).

CALORIES 110; FAT 6.5g (sat 0.9g, mono 4.6g, poly 0.8g); PROTEIN 2.3g; CARB 11.2g; FIBER 0.9g; CHOL 0mg; IRON 0.8mg; SODIUM 285mg; CALC 16mg

Pair this spicy dip with an assortment of vegetables, such as carrots, bell peppers, green beans, celery, cucumbers, radishes, or whatever fresh seasonal vegetables you have on hand.

Curried Yogurt Dip
Prep: 5 minutes

½ cup plain 2% reduced-fat Greek yogurt
½ cup canola mayonnaise
1½ tablespoons chopped fresh cilantro

1 tablespoon fresh lime juice
1½ teaspoons hot curry powder
1 garlic clove, minced

1. Combine all ingredients in a small bowl. Yield: 4 servings (serving size: ¼ cup).

CALORIES 113; FAT 9.7g (sat 0.4g, mono 5.2g, poly 3g); PROTEIN 2.5g; CARB 2.1g; FIBER 0.3g; CHOL 2mg; IRON 0.2mg; SODIUM 190mg; CALC 24mg

Walnuts are a delicious substitute if you don't have honey-roasted peanuts on hand.

Curried Chutney–Stuffed Celery
Prep: 10 minutes

6 tablespoons (4 ounces) ⅓-less-fat cream cheese, softened
2 tablespoons mango chutney
1 teaspoon grated onion

½ teaspoon red curry powder
9 celery stalks, each cut into 3 pieces
2 tablespoons finely chopped honey-roasted peanuts

1. Combine first 4 ingredients in a small bowl; stir well. Spread about 1½ teaspoons cheese mixture into each celery piece. Sprinkle cheese mixture evenly with peanuts. Serve immediately, or cover and chill. Yield: 9 servings (serving size: 3 stuffed celery pieces).

CALORIES 66; FAT 3.8g (sat 1.8g, mono 1.2g, poly 0.4g); PROTEIN 2.2g; CARB 6.2g; FIBER 1.2g; CHOL 9mg; IRON 0.3mg; SODIUM 134mg; CALC 35mg

Curried Yogurt Dip

Dill Snack Mix

Make this tasty snack mix using wheat, rice, or corn cereal squares.

Dill Snack Mix
Prep: 4 minutes • Cook: 5 minutes

2 cups crispy wheat cereal squares
1 cup mini pretzels
½ cup slivered almonds, toasted
½ cup lightly salted dry-roasted peanuts

2 tablespoons olive oil
2 tablespoons chopped fresh dill
¼ teaspoon kosher salt

1. Combine first 4 ingredients in large bowl.
2. Heat oil in small skillet over medium heat. Add dill and salt; cook, stirring constantly, 1 minute. Pour dill mixture over cereal mixture; toss to coat. Yield: 12 servings (serving size: ⅓ cup).

CALORIES 136; FAT 8g (sat 1g, mono 3.7g, poly 1.9g); PROTEIN 4.1g; CARB 13.5g; FIBER 2.3g; CHOL 0mg; IRON 3.5mg; SODIUM 223mg; CALC 37mg

If you can, make this dip the day before, and refrigerate it overnight to allow the yogurt to fully absorb the flavors from the onions, lemon rind, and feta cheese. Serve with fresh seasonal vegetables or whole-grain flaxseed crackers.

Feta-Mint Dip
Prep: 7 minutes

1 cup plain 2% reduced-fat Greek yogurt
½ cup (2-ounces) crumbled feta cheese
½ cup finely chopped English cucumber
3 tablespoons chopped fresh mint

2 tablespoons sliced green onions
¼ teaspoon grated lemon rind
¼ teaspoon salt
⅛ teaspoon freshly ground black pepper

1. Place yogurt and feta in a food processor; process until smooth. Transfer to a small bowl. Stir in cucumber and next 5 ingredients. Sprinkle with additional black pepper, if desired. Yield: 8 servings (serving size: about 3½ tablespoons).

CALORIES 40; FAT 2g (sat 1.2g, mono 0.6g, poly 0.1g); PROTEIN 4g; CARB 2g; FIBER 0.4g; CHOL 7mg; IRON 0.2mg; SODIUM 165mg; CALC 43mg

Serve this spread at room temperature with pita chips or apple slices.

Fig–Goat Cheese Spread
Prep: 10 minutes

1 (8-ounce) package ⅓-less-fat cream cheese, softened
⅓ cup (2.65 ounces) goat cheese
¼ cup fig preserves
¼ cup chopped dried figs
1 teaspoon grated lemon rind
2 teaspoons fresh lemon juice
¼ cup chopped walnuts, toasted

1. Combine all ingredients in large bowl, stirring until blended. Yield: 15 servings (serving size: 2 tablespoons).

CALORIES 82; FAT 5.6g (sat 3g, mono 1.2g, poly 1.1g); PROTEIN 2.4g; CARB 5.9g; FIBER 0.4g; CHOL 13mg; IRON 0.2mg; SODIUM 78mg; CALC 24mg

Tomato seeds can be bitter, so remove them. Seeding a tomato is easy: Cut it in half horizontally, and use a spoon or your finger to quickly scrape out the seeds.

Fresh Salsa
Prep: 13 minutes

1⅔ cups chopped seeded tomato (1 large)
½ cup chopped onion
¼ cup chopped fresh cilantro
2 tablespoons fresh lime juice
¼ teaspoon salt
2 garlic cloves, minced
1 jalapeño pepper, seeded and minced

1. Combine all ingredients in a medium bowl. Yield: 14 servings (serving size: 2 tablespoons).

CALORIES 8; FAT 0.1g (sat 0g, mono 0g, poly 0g); PROTEIN 0.3g; CARB 1.8g; FIBER 0.4g; CHOL 0mg; IRON 0.1mg; SODIUM 44mg; CALC 5mg

Fresh Salsa

Pretty and light, these pops are a refreshing treat on a warm afternoon.

Lemon-Basil Ice Pops

Prep: 6 minutes • Cook: 2 minutes • Other: 8 hours and 30 minutes

1   cup water
¾   cup sugar
3   tablespoons chopped fresh basil

1   tablespoon grated lemon rind
1   cup fresh lemon juice
6   fresh basil leaves

1. Combine first 4 ingredients in a small saucepan. Bring to a boil; remove from heat, and let stand 30 minutes. Strain lemon mixture through a sieve into a bowl. Stir in lemon juice. Pour mixture evenly into 6 (3-ounce) ice pop molds. Place one basil leaf into each mold. Freeze 8 hours or until firm. Yield: 6 servings (serving size: 1 pop).

CALORIES 109; FAT 0g (sat 0g, mono 0g, poly 0g); PROTEIN 0.2g; CARB 28.9g; FIBER 0.3g; CHOL 0mg; IRON 0.1mg; SODIUM 1mg; CALC 8mg

You can make this dip in advance, and store it in an airtight container in the refrigerator up to one week.

Lemon, Mint, and White Bean Dip

Prep: 5 minutes

1   garlic clove
1   (15-ounce) can no-salt-added cannellini
     beans, rinsed and drained
2   tablespoons chopped fresh mint
1   teaspoon grated lemon rind

1½   tablespoons fresh lemon juice
1   tablespoon extra-virgin olive oil
¼   teaspoon salt
¼   teaspoon freshly ground black pepper

1. Drop garlic through food chute with processor on; process until minced. Add beans and remaining ingredients; process until smooth. Cover and chill until ready to serve. Yield: 10 servings (serving size: 2 tablespoons).

CALORIES 35; FAT 1.6g (sat 0.2g, mono 1g, poly 0.2g); PROTEIN 1.4g; CARB 4.1g; FIBER 1.2g; CHOL 0mg; IRON 0.4mg; SODIUM 67mg; CALC 10mg

Lemon-Basil Ice Pops

Melon Kebabs with Lime and Chiles

These spicy kebabs, sold in the streets of Mexico, are a snack that's popular with schoolchildren. You can serve this recipe in a bowl as a side salad as well.

Melon Kebabs with Lime and Chiles
Prep: 4 minutes

5 cups cubed cantaloupe, honeydew, and watermelon
1 teaspoon grated lime rind
¼ cup fresh lime juice

1 teaspoon agave syrup
1 teaspoon crushed chipotle chile flakes (such as Williams-Sonoma Crushed Chipotle Chili)
¼ teaspoon kosher salt

1. Thread 1 cup fruit onto each of 5 (8-inch) skewers, alternating cantaloupe, honeydew, and watermelon.
2. Combine lime rind, lime juice, and agave syrup in a small bowl, stirring with a small whisk. Brush syrup over fruit. Combine chile flakes and salt; sprinkle over skewers. Yield: 5 servings (serving size 1 kebab).

CALORIES 175; FAT 0.3g (sat 0.1g, mono 0g, poly 0.1g); PROTEIN 1.2g; CARB 15.6g; FIBER 1.3g; CHOL 0mg; IRON 0.4mg; SODIUM 116mg; CALC 15mg

Serve this protein-packed dip with apple slices, crackers, or pretzels for an afternoon snack. If you do not want the extra crunch, substitute creamy peanut butter.

Peanut Butter–Banana Dip
Prep: 4 minutes

½ cup chunky peanut butter
⅓ cup mashed ripe banana
1 tablespoon honey

¼ teaspoon ground cinnamon
1 (6-ounce) carton vanilla fat-free organic yogurt

1. Combine all ingredients in a medium bowl. Yield: 8 servings (serving size: 3 tablespoons).

CALORIES 127; FAT 8g (sat 1.3g, mono 3.9g, poly 2.4g); PROTEIN 4.8g; CARB 10.9g; FIBER 1.7g; CHOL 1mg; IRON 0.3mg; SODIUM 91mg; CALC 37mg

Peanut Butter–Chocolate Chip Granola Squares

Prep: 7 minutes • Cook: 25 minutes

Cooking spray
2 cups old-fashioned rolled oats, divided
⅓ cup sugar
¾ cup semisweet chocolate chips

⅓ cup creamy peanut butter
¼ cup honey
3 tablespoons canola oil

1. Preheat oven to 350°. Coat an 8-inch square metal baking pan with cooking spray. Line pan with parchment paper, allowing parchment paper to extend over edge of pan. Coat parchment paper with cooking spray.
2. Place ½ cup oats in a food processor; process until finely ground. Combine ground oats, remaining 1½ cups oats, sugar, and chocolate chips in a bowl. Add peanut butter, honey, and oil; stir until a stiff dough forms. Press mixture evenly into prepared pan.
3. Bake at 350° for 25 minutes or until golden. Cool completely in pan on a wire rack. Lift mixture from pan using edges of parchment paper. Cut into 16 squares. Yield: 16 servings (serving size: 1 square).

CALORIES 177; FAT 9.1g (sat 2.8g, mono 4.2g, poly 1.8g); PROTEIN 3.4g; CARB 23g; FIBER 2.1g; CHOL 0mg; IRON 0.6mg; SODIUM 25mg; CALC 3mg

Keep a container of this snack mix at the office to curb afternoon munchies.

Peanut-Raisin Snack Mix

Prep: 6 minutes • Cook: 3 minutes

1½ cups oatmeal squares cereal
1 cup toasted multigrain cereal (such as Cheerios)
½ cup honey-roasted peanuts
½ cup classic granola

2 tablespoons butter, melted
½ teaspoon ground cinnamon
Cooking spray
⅓ cup raisins
⅓ cup golden raisins

1. Combine first 4 ingredients in large microwave-safe bowl. Combine butter and cinnamon in a small bowl. Drizzle butter mixture over cereal mixture; toss to coat. Coat mixture with cooking spray. Microwave at HIGH 3 minutes, stirring every 45 seconds. Stir in raisins. Spread snack mix on wax paper to cool completely. Yield: 10 servings (serving size: about 6 tablespoons).

CALORIES 157; FAT 6.6g (sat 2.2g, mono 2.5g, poly 1.5g); PROTEIN 3.9g; CARB 22.3g; FIBER 2.4g; CHOL 6mg; IRON 4.9mg; SODIUM 103mg; CALC 35mg

There's nothing like the combination of peanut butter and chocolate for an afternoon pick-me-up. With these homemade granola bars, you can control the amount of sugar and avoid the preservatives found in store-bought counterparts.

Peanut Butter-Chocolate Chip Granola Squares

These nutty biscotti are a delicious
accompaniment to a cup of coffee or tea.
Store them for up to two weeks in an airtight container.

Pecan Biscotti

Pecan Biscotti

Prep: 15 minutes • Cook: 50 minutes • Other: 10 minutes

1½ cups coarsely chopped pecans, toasted
and divided
¾ cup sugar

9 ounces self-rising flour (about 2 cups)
1 teaspoon vanilla extract
3 large eggs

1. Preheat oven to 350°.
2. Line a large baking sheet with parchment paper.
3. Place ½ cup pecans and sugar in a food processor; process until finely ground. Transfer pecan mixture to a large bowl. Weigh or lightly spoon flour into dry measuring cups, and level with a knife. Add flour, vanilla and eggs to bowl. Beat with a heavy-duty mixer at medium speed just until a soft dough forms. Stir in 1 cup pecans.
4. Using floured hands, divide dough in half. Form each half into a 10 x 2–inch log. Place logs 3 inches apart on prepared baking sheet.
5. Bake at 350° for 30 minutes or until lightly browned. Cool logs on pan 10 minutes.
6. Cut logs diagonally into ¼-inch-thick slices with a serrated knife. Arrange slices on baking sheet. Bake at 350° for 10 minutes. Turn slices over; bake an additional 10 minutes or until golden and crisp. Remove slices from pan. Cool completely on a wire rack. Yield: 32 servings (serving size: 1 biscotto).

CALORIES 88; FAT 4.2g (sat 0.5g, mono 2.3g, poly 1.2g); PROTEIN 1.8g; CARB 11.3g; FIBER 0.7g; CHOL 20mg; IRON 0.6mg; SODIUM 106mg; CALC 33mg

Pimiento cheese is a great snack with any fresh veggie. Try it with celery sticks or bell pepper wedges.

Pimiento Cheese Poppers

Prep: 9 minutes

3 ounces ⅓-less-fat cream cheese, softened
3 ounces fat-free cream cheese, softened
8 ounces reduced-fat extra-sharp cheddar
cheese, shredded
¼ cup canola mayonnaise

1 (4-ounce) jar diced pimientos, drained
2 tablespoons finely diced onion
Ground red pepper (optional)
24 tricolor sweet mini peppers, cut in half

1. Combine first 6 ingredients and ground red pepper, if desired, in a medium bowl. Stuff each pepper half with 2 teaspoons cheese mixture. Refrigerate until ready to serve. Yield: 24 servings (serving size: 2 stuffed pepper halves).

CALORIES 72; FAT 5.3g (sat 2g, mono 2.4g, poly 0.9g); PROTEIN 3.5g; CARB 2.1g; FIBER 0.4g; CHOL 11mg; IRON 0.1mg; SODIUM 142mg; CALC 84mg

Don't be tempted to stir the edamame too frequently—it's more flavorful when it's lightly charred.

Roasted Edamame
Prep: 4 minutes • Cook: 15 minutes

1 (16-ounce) package frozen unshelled edamame (green soybeans), thawed
4 teaspoons olive oil
¼ teaspoon ground red pepper
2 garlic cloves, minced
½ teaspoon coarse sea salt

1. Preheat oven to 500°.
2. Pat edamame dry with paper towels. Place edamame, oil, red pepper, and garlic on a rimmed baking sheet, tossing to coat.
3. Bake at 500° for 15 minutes or until browned, stirring once. Sprinkle with salt. Yield: 8 servings (serving size: ½ cup).

CALORIES 101; FAT 5.6g (sat 0.7g, mono 2.8g, poly 1.6g); PROTEIN 6.7g; CARB 6.3g; FIBER 2g; CHOL 0mg; IRON 1.2mg; SODIUM 149mg; CALC 68mg

Spicy ginger is the perfect pairing with strawberries in these refreshing yogurt pops.

Strawberry-Ginger Yogurt Pops
Prep: 5 minutes • Cook: 5 minutes • Other: 8 hours

2 cups quartered strawberries
¼ cup sugar
2 tablespoons water
½ teaspoon grated peeled fresh ginger
1 cup plain low-fat Greek yogurt
1 teaspoon fresh lime juice

1. Combine first 4 ingredients in a medium saucepan. Bring to a boil; reduce heat, and simmer, uncovered, 5 minutes or until berries are softened, stirring occasionally. Place strawberry mixture in a blender; process until smooth. Add yogurt and lime juice. Process just until blended.
2. Fill 8 (3-ounce) ice pop molds with strawberry mixture, according to manufacturer's instructions. Freeze 8 hours or until firm. Yield: 8 servings (serving size: 1 pop).

CALORIES 91; FAT 1.1g (sat 0.6g, mono 0.3g, poly 0.1g); PROTEIN 4.3g; CARB 17.1g; FIBER 1.3g; CHOL 3mg; IRON 0.3mg; SODIUM 16mg; CALC 41mg

Strawberry-Ginger Yogurt Pops

Strawberry-Cereal Snack Bars

Strawberry-Cereal Snack Bars

Prep: 7 minutes • Cook: 2 minutes • Other: 5 minutes

1 (10.5-ounce) package miniature marshmallows
¼ cup butter
6 cups bran twigs, soy grahams, and puffed whole grain cereal (such as Kashi Go Lean)

1 (5-ounce) package dried strawberries, chopped
Cooking spray

1. Place marshmallows and butter in a large microwave-safe bowl. Microwave at HIGH 2 minutes. Stir until marshmallows melt. Stir in cereal and strawberries until completely coated.

2. Press mixture into a 13 x 9–inch pan coated with cooking spray. Let stand until firm. Cut into 16 bars. Yield: 16 servings (serving size: 1 bar).

CALORIES 181; FAT 3.3g (sat 1.9g, mono 0.8g, poly 0.3g); PROTEIN 5.3g; CARB 34.1g; FIBER 4.5g; CHOL 7.6mg; IRON 1.1mg; SODIUM 81mg; CALC 33mg

Popped corn keeps fresh for a day or two if stored in a paper bag with the top folded down. Use other spices you like, such as coriander, cumin, or paprika.

Sweet and Spicy Kettle Corn

Prep: 2 minutes • Cook: 5 minutes

½ teaspoon ground red pepper
1¼ teaspoons fine sea salt
¼ teaspoon ground chipotle chile pepper

3 tablespoons canola oil
½ cup popcorn, unpopped
¼ cup sugar

1. Combine first 3 ingredients in a small bowl.

2. Heat oil in a large Dutch oven over medium heat. Add popcorn; cover and cook 30 seconds. Sprinkle popcorn with sugar; cover. As soon as kernels begin to pop, begin shaking pan. Cook, shaking pan constantly, 4 minutes or until popping slows to 2 to 3 seconds between pops. Transfer popped corn to a large bowl. Sprinkle with red pepper mixture; toss well. Yield: 16 servings (serving size: 1 cup).

CALORIES 57; FAT 2.9g (sat 0.2g, mono 1.7g, poly 0.9g); PROTEIN 0.6g; CARB 7.4g; FIBER 0.9g; CHOL 0mg; IRON 0.2mg; SODIUM 175mg; CALC 0mg

Toasted Cashew
Hummus

Toasting the already roasted cashews deepens their flavor. Serve with pita chips or raw veggies.

Toasted Cashew Hummus

Prep: 6 minutes • Cook: 7 minutes

 1 cup jumbo cashews, roasted in sea salt
 2 garlic cloves
 ¾ cup water
 ¼ cup tahini (roasted sesame seed paste)
 2 tablespoons fresh lime juice
 1 tablespoon olive oil
 1 teaspoon ground cumin
 ¼ teaspoon salt
 1 (15.5-ounce) can chickpeas (garbanzo beans), rinsed and drained
 2 teaspoons chopped fresh cilantro (optional)

1. Preheat oven to 350°.
2. Spread cashews in a shallow pan. Bake at 350° for 7 minutes, stirring occasionally.
3. Drop garlic through food chute with processor on; process until minced. Add cashews, water, and next 6 ingredients; process until smooth. Garnish with cilantro, if desired. Yield: 10 servings (serving size: ¼ cup).

CALORIES 162; FAT 11.3g (sat 1.9g, mono 6g, poly 2.8g); PROTEIN 4.6g; CARB 12.7g; FIBER 2g; CHOL 0mg; IRON 1.6mg; SODIUM 234mg; CALC 27mg

This dip's smooth texture makes it an ideal sandwich spread or taco topping.

Tomato-Avocado Dip

Prep: 5 minutes

 1 cup chopped tomato
 1½ teaspoons chopped fresh cilantro
 1 tablespoon fresh lime juice
 ¼ teaspoon salt
 ¼ teaspoon ground cumin
 1 ripe peeled avocado, coarsely mashed
 1 garlic clove, minced
 36 baked tortilla chips

1. Combine first 7 ingredients in a medium bowl. Serve immediately with chips. Yield: 6 servings (serving size: ¼ cup dip and 6 tortilla chips).

CALORIES 103; FAT 5.4g (sat 0.7g, mono 3.3g, poly 0.6g); PROTEIN 2.1g; CARB 13.6g; FIBER 3.4g; CHOL 0mg; IRON 0.4mg; SODIUM 177mg; CALC 24mg

Toss a few of these nutrient-packed poppers in a zip-top plastic bag, and you're ready to roll with snack in hand. Pair them with yogurt for a quick breakfast, too. Create a more complex flavor by adding three slices of crystallized ginger when mincing the fruit bits.

Trail Mix Poppers
Prep: 11 minutes

⅔ cup sliced almonds
¼ cup flaked sweetened coconut
1 (7-ounce) bag dried fruit bits (such as SunMaid)

1½ tablespoons honey

1. Place almonds in a food processor; pulse 10 times or until minced. Transfer half of almonds to a medium bowl. Add coconut and fruit bits to remaining almonds in processor; process 30 seconds or until minced. Add honey. Pulse 10 times or just until blended.
2. Using a 1-inch scoop, shape mixture into 18 (1-inch) balls. Roll balls in reserved almonds. Store in an airtight container. Yield: 9 servings (serving size: 2 poppers).
Note: The bag of dried fruit bits we used in testing contained raisins, apples, apricots, peaches, plums, and cherries.

CALORIES 119; FAT 3.4g (sat 0.8g, mono 1.7g, poly 0.7g); PROTEIN 1.8g; CARB 21.3g; FIBER 2.6g; CHOL 0mg; IRON 0.7mg; SODIUM 18mg; CALC 26mg

cocktail
hour

Wonton wrappers become a crispy golden shell for fresh crab salad: Simply coat them with cooking spray, mold them into mini muffin cups, and bake.

Crab Salad in Wonton Cups
Prep: 3 minutes • Cook: 12 minutes

Cooking spray
18 wonton wrappers
Chile-Lime Dressing
½ pound jumbo lump crabmeat, drained and
   shell pieces removed
½ cup finely chopped celery (2 stalks)
⅓ cup finely chopped red onion

1. Preheat oven to 375°.
2. Coat 18 miniature muffin cups with cooking spray. Coat wonton wrappers with cooking spray; press 1 wrapper into each muffin cup. Bake at 375° for 12 minutes or until browned and crisp. Remove wonton cups from muffin cups.
3. While wonton cups bake, prepare Chile-Lime Dressing in a medium bowl. Add crab, celery, and onion to dressing, tossing to coat. Fill wonton cups evenly with crab mixture. Serve immediately. Yield: 9 servings (serving size: 2 filled wonton cups).

CALORIES 104; FAT 3g (sat 0.4g, mono 1.7g, poly 0.4g); PROTEIN 7.7g; CARB 10.8g; FIBER 0.7g; CHOL 28mg; IRON 0.9mg; SODIUM 227mg; CALC 39mg

Chile-Lime Dressing
Prep: 4 minutes

1 teaspoon grated lime rind
2½ tablespoons fresh lime juice
2 tablespoons minced green onions
1½ tablespoons olive oil
½ teaspoon chopped dried Thai chiles
   (2 chiles)
¼ teaspoon freshly ground black pepper
⅛ teaspoon salt

1. Combine all ingredients in a medium bowl, stirring with a whisk. Cover and chill until ready to serve. Yield: 9 servings (serving size: 2 teaspoons).

CALORIES 23; FAT 2.3g (sat 0.3g, mono 1.7g, poly 0.3g); PROTEIN 0.1g; CARB 0.7g; FIBER 0.2g; CHOL 0mg; IRON 0.1mg; SODIUM 34mg; CALC 2mg

This simple appetizer is also delicious with white Stilton or a white Stilton blend with ginger. You can substitute honey for the agave syrup, if you like. A glass of Vouvray would complement these snacks.

Apricot-Stilton Bites

Apricot-Stilton Bites

Prep: 6 minutes

¼ cup (1 ounce) crumbled blue Stilton cheese
12 dried apricot halves
2 tablespoons coarsely chopped pistachios

1 tablespoon agave syrup
½ teaspoon chopped fresh thyme

1. Place 1 teaspoon cheese on each apricot; top each with ½ teaspoon pistachios. Drizzle evenly with syrup. Sprinkle evenly with thyme. Yield: 4 servings (serving size: 3 topped apricots).

CALORIES 92; FAT 4.3g (sat 1.9g, mono 1.6g, poly 0.6g); PROTEIN 2.8g; CARB 11.8g; FIBER 1.2g; CHOL 6.3mg; IRON 0.4mg; SODIUM 144mg; CALC 51mg

Take inspiration from these bruschetta, and spread leftover broccoli pesto on a sandwich.

Broccoli Pesto Bruschetta

Prep: 4 minutes • Cook: 6 minutes

12 (½-ounce) slices diagonally cut French bread baguette
Cooking spray
2 cups broccoli florets
1 garlic clove

¼ cup (1 ounce) grated fresh Parmesan cheese
2 tablespoons pine nuts
2 tablespoons olive oil
1½ ounces shaved pecorino Romano cheese
¼ teaspoon freshly ground black pepper

1. Preheat oven to 450°.
2. Lightly coat bread slices with cooking spray; place on a baking sheet. Bake at 450° for 5 minutes or until crisp.
3. While bread bakes, cook broccoli in boiling water 6 minutes or just until tender; drain.
4. Drop garlic through food chute with processor on; process until minced. Add broccoli, Parmesan cheese, pine nuts, and olive oil. Process until smooth.
5. Top toast slices evenly with broccoli mixture and pecorino Romano cheese. Sprinkle evenly with pepper. Serve immediately. Yield: 12 servings (serving size: 1 bruschetta).

CALORIES 79; FAT 4.4g (sat 1g, mono 1.9g, poly 0.8g); PROTEIN 3g; CARB 7.5g; FIBER 0.7g; CHOL 3mg; IRON 0.6mg; SODIUM 149mg; CALC 52mg

A classy twist on onion dip, these tarts pair the complex flavor of caramelized onion with goat cheese in a pretty shell.

Caramelized Onion and Goat Cheese Tartlets

Prep: 10 minutes • Cook: 22 minutes

1 (1.9-ounce) package mini phyllo shells
Cooking spray
1 cup diced onion
2 tablespoons reduced-fat sour cream

½ teaspoon freshly ground black pepper
1 (4-ounce) package herbed goat cheese
Thyme sprigs (optional)

1. Preheat oven to 400°.
2. Arrange phyllo shells on a baking sheet. Heat a medium skillet over medium-high heat. Coat pan with cooking spray. Add onion to pan; coat with cooking spray. Cook onion, stirring frequently, 10 minutes or until golden brown and tender.
3. Combine sour cream, pepper, and cheese. Place 1 tablespoon cheese mixture into each mini phyllo shell. Top each with 1 teaspoon onion.
4. Bake at 400° for 10 to 12 minutes or until golden. Let cool on a wire rack. Garnish with thyme sprigs, if desired. Yield: 15 servings (serving size: 1 tartlet).

CALORIES 42; FAT 2.8g (sat 1.2g, mono 1.1g, poly 0.3g); PROTEIN 1.3g; CARB 3.2g; FIBER 0.2g; CHOL 3.7mg; IRON 0.2mg; SODIUM 48mg; CALC 11mg

Carrot Soup Shots

Prep: 3 minutes • Cook: 5 minutes

2 cups frozen sliced carrots
2 tablespoons water
1½ teaspoons unsalted butter
2 tablespoons chopped shallots
  (1 medium shallot)

2 cups organic vegetable broth, divided
Ginger Crème Fraîche

1. Place carrots and 2 tablespoons water in a medium microwave-safe bowl. Cover tightly with heavy-duty plastic wrap. Microwave at HIGH 5 minutes or until carrots are tender.

2. While carrots cook, melt butter in a 2-quart saucepan over medium-high heat. Add shallots; cook, stirring often, 3 minutes or just until tender.

3. Place shallots, half of cooked carrots, and 1 cup broth in a blender. Remove center piece of blender lid (to allow steam to escape); secure blender lid on blender. Place a clean towel over opening in blender lid (to avoid splatters). Blend until smooth. Pour into a large bowl. Repeat procedure with remaining carrots and broth. Stir to blend.

4. Serve soup, warm or chilled, in shot glasses with a dollop of Ginger Crème Fraîche. Yield: 20 servings (serving size: 2 tablespoons soup and about ½ teaspoon crème fraîche).

CALORIES 15; FAT 0.9g (sat 0.5g, mono 0.3g, poly 0g); PROTEIN 0.1g; CARB 1.5g; FIBER 0.4g; CHOL 3mg; IRON 0.1mg; SODIUM 64mg; CALC 6mg

Ginger Crème Fraîche

Prep: 2 minutes

2 tablespoons crème fraîche
1 teaspoon chopped green onions

¾ teaspoon grated peeled fresh ginger
¼ teaspoon fresh lemon juice

1. Combine all ingredients in a small bowl. Chill until ready to serve. Yield: 20 servings (serving size: about ½ teaspoon).

CALORIES 6; FAT 0.6g (sat 0.4g, mono 0.2g, poly 0g); PROTEIN 0g; CARB 0g; FIBER 0g; CHOL 2mg; IRON 0mg; SODIUM 0.6mg; CALC 1mg

Ginger and carrots are a classic combo. Here, the ginger blends with crème fraîche, a thick, mild-flavored dairy product that is popular in France. If you can't find it, you can substitute sour cream.

Sour cream makes this dip extra smooth. Experiment with different chips: You might try plaintain chips or taro root chips in place of the store-bought sweet potato chips.

Creamy Avocado Dip with Sweet Potato Chips

Prep: 6 minutes

1 ripe peeled avocado, coarsely mashed	¼ teaspoon salt
⅓ cup light sour cream	¼ teaspoon freshly ground black pepper
2 tablespoons fresh lemon juice	32 sweet potato chips
½ teaspoon ground cumin	

1. Combine first 6 ingredients in a medium bowl. Serve with chips. Yield: 8 servings (serving size: 2 tablespoons dip and 4 chips).

CALORIES 78; FAT 5.2g (sat 1.1g, mono 2.4g, poly 0.9g); PROTEIN 1.3g; CARB 7g; FIBER 1.5g; CHOL 3.3mg; IRON 0.3mg; SODIUM 85mg; CALC 29mg

use extra avocado in

Shredded Chicken Tacos, page **271**

Black Bean Omelet with Tomato-Avocado Salsa, page **67**

Avocado BLT, page **138**

Hummus, a Mediterranean classic, gets an Indian twist with curry.

Curried Hummus
Prep: 4 minutes

2 (15-ounce) cans no-salt-added chickpeas (garbanzo beans), drained
2 tablespoons water
2 tablespoons extra-virgin olive oil
1 tablespoon fresh lemon juice
2 teaspoons curry powder
½ teaspoon salt

1. Place all ingredients in a food processor; process until smooth. Yield: 8 servings (serving size: ⅓ cup).

CALORIES 94; FAT 4.7g (sat 0.5g, mono 3g, poly 0.9g); PROTEIN 3.3g; CARB 10.2g; FIBER 2.9g; CHOL 0mg; IRON 1.1mg; SODIUM 224mg; CALC 24mg

serve with
Spicy Cilantro Naan Chips
Prep: 5 minutes • Cook: 7 minutes

1 (9-ounce) package whole-wheat naan (2 naan)
Olive oil-flavored cooking spray
½ teaspoon smoked paprika
¼ teaspoon kosher salt
¼ teaspoon ground red pepper
2 tablespoons chopped fresh cilantro

1. Preheat oven to 425°.
2. Cut each naan into 8 wedges. Arrange wedges in a single layer on a baking sheet. Coat wedges with cooking spray.
3. Combine smoked paprika, salt, and ground red pepper in a small bowl; sprinkle evenly over wedges. Lightly coat wedges with cooking spray. Sprinkle with cilantro.
4. Bake at 425° for 7 minutes or until browned and crisp. Yield: 8 servings (serving size: 2 chips).

CALORIES 87; FAT 2.6g (sat 0.5g, mono 0.8g, poly 0.8g); PROTEIN 2.6g; CARB 10.8g; FIBER 2.1g; CHOL 2.5mg; IRON 0.9mg; SODIUM 263mg; CALC 21mg

Straight from the oven, this sweet and savory flatbread wins rave reviews. Balsamic glaze is a sweet, tangy syrup made from balsamic vinegar. Look for it in grocery stores. You can substitute feta cheese or a young sheep's milk cheese for the ricotta salata.

Fig and Caramelized Onion Flatbread

Prep: 10 minutes • Cook: 27 minutes • Other: 5 minutes

1 tablespoon olive oil
1 large onion, thinly sliced
⅛ teaspoon freshly ground black pepper
1 cup water
¾ cup dried Mission figs, stems removed

1 (11-ounce) can refrigerated thin pizza
   crust dough
Cooking spray
⅔ cup ricotta salata
1 tablespoon balsamic glaze

1. Preheat oven to 425°.
2. Heat oil in a medium nonstick skillet over medium heat. Add onion; cook 10 minutes or until very soft and golden, stirring frequently. Stir in pepper, and remove from heat.
3. While onion cooks, combine water and figs in a small microwave-safe bowl. Microwave at HIGH 1 minute. Let stand 5 minutes.
4. While figs stand, unroll dough. Shape dough into a 15 x 12–inch rectangle on a baking sheet coated with cooking spray. Bake at 425° for 5 minutes.
5. Drain figs, and coarsely chop. Top crust with onion and figs; sprinkle with ricotta salata.
6. Bake at 425° for 10 minutes or until golden. Drizzle with balsamic glaze. Cut into pieces. Serve immediately. Yield: 18 servings (serving size: 1 piece).

CALORIES 89; FAT 3.1g (sat 1g, mono 1g, poly 0.8g); PROTEIN 2.3g; CARB 13.4g; FIBER 1.1g; CHOL 0mg; IRON 0.6mg; SODIUM 174mg; CALC 18mg

use extra dried figs in

Beef Tenderloin with Peppery
Fig-Port Sauce, page **310**

Fig-Goat Cheese Spread,
page **200**

Fig-Maple Drop Biscuits,
page **41**

Goat Cheese–Stuffed Piquillo Peppers
Prep: 10 minutes

4 teaspoons olive oil, divided
2 tablespoons chopped pitted kalamata olives
¼ teaspoon garlic pepper
1 (4-ounce) package goat cheese

1½ teaspoons sherry vinegar
1 (9.5-ounce) jar pimientos del piquillo peppers
2 teaspoons chopped fresh chives

1. Combine 1 teaspoon oil and next 3 ingredients in a small bowl.
2. Combine 3 teaspoons oil and vinegar in another small bowl, stirring with a whisk.
3. Drain peppers, and pat dry. Carefully make a vertical slit down 1 side of each pepper. Open peppers and fill evenly with cheese mixture. Close edges of pepper over filling to seal. Place stuffed peppers, seam sides down, on a serving platter. Drizzle evenly with vinaigrette, and sprinkle evenly with chives. Serve immediately. Yield: 12 servings (serving size: 1 pepper).

CALORIES 52; FAT 3.9g (sat 1.6g, mono 1.9g, poly 0.3g); PROTEIN 1.8g; CARB 2g; FIBER 0.9g; CHOL 4.4mg; IRON 0.2mg; SODIUM 128mg; CALC 14mg

Use green, white, and purple asparagus for a stunning pizza.

Grilled Asparagus Pizzas
Prep: 7 minutes • Cook: 4 minutes

¼ pound asparagus spears, trimmed
1½ teaspoons olive oil
½ teaspoon freshly ground black pepper, divided
¼ teaspoon salt
1 lemon

½ cup part-skim ricotta cheese
¼ cup (2 ounces) herbed goat cheese
½ (12-ounce) package whole-wheat naan (2 naan)
Cooking spray

1. Preheat grill to medium-high heat.
2. Place asparagus in a bowl. Add oil, ¼ teaspoon pepper, and salt; toss to coat.
3. Grate 1 teaspoon rind and squeeze 1 tablespoon juice from lemon. Combine ¼ teaspoon pepper, lemon rind, lemon juice, ricotta cheese, and goat cheese in a small bowl. Spread each naan with half of cheese mixture.
4. Place pizzas and asparagus on grill rack coated with cooking spray. Grill 4 minutes or until pizzas are crisp and asparagus is crisp-tender. Chop asparagus, and sprinkle evenly over pizzas. Cut each pizza into 8 wedges. Yield: 8 servings (serving size: 2 wedges).

CALORIES 111; FAT 4.5g (sat 1.9g, mono 1.4g, poly 0.6g); PROTEIN 5.6g; CARB 12.9g; FIBER 2.4g; CHOL 7.3mg; IRON 1.1mg; SODIUM 204mg; CALC 53mg

For an easy make-ahead option, chill the stuffed peppers, covered, on the serving platter. When ready to serve, let them stand at room temperature 30 minutes, and then drizzle with the vinaigrette and sprinkle with chives.

Goat Cheese-Stuffed
Piquillo Peppers

A tangy spread gets a kick from cumin-dusted pita crisps. Make it while the pita crisps bake.

Lemon-Artichoke Spread with Spicy Pita Crisps

Prep: 10 minutes • Cook: 5 minutes

1 (10-ounce) package frozen artichoke hearts, thawed and chopped
2 tablespoons chopped fresh flat-leaf parsley
6 ounces $\frac{1}{3}$-less-fat cream cheese, softened
2 tablespoons fresh lemon juice
$\frac{1}{4}$ teaspoon freshly ground black pepper
Spicy Pita Crisps

1. Combine first 5 ingredients in a small bowl. Serve with Spicy Pita Crisps. Yield: 8 servings (serving size: 2 tablespoons spread and 4 crisps).

CALORIES 116; FAT 5.5g (sat 2.8g, mono 1.3g, poly 0.5g); PROTEIN 4.4g; CARB 13g; FIBER 3.4g; CHOL 16mg; IRON 0.8mg; SODIUM 210mg; CALC 47mg

serve with
Spicy Pita Crisps

Prep: 5 minutes • Cook: 5 minutes

2 (6-inch) whole-wheat pitas
Olive oil-flavored cooking spray
$\frac{1}{2}$ teaspoon ground cumin
$\frac{1}{4}$ teaspoon freshly ground black pepper
$\frac{1}{8}$ teaspoon kosher salt
$\frac{1}{8}$ teaspoon ground red pepper

1. Preheat oven to 425°.
2. Cut each pita into 8 wedges. Split each wedge in half. Place in single layer on a baking sheet coated with cooking spray.
3. Combine cumin and next 3 ingredients in small bowl. Sprinkle evenly over pita wedges. Lightly coat pita wedges with cooking spray.
4. Bake at 425° for 5 minutes or until browned and crisp. Yield: 8 servings (serving size: 4 crisps).

CALORIES 44; FAT 0.5g (sat 0.1g, mono 0.1g, poly 0.2g); PROTEIN 1.6g; CARB 8.9g; FIBER 1.3g; CHOL 0mg; IRON 0.5mg; SODIUM 115mg; CALC 4mg

Lime is the flavor star in both the vinaigrette
and the dipping sauce for these crisp shrimp.

Grilled Bacon-Wrapped Shrimp

Prep: 8 minutes • Cook: 7 minutes

3 ounces thinly sliced pancetta (about 16 slices)	2 teaspoons olive oil
16 large shrimp, peeled and deveined (about ¾ pound)	¼ teaspoon freshly ground black pepper
1 tablespoon fresh lime juice	1 large garlic clove, minced
	Cooking spray
	Apricot-Lime Dipping Sauce

1. Preheat grill pan.

2. Wrap pancetta around shrimp.

3. Combine lime juice and next 3 ingredients in a small bowl. Brush mixture over shrimp. Coat hot grill pan with cooking spray. Place shrimp on pan; cook 3 minutes on each side or until shrimp are done and pancetta is crisp, brushing with remaining lime juice mixture. Serve with Apricot-Lime Dipping Sauce. Yield: 8 servings (serving size: 2 shrimp and about 2 teaspoons sauce).

CALORIES 128; FAT 4.9g (sat 1.4g, mono 2.2g, poly 0.7g); PROTEIN 11g; CARB 9.5g; FIBER 0.1g; CHOL 72mg; IRON 1.3mg; SODIUM 310mg; CALC 24mg

Apricot-Lime Dipping Sauce

Prep: 2 minutes

⅓ cup apricot preserves	½ teaspoon grated lime rind
2 teaspoons fresh lime juice	½ teaspoon grated peeled fresh ginger
1½ teaspoons lower-sodium soy sauce	

1. Combine all ingredients in a small bowl. Yield: 8 servings (serving size: about 2 teaspoons).

CALORIES 143; FAT 5.1g (sat 1.5g, mono 2.2g, poly 0.8g); PROTEIN 13.9g; CARB 9.7g; FIBER 0.1g; CHOL 94mg; IRON 1.7mg; SODIUM 328mg; CALC 31mg

Great for serving at small parties, this recipe can also be made into full-sized burgers for dinner.

Barbecue Turkey Burger Sliders
Prep: 15 minutes • Cook: 10 minutes

1 pound ground turkey breast
3 tablespoons chopped fresh cilantro
2 tablespoons barbecue sauce

Cooking spray
12 (1.2-ounce) whole-wheat slider buns
Mustard Coleslaw

1. Combine first 3 ingredients in a medium bowl. Divide meat mixture into 12 equal portions; shape portions into ¼-inch-thick patties.
2. Heat a large nonstick skillet over medium-high heat. Coat pan with cooking spray. Add half of patties to pan; cook 3 minutes. Turn patties over; cook 2 minutes or until done. Transfer patties to a plate; keep warm. Repeat procedure with remaining patties.
3. Place 1 patty on bottom half of each bun. Top each patty with about 3 tablespoons Mustard Coleslaw and 1 bun top. Yield: 12 servings (serving size: 1 burger).

CALORIES 149; FAT 2.5g (sat 0.1g, mono 0.2g, poly 1.1g); PROTEIN 14.5g; CARB 19g; FIBER 1.3g; CHOL 15mg; IRON 0.5mg; SODIUM 207mg; CALC 47mg

Mustard Coleslaw
Prep: 5 minutes

¼ cup creamy mustard blend (such as Dijonnaise)
2 tablespoons white wine vinegar
¾ teaspoon sugar

¼ teaspoon freshly ground black pepper
¼ cup chopped red onion
1 (5-ounce) package cabbage-and-carrot coleslaw

1. Combine first 4 ingredients in a medium bowl, stirring with a whisk.
2. Add onion and coleslaw; toss to coat. Yield: 12 servings (serving size: about 3 tablespoons).

CALORIES 8; FAT 0g (sat 0g, mono 0g, poly 0g); PROTEIN 0.2g; CARB 1.6g; FIBER 0.3g; CHOL 0mg; IRON 0mg; SODIUM 27mg; CALC 7mg

Your kitchen will be fragrant with the aroma of fennel while these meatballs bake. The Simple Tomato-Basil Sauce is nice to have on hand to dress pasta for lunch or dinner.

Fennel-Sausage Meatballs

Prep: 17 minutes • Cook: 10 minutes

1 pound hot turkey Italian sausage, casings removed
¼ cup freshly grated Parmigiano-Reggiano cheese

1 teaspoon fennel seeds
2 garlic cloves, minced
2 teaspoons olive oil
2 cups Simple Tomato-Basil Sauce

1. Preheat oven to 450°.
2. Combine first 4 ingredients in a medium bowl; shape mixture into 32 meatballs (about 1 inch thick).
3. Heat oil in a large nonstick skillet over medium-high heat. Add meatballs to pan. Cook 2 minutes on each side or until browned. Place meatballs on a jelly-roll pan.
4. Bake at 450° for 6 minutes or until done. Add Simple Tomato-Basil Sauce, stirring to coat. Yield: 16 servings (serving size: 2 meatballs and 2½ tablespoons sauce).

CALORIES 81; FAT 4.6g (sat 1.7g, mono 1.7g, poly 0.6g); PROTEIN 6.1g; CARB 3.2g; FIBER 0.9g; CHOL 18mg; IRON 1.2mg; SODIUM 220mg; CALC 34mg

Simple Tomato-Basil Sauce

Prep: 2 minutes • Cook: 3 minutes

2 teaspoons olive oil
2 garlic cloves, sliced
1 (28-ounce) can crushed tomatoes

¼ teaspoon freshly ground black pepper
⅛ teaspoon salt
¼ cup torn fresh basil leaves

1. Heat oil in a large nonstick skillet over medium heat. Add garlic to pan. Sauté 1 minute or until lightly browned. Add tomatoes, pepper, and salt. Bring to a boil; remove from heat, and stir in basil. Yield: 16 servings (serving size: 2½ tablespoons).

CALORIES 22; FAT 0.6g (sat 0.1g, mono 0.4g, poly 0.1g); PROTEIN 0.9g; CARB 2.6g; FIBER 0.8g; CHOL 0mg; IRON 0.6mg; SODIUM 18mg; CALC 18mg

This refreshing gin cocktail gains its herbal notes from an infusion of cucumber and shiso, as well as a touch of Pimm's No. 1. Shiso, also known as perilla, is an herb widely used in Japanese cuisine. The anise-flavored herb comes in both a red and a green variety; you can find it at Asian markets. Use a vegetable peeler to make the cucumber ribbon. The drink is best with a lighter-style gin, such as Beefeater or Hendrick's.

Cucumber-Gin Sipper
Prep: 5 minutes

4 (¼-inch-thick) slices English cucumber
4 green shiso leaves, divided
2 teaspoons Pimm's No. 1
2 tablespoons gin
1 teaspoon lime juice

Crushed ice
¼ cup club soda
1 (6 x 2-inch) English cucumber ribbon (⅛ inch thick)

1. Place cucumber slices, 3 shiso leaves, and Pimm's in a martini shaker; crush leaves with back of a long spoon. Add gin and lime juice. Fill shaker with crushed ice; shake. Fill an old-fashioned glass with crushed ice. Strain mixture over ice in glass. Stir in club soda. Garnish with 1 shiso leaf and a cucumber ribbon. Yield: 1 serving.

CALORIES 89; FAT 0g (sat 0g, mono 0g, poly 0g); PROTEIN 0.2g; CARB 0.9g; FIBER 0.1g; CHOL 0mg; IRON 0.1mg; SODIUM 1mg; CALC 6mg

use extra cucumber in

Mini Pork Buns, page **177**

Greek Lamb Salad, page **186**

Feta-Mint Dip, page **199**

A twist on the Moscow Mule, which is traditionally made with vodka and ginger ale, this cocktail steps up the game with bourbon and ginger beer.

Kentucky Mule
Prep: 3 minutes • Other: 10 minutes

½ cup bourbon
2 tablespoons Cointreau (orange-flavored liqueur)

3 cups ginger beer
Icy Ginger Oranges

1. Fill 6 (8-ounce) glasses one-third full with ice. Combine bourbon and Cointreau; pour 1⅔ tablespoons bourbon mixture in each glass. Add ½ cup ginger beer to each glass. Garnish with Icy Ginger Oranges. Yield: 6 servings (serving size: about ⅔ cup and 1 orange slice).

CALORIES 171; FAT 0g (sat 0g, mono 0g, poly 0g); PROTEIN 0.2g; CARB 23g; FIBER 0.5g; CHOL 0mg; IRON 0.3mg; SODIUM 2mg; CALC 18mg

Icy Ginger Oranges
Prep: 2 minutes • Other: 10 minutes

1 tablespoon chopped crystallized ginger
2 tablespoons sugar

6 (⅛-inch-thick) slices navel orange

1. Place ginger and sugar in small food processor or spice grinder; pulse until minced. Dredge orange slices in ginger mixture; place in a single layer on a parchment paper–lined baking sheet. Freeze 10 minutes or until ready to use. Yield: 6 servings (serving size: 1 orange slice).

CALORIES 48; FAT 0.3g (sat 0g, mono 0g, poly 0g); PROTEIN 0.2g; CARB 12.3g; FIBER 0.5g; CHOL 0mg; IRON 0.3mg; SODIUM 2mg; CALC 18mg

What do you get when you combine the best of
two favorites: a mojito and a margarita? A festive mo-rita!

Mango Mo-rita

Mango Mo-rita

Prep: 7 minutes

1 cup cubed peeled ripe mango
¼ cup fresh mint leaves
2 tablespoons superfine sugar
2 tablespoons fresh lime juice
½ cup tequila

1 tablespoon Triple Sec (orange-flavored liqueur)
Crushed ice
1 cup club soda
Mint sprigs (optional)

1. Place first 4 ingredients in a blender; process until smooth. Stir in tequila and Triple Sec.
2. Fill each of 4 glasses with ½ cup crushed ice. Pour mango mixture evenly over ice, and fill each glass with ¼ cup club soda. Garnish with mint sprigs, if desired. Yield: 4 servings (serving size: about ⅔ cup).

CALORIES 130; FAT 0.1g (sat 0g, mono 0g, poly 0g); PROTEIN 0.3g; CARB 15.7g; FIBER 0.9g; CHOL 0mg; IRON 0.2mg; SODIUM 14mg; CALC 12mg

Use your favorite brand of green tea for this refreshing drink; they often vary in strength and flavor. Add a lemon wedge, if you like.

Mint Vodka and Iced Green Tea

Prep: 5 minutes • Cook: 8 minutes • Other: 2 hours and 10 minutes

4 cups water
2 tablespoons agave syrup
6 mint green tea bags

4 (5-inch) mint sprigs
1 cup sweet tea vodka

1. Place first 4 ingredients in a large saucepan; bring to a boil. Boil 5 minutes, stirring occasionally. Remove pan from heat; cover and let stand 10 minutes. Remove and discard tea bags and mint, squeezing tea bags to remove liquid. Stir in vodka; let cool completely. Pour tea mixture into a pitcher; cover and refrigerate until thoroughly chilled.
2. Serve tea over ice. Yield: 5 servings (serving size: about 1 cup).

CALORIES 127; FAT 0g (sat 0g, mono 0g, poly 0g); PROTEIN 0g; CARB 6.4g; FIBER 0g; CHOL 0mg; IRON 0mg; SODIUM 1mg; CALC 0mg

To ramp up the raspberry flavor, use raspberry-flavored sparkling water.

Raspberry Lemon Drop

Raspberry Lemon Drop

Prep: 5 minutes • Cook: 3 minutes

½ cup sugar
½ cup water
¼ cup fresh lemon juice
6 lemon thyme sprigs
1 cup fresh raspberries

6 ounces raspberry-flavored vodka
1 cup club soda
4 lemon slices
Additional fresh raspberries (optional)

1. Combine first 4 ingredients in a small heavy saucepan. Cook over medium heat, stirring gently until sugar dissolves. Remove pan from heat. Remove and discard thyme sprigs.

2. Place ¼ cup raspberries in a cocktail shaker; crush with back of a wooden spoon. Add 1½ ounces vodka and 1 tablespoon thyme syrup. Fill shaker with crushed ice; shake until outside of glass is frosted. Pour mixture through a fine-mesh sieve into a glass; gently stir in ¼ cup soda. Repeat procedure with remaining raspberries, vodka, syrup, ice, and club soda, reserving remaining syrup for another use. Serve each drink with a lemon slice and additional raspberries, if desired. Yield: 4 servings (serving size: ½ cup).

CALORIES 152; FAT 0.3g (sat 0g, mono 0g, poly 0.1g); PROTEIN 0.5g; CARB 13.5g; FIBER 2.5g; CHOL 0mg; IRON 1.2mg; SODIUM 1.4mg; CALC 24mg

Muddle mint leaves in the bottom of each glass for more flavor, or add 1⅓ cups citrus vodka for a spiked cocktail.

Sparkling Peach Lemonade

Prep: 5 minutes • Cook: 4 minutes

¼ cup fresh lemon juice
3 tablespoons sugar
2 cups lemon-flavored sparkling water, chilled

2 cups ginger ale, chilled
1½ cups peach nectar, chilled
Mint sprigs (optional)

1. Combine lemon juice and sugar in a small saucepan. Cook over medium heat, stirring constantly, 4 minutes or just until sugar dissolves. Pour into a large pitcher. Cover and chill.

2. Stir in sparkling water, ginger ale, and peach nectar just before serving. Serve over ice, and garnish with mint sprigs, if desired. Yield: 6 servings (serving size: about 1 cup).

CALORIES 88; FAT 0g (sat 0g, mono 0g, poly 0g); PROTEIN 0.2g; CARB 23g; FIBER 0.4g; CHOL 0mg; IRON 0.3mg; SODIUM 13mg; CALC 19mg

Spicy Carrot Bloody Mary

Prep: 3 minutes

1 cup carrot juice, chilled
½ cup vodka
¼ teaspoon ground cumin
1 (15-ounce) can diced tomatoes with celery, onion, and green pepper

1 jalapeño pepper, coarsely chopped
5 small serrano peppers (optional)
5 carrot ribbons (optional)

1. Place first 5 ingredients in a blender. Blend until smooth. Serve over ice. Garnish with serrano peppers and carrot ribbons, if desired. Yield: 5 servings (serving size: about ¾ cup).

CALORIES 103; FAT 0.1g (sat 0g, mono 0g, poly 0g); PROTEIN 1.2g; CARB 11.5g; FIBER 1.9g; CHOL 0mg; IRON 0.8mg; SODIUM 187mg; CALC 40mg

These spritzers combine white cranberry–peach juice and citrusy, herbal Lillet Blanc, a white aperitif wine, with seasonal fresh peaches and lime-flavored sparkling water to create a light, summery drink.

White Cranberry–Peach Spritzers

Prep: 7 minutes

2 cups white cranberry-peach juice
1 cup Lillet Blanc (French aperitif wine)
1 peach, halved

1½ cups lime-flavored sparkling water
4 lime slices

1. Combine juice and wine in a pitcher. Peel half of peach and cut into slices. Add peach slices to juice mixture; muddle with liquid. Divide peach mixture evenly among 4 ice-filled glasses. Add 6 tablespoons (⅜ cup) lime-flavored sparkling water to each glass. Cut remaining peach half into 4 slices. Garnish each drink with 1 peach slice and 1 lime slice. Yield: 4 servings (serving size: 1¼ cups).

CALORIES 120; FAT 0.1g (sat 0g, mono 0g, poly 0g); PROTEIN 0.3g; CARB 20g; FIBER 0.6g; CHOL 0mg; IRON 0.1mg; SODIUM 20mg; CALC 11mg

This version of a Bloody Mary mixes the heat of jalapeño with sweet carrot juice. Make the cocktails spicier by using jalapeño or black pepper vodka. Use a vegetable peeler to make the carrot ribbons. You can also dress them up with lime wedges, preserved lemon slices, or green olives.

Spicy Carrot Bloody Mary

weeknight
dinners

Horseradish gives grilled flank steak a tangy kick of spiciness.

Horseradish-Garlic Flank Steak

Prep: 3 minutes • Cook: 12 minutes • Other: 5 minutes

2 tablespoons prepared horseradish
1 tablespoon olive oil
½ teaspoon salt
4 garlic cloves, minced
1 (1-pound) flank steak, trimmed
Cooking spray

1. Preheat grill to medium-high heat.
2. Combine first 4 ingredients in a bowl, stirring with a whisk. Spread mixture onto both sides of steak.
3. Place steak on grill rack coated with cooking spray. Grill 4 to 5 minutes on each side or until desired degree of doneness. Remove from grill; let stand 5 minutes. Cut steak diagonally across grain into thin slices. Yield: 4 servings (serving size: 3 ounces).

CALORIES 198; FAT 9.6g (sat 2.8g, mono 4.7g, poly 0.6g); PROTEIN 24.7g; CARB 1.8g; FIBER 0.3g; CHOL 37mg; IRON 1.9mg; SODIUM 377mg; CALC 37mg

serve with
Lemony Arugula Salad

Prep: 4 minutes

2 tablespoons extra-virgin olive oil
1 tablespoon fresh lemon juice
1 tablespoon water
½ teaspoon Dijon mustard
⅛ teaspoon salt
¼ teaspoon freshly ground black pepper
1 (5-ounce) bag arugula
¼ cup (1 ounce) shaved Parmesan cheese

1. Combine first 6 ingredients in a large bowl, stirring with a whisk. Add arugula; toss to coat. Divide arugula mixture evenly among 4 plates; top evenly with cheese. Yield: 4 servings (serving size: 1 cup salad and 1 tablespoon cheese).

CALORIES 102; FAT 9.1g (sat 2.2g, mono 5.9g, poly 0.8g); PROTEIN 3.5g; CARB 2.1g; FIBER 0.6g; CHOL 4.8mg; IRON 0.6mg; SODIUM 211mg; CALC 142mg

Balsamic Vegetable Pita Pizzas

Prep: 6 minutes • Cook: 9 minutes

4 (6-inch) whole-wheat pitas
Balsamic Vegetables

½ cup hummus
½ cup (2 ounces) crumbled goat cheese

1. Preheat oven to 450°.
2. Arrange pitas on a large baking sheet. Bake at 450° for 2 to 3 minutes or until pitas are toasted.
3. Prepare Balsamic Vegetables.
4. Spread 2 tablespoons hummus over each pita. Top evenly with Balsamic Vegetables and goat cheese. Yield: 4 servings (serving size: 1 pizza).

CALORIES 326; FAT 11.3g (sat 3.3g, mono 4.6g, poly 2.3g); PROTEIN 12g; CARB 48.4g; FIBER 7.8g; CHOL 7mg; IRON 3.3mg; SODIUM 709mg; CALC 53mg

Balsamic Vegetables

Prep: 3 minutes • Cook: 7 minutes

1 tablespoon olive oil
1 medium zucchini, halved lengthwise and sliced
1 medium yellow squash, halved lengthwise and sliced
1 cup sliced fresh cremini mushrooms

½ cup red bell pepper strips
½ cup sliced red onion
2 tablespoons balsamic vinegar
¼ teaspoon salt
¼ teaspoon freshly ground black pepper

1. Heat oil in a large nonstick skillet over medium-high heat. Add zucchini and next 4 ingredients. Sauté 5 minutes or until vegetables are tender. Stir in vinegar, salt, and pepper; sauté 1 additional minute. Yield: 4 servings (serving size: ¾ cup).

CALORIES 68; FAT 3.7g (sat 0.5g, mono 2.5g, poly 0.5g); PROTEIN 2.1g; CARB 8.1g; FIBER 2.1g; CHOL 0mg; IRON 0.7mg; SODIUM 156mg; CALC 24mg

use extra ingredients

Pitas

Goat Cheese

Red Bell Peppers

Turkey-Hummus Pitas, page **132**

Pistachio-Crusted Chicken and Strawberry Salad, page **307**

Mediterranean Hash Brown Cakes, page **78**

If you want to make the cheese gooey, place the assembled pizzas under the broiler for one minute or until browned.

The name of this South-Asian curry sauce translates literally to "two onions" because onions are added in two stages as it cooks. Skip the slow simmer time and take advantage of a prepared sauce, which gets these pizzas in the oven in under 10 minutes. You can find dopiaza sauce in the international aisle of your supermarket.

Pizza Dopiaza

Prep: 9 minutes • Cook: 10 minutes

1 (8.8-ounce) package whole-grain naan (2 naan)
⅔ cup dopiaza curry cooking sauce
1 cup bagged baby spinach leaves, chopped
1 cup rinsed and drained canned chickpeas (garbanzo beans)
1 cup (2 ounces) shredded paneer or crumbled queso blanco
2 tablespoons fresh cilantro (optional)

1. Preheat oven to 450°.
2. Place naan on a baking sheet. Spread ⅓ cup cooking sauce over each naan. Top each pizza with ½ cup spinach leaves, ½ cup chickpeas, and ½ cup cheese.
3. Bake at 450° for 10 minutes or until thoroughly heated. Sprinkle with cilantro, if desired. Yield: 4 servings (serving size: ½ pizza).

CALORIES 311; FAT 8.8g (sat 1.8g, mono 4.6g, poly 2g); PROTEIN 10.5g; CARB 40.6g; FIBER 7.9g; CHOL 9.6mg; IRON 3mg; SODIUM 736mg; CALC 111mg

use extra ingredients

Baby Spinach	Chickpeas	Paneer or Queso Blanco

Prosciutto-Fig Salad, page **142**	Chickpea, Fennel, and Olive Chicken Salad, page **122**	Curried Paneer and Spinach-Stuffed Potatoes, page **146**

Serve these hearty meatless patties with Cucumber-Tomato Relish or Greek yogurt spiked with fresh cilantro and cumin.

Tofu-Chickpea Patties
Prep: 10 minutes • Cook: 16 minutes

1 (16-ounce) package cilantro-flavored firm tofu, drained
3 garlic cloves
1 (15-ounce) can lower-sodium chickpeas (garbanzo beans), rinsed and drained
4 teaspoons olive oil, divided
1 large egg
½ cup dry breadcrumbs
½ teaspoon freshly ground black pepper
¼ teaspoon salt

1. Place tofu between paper towels until barely moist. Cut tofu into 1-inch cubes.
2. With food processor running, drop garlic through food chute; process until minced. Add tofu and chickpeas. Pulse twice; scrape sides. Add 1 teaspoon oil, egg, and next 3 ingredients; pulse 4 times or just until beans are finely chopped (do not overprocess). Shape mixture into 8 (4-inch-round, ½-inch-thick) patties.
3. Heat 1½ teaspoons oil in a large nonstick skillet over medium heat. Add half of patties to pan; cook 4 minutes. Carefully turn patties over; cook 4 minutes or until browned. Repeat procedure with remaining oil and patties. Serve immediately. Yield: 4 servings (serving size: 2 patties).

CALORIES 312; FAT 15.5g (sat 2.4g, mono 6.3g, poly 6.5g); PROTEIN 19.4g; CARB 23.1g; FIBER 4.5g; CHOL 46.5mg; IRON 2mg; SODIUM 327mg; CALC 54mg

serve with
Cucumber-Tomato Relish
Prep: 9 minutes

2 cups chopped English cucumber
½ cup chopped red onion
2 tablespoons chopped fresh mint
3 tablespoons fresh lemon juice
1½ tablespoons olive oil
½ teaspoon ground cumin
⅛ teaspoon salt
⅛ teaspoon freshly ground black pepper
1 (8-ounce) tomato, chopped

1. Place all ingredients except tomato in a food processor; pulse twice. Transfer mixture to a medium bowl, and stir in tomato. Yield: 4 servings (serving size: ¾ cup).

CALORIES 75; FAT 5.3g (sat 0.7g, mono 3.7g, poly 0.6g); PROTEIN 1.6g; CARB 6.6g; FIBER 2g; CHOL 0mg; IRON 0.4mg; SODIUM 78mg; CALC 15mg

Waffles aren't just for breakfast. Enjoy this savory version for a fun, light dinner. Take advantage of summer tomatoes and corn, when you can get them, to make the topping.

Savory Cornmeal Waffles
Prep: 5 minutes • Cook: 10 minutes

1 cup 10-grain whole-grain pancake and waffle mix
⅓ cup yellow cornmeal
1 cup club soda

1 tablespoon canola oil
2 large egg whites
Cooking spray
Tomato-Corn Topping

1. Preheat waffle iron.
2. Combine pancake and waffle mix and cornmeal in a large bowl, stirring with a whisk. Combine club soda, oil, and egg whites in a medium bowl, stirring well with a whisk. Add egg white mixture to cornmeal mixture, stirring just until smooth.
3. Coat waffle iron with cooking spray. Spoon about ⅓ cup batter per 4-inch waffle onto hot waffle iron, spreading batter to edges. Cook 2 minutes or until steaming stops and waffles are golden; repeat procedure with remaining batter. Serve with Tomato-Corn Topping. Yield: 5 servings (serving size: 2 waffles and ⅓ cup topping).

CALORIES 206; FAT 6.2g (sat 2g, mono 2.7g, poly 1.3g); PROTEIN 7.1g; CARB 31.9g; FIBER 3.8g; CHOL 8mg; IRON 1.4mg; SODIUM 410mg; CALC 79mg

Tomato-Corn Topping
Prep: 3 minutes • Cook: 4 minutes

1 tablespoon butter
2 cups chopped plum tomato
1 cup fresh corn kernels
⅓ cup thinly sliced fresh basil

¼ cup sliced green onions
¼ teaspoon salt
¼ teaspoon freshly ground black pepper

1. Melt butter in a medium nonstick skillet. Add tomato and corn; sauté 4 minutes or until tomato begins to soften. Stir in basil and remaining ingredients. Yield: 5 servings (serving size: ⅓ cup).

CALORIES 63; FAT 2.8g (sat 1.5g, mono 0.7g, poly 0.3g); PROTEIN 1.8g; CARB 9.2g; FIBER 2g; CHOL 6mg; IRON 0.6mg; SODIUM 127mg; CALC 18mg

Chinese long beans usually come in a bunch secured with a rubber band. To quickly cut the beans, leave the rubber band intact and cut the entire bunch, from the opposite end, into 2-inch pieces.

Tofu and Chinese Long Beans
Prep: 3 minutes • Cook: 10 minutes

1 (14-ounce) package extra-firm tofu, drained
1 tablespoon canola oil
1 pound Chinese long beans, cut into 2-inch pieces
1 tablespoon water
1 large-size zip-top plastic steam-cooking bag
1 (8.8-ounce) package microwaveable precooked whole-grain brown rice

¼ cup lower-sodium soy sauce
2 tablespoons seasoned rice vinegar
1 tablespoon grated peeled fresh ginger
1 teaspoon brown sugar
4 teaspoons dark sesame oil

1. Gently press tofu between paper towels to remove excess moisture; cut into ¾-inch cubes.
2. Heat oil in a large nonstick skillet over medium-high heat. Add tofu cubes. Cook 8 minutes or until browned on all sides, turning carefully with a spatula to keep cubes intact.
3. While tofu cooks, place long beans and water in steam-cooking bag according to package directions. Seal bag. Microwave at HIGH 3 minutes. Microwave rice according to package directions.
4. Combine soy sauce and next 4 ingredients in a small bowl, stirring with a whisk. Drain beans. Add steamed beans and sauce mixture to tofu; stir-fry 1 minute. Serve over rice. Yield: 4 servings (serving size: 1¼ cups tofu mixture and ½ cup rice).

CALORIES 298; FAT 14.2g (sat 1.6g, mono 6.2g, poly 6.3g); PROTEIN 13.9g; CARB 31.6g; FIBER 5.1g; CHOL 0mg; IRON 3mg; SODIUM 771mg; CALC 109mg

Toss halibut fillets and orange slices in a quick vinaigrette of lemon juice, honey, mint and ginger, and then grill. Place orange halves on the grill alongside the fish, and squeeze their sweet juice over the fish right before serving.

Grilled Citrus Halibut

Prep: 5 minutes • Cook: 8 minutes

2 large navel oranges, divided
2 tablespoons fresh lemon juice
1 tablespoon chopped fresh mint
1 tablespoon olive oil
2 teaspoons grated peeled fresh ginger
1 teaspoon honey

¼ teaspoon salt
¼ teaspoon freshly ground black pepper
4 skinless halibut fillets (about 1¼ pounds)
Cooking spray
Mint sprigs (optional)

1. Preheat grill to medium-high heat.
2. Cut 1 orange in half. Cut remaining orange into 8 slices. Combine lemon juice and next 6 ingredients in a large bowl. Add fish and orange slices; toss gently to coat.
3. Place fish and orange slices on grill rack coated with cooking spray, discarding lemon mixture. Place orange halves, cut sides down, on grill rack. Grill 8 minutes or until fish flakes easily when tested with a fork, turning fish and orange slices after 4 minutes. Place 1 fillet on each of 4 plates. Top each with 2 orange slices. Squeeze orange halves evenly over fish and orange slices. Garnish with mint sprigs, if desired. Yield: 4 servings (serving size: 1 fillet, 2 orange slices, and about 1 tablespoon orange juice).

CALORIES 231; FAT 7g (sat 1g, mono 3.7g, poly 1.4g); PROTEIN 30.2g; CARB 11.2g; FIBER 1.7g; CHOL 45mg; IRON 1.4mg; SODIUM 223mg; CALC 99mg

use extra ingredients

Navel Oranges

Arugula-Orange Salad with Fig-Bacon Dressing, page **135**

Mint

Watermelon-Mint Sorbet, page **375**

Ginger

Orange-Ginger Pork Chops with Sweet and Sour Cabbage, page **308**

The slightly sweet dressing would also be excellent drizzled over fresh fruit.

Grilled Shrimp Salad with Honey-Lime Dressing

Prep: 5 minutes • Cook: 8 minutes

1 pound peeled and deveined shrimp (about 20 shrimp)
1 tablespoon olive oil
1 tablespoon fiery 5-pepper seasoning, divided
1 (1¼-pound) cored fresh pineapple, cut into ½-inch-thick slices

Cooking spray
Honey-Lime Dressing
2 (4-ounce) packages lettuce and herb blend salad greens
¼ cup chopped fresh cilantro (optional)
4 lime wedges (optional)

1. Preheat grill to medium-high heat.
2. Thread shrimp onto 3 (12-inch) metal skewers. Brush shrimp with oil; sprinkle with 1½ teaspoons seasoning. Sprinkle pineapple slices with remaining 1½ teaspoons seasoning.
3. Place skewers and pineapple slices on grill rack coated with cooking spray. Grill 8 minutes or until lightly browned, turning once. Cut each pineapple slice into 4 pieces.
4. While shrimp and pineapple cook, prepare Honey-Lime Dressing.
5. Divide greens evenly among 4 plates, and top evenly with grilled shrimp and pineapple. Drizzle salads with Honey-Lime Dressing. Sprinkle each serving with 1 tablespoon chopped fresh cilantro, and serve with 1 lime wedge, if desired. Yield: 4 servings (serving size: 5 shrimp, 2¼ cups greens, ⅔ cup pineapple, and 2 tablespoons dressing).

CALORIES 366; FAT 16.7g (sat 1.9g, mono 8.9g, poly 4.2g); PROTEIN 25.2g; CARB 30g; FIBER 2.7g; CHOL 177mg; IRON 3.2mg; SODIUM 360mg; CALC 105mg

Honey-Lime Dressing

Prep: 3 minutes

¼ cup organic canola mayonnaise
2 tablespoons honey
1½ tablespoons fresh lime juice

1 tablespoon chopped fresh cilantro
Dash of ground red pepper

1. Combine all ingredients in a small bowl. Yield: 4 servings (serving size: 2 tablespoons).

CALORIES 133; FAT 11g (sat 1g, mono 6g, poly 3g); PROTEIN 0.1g; CARB 9g; FIBER 0g; CHOL 5mg; IRON 0mg; SODIUM 100mg; CALC 1mg

As the tomatoes, wine, and capers cook, the tomatoes begin to burst and release their juices, enhancing the pan sauce.

Pan-Roasted Salmon and Tomatoes

Prep: 3 minutes • Cook: 11 minutes

4 (6-ounce) salmon fillets	2 cups grape tomatoes, halved
¼ teaspoon salt	¼ cup dry white wine
¼ teaspoon freshly ground black pepper	1 tablespoon drained capers
Cooking spray	¼ cup chopped fresh basil

1. Sprinkle salmon with salt and pepper. Heat a large nonstick skillet over medium-high heat. Coat pan with cooking spray. Add fillets, skin side up, to pan. Cook 3 minutes or until browned. Carefully turn fillets over. Add tomatoes, wine, and capers. Cover and cook 7 minutes or until salmon flakes when tested with a fork or until desired degree of doneness. Sprinkle with basil. Yield: 4 servings (serving size: 1 fillet and ¼ cup tomato mixture).

CALORIES 226; FAT 6.1g (sat 1g, mono 1.7g, poly 2.3g); PROTEIN 34.6; CARB 3.6g; FIBER 1.2g; CHOL 89mg; IRON 1.5mg; SODIUM 327mg; CALC 40mg

serve with
Asparagus with Lemon-Basil Yogurt Sauce

Prep: 4 minutes • Cook: 2 minutes

1 pound asparagus spears	2 tablespoons fresh lemon juice
½ cup low-fat Greek yogurt	¼ teaspoon salt
2 tablespoons chopped fresh basil	¼ teaspoon freshly ground black pepper
½ teaspoon grated lemon rind	

1. Snap off tough ends of asparagus. Cook asparagus in boiling water to cover 2 minutes or until crisp-tender; drain. Plunge asparagus into ice water; drain.
2. Combine yogurt and remaining ingredients in a small bowl. Serve over asparagus. Yield: 4 servings (serving size: ¼ of asparagus and 2 tablespoons sauce).

CALORIES 46; FAT 0.6g (sat 0.4g, mono 0.2g, poly 0g); PROTEIN 4.9g; CARB 6.8g; FIBER 2.6g; CHOL 1.9mg; IRON 0.5mg; SODIUM 155mg; CALC 47mg

Slice the onion just before placing it on the grill. If given time to set, the onion rings will begin to separate and will not have good grill marks.

Sautéed Tilapia Tacos with Grilled Peppers and Onion

Prep: 7 minutes • Cook: 18 minutes • Other: 5 minutes

2 (½-inch-thick) slices white onion
1 (8-ounce) package mini sweet bell peppers
Cooking spray
¾ teaspoon salt, divided
½ teaspoon freshly ground black pepper, divided

4 (5-ounce) tilapia fillets
8 (6-inch) corn tortillas
1 small jalapeño pepper, thinly sliced
8 lime wedges (optional)

1. Preheat grill to high heat.
2. Arrange onion slices and bell peppers on grill rack coated with cooking spray. Grill onions 12 minutes, turning after 6 minutes. Grill bell peppers 12 minutes, turning occasionally. Remove onions and bell peppers from grill, and let stand 5 minutes. Slice onion rings in half. Thinly slice bell peppers; discard stems and seeds. Combine onion, bell peppers, ¼ teaspoon salt, and ⅛ teaspoon black pepper in a small bowl.
3. Sprinkle fish evenly with remaining ½ teaspoon salt and remaining ⅜ teaspoon black pepper. Heat a large nonstick skillet over medium-high heat. Coat pan with cooking spray. Add fish to pan, and cook 3 minutes on each side or until fish flakes easily when tested with a fork or until desired degree of doneness.
4. Warm tortillas according to package directions. Divide fish, onion mixture, and jalapeño slices evenly among tortillas. Serve with lime wedges, if desired. Yield: 4 servings (serving size: 2 tacos).

CALORIES 292; FAT 4.4g (sat 1.2g, mono 1.2g, poly 1.3g); PROTEIN 32.6g; CARB 32g; FIBER 4.8g; CHOL 71mg; IRON 1.9mg; SODIUM 526mg; CALC 120mg

Shredded Chicken Tacos

Prep: 17 minutes • Cook: 18 minutes

2	ears shucked corn	2	cups shredded skinless, boneless rotisserie chicken breast
1	(12-ounce) package baby heirloom tomatoes	1	peeled avocado, cut into 16 slices
½	teaspoon freshly ground black pepper	8	lime wedges (optional)
¼	teaspoon salt		
8	(6-inch) corn tortillas		

1. Preheat broiler.

2. Place corn on a jelly-roll pan; broil 18 minutes or until charred on all sides, rotating every 6 minutes. Cut kernels from corn; place kernels in a medium bowl. Cut tomatoes into quarters. Add tomatoes to corn, and sprinkle corn mixture with pepper and salt.

3. Heat tortillas according to package directions. Divide chicken evenly among tortillas; top each taco with ¼ cup corn mixture and 2 avocado slices. Serve with lime wedges, if desired. Yield: 4 servings (serving size: 2 tacos).

CALORIES 420; FAT 13.5g (sat 2.3g, mono 7.1g, poly 2.4g); PROTEIN 39.2g; CARB 40.6g; FIBER 8.4g; CHOL 101mg; IRON 2mg; SODIUM 554mg; CALC 123mg

Shredded Chicken Tacos

Sautéed Tilapia Tacos with Grilled Peppers and Onion

Pick juicy tomatoes at their peak in the summer, or visit a local farmers' market for vegetables until early fall. Small pods of okra are more tender.

Shrimp and Summer Vegetable Sauté

Prep: 1 minute • Cook: 14 minutes

4 bacon slices
2 cups fresh corn kernels
1½ cups chopped tomato (1 large)
1 cup sliced fresh okra
½ cup chopped onion
1¼ pounds peeled and deveined large shrimp
¼ teaspoon salt
¼ teaspoon freshly ground black pepper
Cooking spray
2 tablespoons torn fresh basil
2 teaspoons fresh lemon juice
Lemon wedges (optional)

1. Cook bacon in a large nonstick skillet over medium heat until crisp. Remove bacon from pan; crumble. Increase to medium-high heat. Add corn and next 3 ingredients to drippings in pan; sauté 3 minutes or until browned. Remove corn mixture from pan. Keep warm. Wipe pan with a paper towel.
2. Sprinkle shrimp with salt and pepper. Heat pan over medium-high heat. Coat pan with cooking spray. Add shrimp; sauté 2 minutes or until shrimp are done.
3. Add corn mixture to shrimp. Stir in crumbled bacon, basil, and lemon juice. Serve with lemon wedges, if desired. Yield: 4 servings (serving size: about 1½ cups).

CALORIES 267; FAT 5.6g (sat 1.8g, mono 1.5g, poly 1.5g); PROTEIN 34.5g; CARB 21.4g; FIBER 3.5g; CHOL 223mg; IRON 4.3mg; SODIUM 509mg; CALC 110mg

use extra ingredients

Corn

Steak Taco Salad with Black Bean-Corn Relish, page **185**

Tomatoes

Crab Louis Salad, page **155**

Basil

Pesto Grilled Cheese Panini, page **152**

Moroccan dishes often combine sweet and savory. Enjoy savory, paprika-spiced chicken with squash that has a sweet and spicy twist from orange, ginger, and cumin.

Chicken and Olives
Prep: 1 minute • Cook: 11 minutes

4 (4-ounce) chicken cutlets
½ teaspoon paprika
¼ teaspoon salt
Cooking spray

1¾ cups thin vertical onion slices
½ cup mixed pitted olives, halved
½ cup dry white wine

1. Sprinkle chicken evenly with paprika and salt. Heat a large skillet over medium-high heat. Coat pan with cooking spray. Add chicken to pan. Cook 2 minutes on each side or until done. Transfer chicken to a serving dish, and keep warm.
2. Coat pan with cooking spray; add onion slices. Sauté 4 minutes or until tender. Return chicken to pan; add olives and white wine. Cook 3 minutes or until liquid is reduced by half. Serve warm. Yield: 4 servings (serving size: 1 chicken cutlet and ½ cup onion mixture).

CALORIES 187; FAT 5g (sat 0.7g, mono 0.9g, poly 0.5g); PROTEIN 24.7g; CARB 6.2g; FIBER 0.9g; CHOL 72.6mg; IRON 0.6mg; SODIUM 415mg; CALC 19mg

serve with
Moroccan Squash
Prep: 1 minute • Cook: 4 minutes

1 (12-ounce) package refrigerated
    steam-in-bag cubed butternut squash
2 tablespoons orange marmalade

1 teaspoon grated peeled fresh ginger
¼ teaspoon ground cumin
1 tablespoon chopped fresh cilantro

1. Microwave squash according to package directions. Place squash in a bowl. Add marmalade, ginger, and cumin; toss gently. Sprinkle with cilantro. Serve immediately. Yield: 4 servings (serving size: about ½ cup).

CALORIES 55; FAT 0.1g (sat 0g, mono 0g, poly 0g); PROTEIN 0.7g; CARB 14.4g; FIBER 2.4g; CHOL 0mg; IRON 0.5mg; SODIUM 9mg; CALC 35mg

A spicy sauce of chipotle chiles, onion, and cilantro coats these juicy grilled chicken tenders. Mexican-style corn topped with Cotija cheese and a squeeze of lime completes the meal.

Green Spice Chicken Tenders

Prep: 5 minutes • Cook: 10 minutes

½ cup chopped onion
¼ cup packed fresh cilantro leaves
1 tablespoon olive oil
4 chipotle chiles in adobo sauce

12 chicken breast tenders (about 1½ pounds)
¼ teaspoon salt
Cooking spray

1. Preheat grill to medium-high heat.
2. Place first 4 ingredients in a food processor. Process 30 seconds or until minced, scraping sides of bowl once; transfer mixture to a large bowl. Add chicken to marinade, turning to coat. Sprinkle salt evenly over chicken.
3. Coat chicken with cooking spray. Place on grill rack coated with cooking spray. Grill 5 minutes on each side or until done. Yield: 4 servings (serving size: 3 chicken tenders).

CALORIES 219; FAT 8.2g (sat 1.4g, mono 4g, poly 1.1g); PROTEIN 36.3g; CARB 4.7g; FIBER 2.5g; CHOL 109mg; IRON 1.1mg; SODIUM 617mg; CALC 13mg

serve with

Mexican-Style Grilled Corn

Prep: 5 minutes • Cook: 8 minutes

1½ tablespoons canola mayonnaise
1½ tablespoons butter, softened
4 ears shucked corn
Cooking spray

½ cup (4 ounces) crumbled Cotija cheese
⅛ teaspoon freshly ground black pepper
4 lime wedges

1. Preheat grill to medium-high heat.
2. Combine mayonnaise and butter in a small bowl. Coat corn with cooking spray; place on grill rack coated with cooking spray. Grill 4 minutes on each side or until grill marks appear.
3. Spread 2 heaping teaspoons butter mixture on each ear of corn; sprinkle each with 2 tablespoons cheese. Sprinkle corn evenly with pepper. Serve with lime wedges. Yield: 4 servings (serving size: 1 ear of corn and 1 lime wedge).

CALORIES 267; FAT 17.9g (sat 8.3g, mono 6.6g, poly 2.2g); PROTEIN 10.6g; CARB 19.8g; FIBER 2.3g; CHOL 34mg; IRON 0.6mg; SODIUM 526mg; CALC 5mg

The orzo takes on a creamy, almost risotto-like texture from cooking in a small amount of liquid. Stir it often so it doesn't stick.

Pan-Seared Chicken Thighs with Lemon and Tomatoes

Prep: 1 minute • Cook: 14 minutes

2 teaspoons canola oil
8 (4-ounce) bone-in chicken thighs, skinned
¼ teaspoon salt
½ teaspoon freshly ground black pepper
¼ cup sliced pimiento-stuffed olives

1 (14.5-ounce) can organic fire-roasted diced tomatoes
2 garlic cloves, minced
1 lemon, thinly sliced

1. Heat canola oil in a large nonstick skillet over medium-high heat. Sprinkle chicken with salt and pepper. Add chicken to pan, and cook 4 minutes on each side or until browned.
2. Add olives, tomatoes, and garlic to pan, spooning mixture over and around chicken. Place lemon slices on chicken. Reduce heat to medium-low. Cover and cook 4 minutes or until chicken is done. Yield: 4 servings (serving size: 2 chicken thighs and ½ cup tomato mixture).

CALORIES 340; FAT 12.7g (sat 2.4g, mono 5g, poly 3.6g); PROTEIN 45.5g; CARB 7.4g; FIBER 1.4g; CHOL 188.2mg; IRON 3mg; SODIUM 607mg; CALC 47mg

serve with
Herb-Feta Orzo

Prep: 2 minutes • Cook: 17 minutes

1 (14.5-ounce) can fat-free, lower-sodium chicken broth
½ cup water
1 cup uncooked orzo

2 tablespoons chopped fresh oregano
1 teaspoon grated lemon rind
¼ teaspoon freshly ground black pepper
¼ cup crumbled feta cheese

1. Bring broth and water to a boil in a medium saucepan; add orzo. Reduce heat and simmer 10 minutes or until orzo is tender, stirring frequently. Drain. Combine orzo, oregano, lemon rind, and pepper. Sprinkle with cheese. Yield: 4 servings (serving size: about ½ cup).

CALORIES 207; FAT 2.5g (sat 1.2g, mono 0.1g, poly 0.3g); PROTEIN 9.9g; CARB 37.1g; FIBER 1.8g; CHOL 6.3mg; IRON 1.7mg; SODIUM 396mg; CALC 44mg

Sun-dried tomatoes pack flavor into this aioli-topped chicken burger. Just a couple tablespoons of oats in the patty keep the burger juicy.

Spinach-Chicken Burgers

Prep: 5 minutes • Cook: 6 minutes

1 pound ground chicken breast	Cooking spray
1/3 cup frozen chopped spinach, thawed, drained, and squeezed dry	4 Bibb lettuce leaves (optional)
2 tablespoons old-fashioned rolled oats	4 (1.5-ounce) 100% whole-wheat hamburger buns
1/4 teaspoon salt	Sun-Dried Tomato Aioli
1/4 teaspoon freshly ground black pepper	

1. Combine first 5 ingredients. Divide chicken mixture into 4 equal portions, shaping each into a ½-inch-thick patty.
2. Heat a large nonstick skillet over medium-high heat; coat pan with cooking spray. Add patties; cook 3 minutes on each side or until thermometer registers 165°.
3. Place 1 lettuce leaf on bottom half of each bun, if using. Place 1 burger on bottom half of each bun. Spread 2½ tablespoons Sun-Dried Tomato Aioli on inside of each bun top; place tops on burgers. Yield: 4 servings (serving size: 1 burger and 2½ tablespoons aioli).

CALORIES 374; FAT 18.2g (sat 1.8g, mono 9g, poly 5.1g); PROTEIN 29.1g; CARB 25.8g; FIBER 4.2g; CHOL 72mg; IRON 1.6mg; SODIUM 654mg; CALC 67mg

Sun-Dried Tomato Aioli

Prep: 3 minutes

1 garlic clove	1 tablespoon fresh lemon juice
1/3 cup canola mayonnaise	1/8 teaspoon salt
3 tablespoons drained oil-packed sun-dried tomatoes	

1. Drop garlic through food chute with food processor on; process until minced. Add remaining ingredients; process until smooth. Yield: 4 servings (serving size: 2½ tablespoons).

CALORIES 146; FAT 15.4g (sat 1.4g, mono 8.5g, poly 4.1g); PROTEIN 0.3g; CARB 1.8g; FIBER 0.3g; CHOL 7mg; IRON 0.2mg; SODIUM 220mg; CALC 4mg

Fruity apple juice and tangy mustard are a perfect flavor combo for these grilled pork chops.

Apple-Mustard–Glazed Pork Chops

Prep: 5 minutes • Cook: 10 minutes • Other: 3 minutes

1 tablespoon canola oil
4 (4-ounce) boneless center-cut loin pork chops (about ½ inch thick)
½ teaspoon salt
¼ teaspoon ground red pepper, divided
¼ cup thawed apple juice concentrate, undiluted

1 tablespoon cider vinegar
1 tablespoon water
2 teaspoons stone-ground mustard
Cooking spray

1. Preheat grill to medium-high heat.
2. Rub oil over both sides of pork; sprinkle with salt and ⅛ teaspoon red pepper.
3. Combine remaining ⅛ teaspoon red pepper, apple juice concentrate, and next 3 ingredients. Place pork on grill rack coated with cooking spray; grill 5 minutes on each side or until a meat thermometer inserted into thickest portion registers 145°, basting frequently with apple juice mixture. Let chops stand 3 minutes before serving. Yield: 4 servings (serving size: 1 pork chop).

CALORIES 208; FAT 7.9g (sat 1.5g, mono 3.9g, poly 1.5g); PROTEIN 25g; CARB 7.4g; FIBER 0g; CHOL 78mg; IRON 0.8mg; SODIUM 389mg; CALC 21mg

serve with
Broccolini with Bacon

Prep: 2 minutes • Cook: 10 minutes

3 quarts water
1 pound Broccolini
2 center-cut bacon slices
½ cup coarsely chopped sweet onion

¼ cup fat-free, lower-sodium chicken broth
⅛ teaspoon salt
⅛ teaspoon freshly ground black pepper

1. Bring 3 quarts water to a boil. Add Broccolini to boiling water; cook 4 minutes or until crisp-tender. Drain.
2. Cook bacon in a large nonstick skillet over medium heat until crisp. Remove bacon from pan; crumble. Add onion to drippings in pan; sauté 4 minutes or until tender. Stir in broth, salt, and pepper, scraping pan to loosen browned bits. Add Broccolini; toss well. Sprinkle with bacon. Yield: 4 servings.

CALORIES 66; FAT 0.8g (sat 0.3g, mono 0.3g, poly 0.1g); PROTEIN 5.3g; CARB 10g; FIBER 1.7g; CHOL 3mg; IRON 1.1mg; SODIUM 187mg; CALC 85mg

Frozen cranberries work well when you cannot find fresh. The sweetness of the cranberry sauce complements the slightly bitter taste of the chard.

Pork Medallions with Cranberry Sauce

Prep: 6 minutes • Cook: 9 minutes

1 (1-pound) pork tenderloin, trimmed
¼ teaspoon salt
½ teaspoon freshly ground black pepper
1 cup fresh or frozen cranberries
½ cup fat-free, lower-sodium chicken broth
¼ cup sugar
1 teaspoon chopped fresh sage
   Cooking spray

1. Cut pork crosswise into 8 pieces. Place pork between 2 sheets of heavy-duty plastic wrap; pound to ¼-inch thickness using a meat mallet or small heavy skillet. Sprinkle both sides of pork evenly with salt and pepper.
2. Combine cranberries, broth, and sugar in a small saucepan. Bring to a boil; boil 6 minutes or until berries burst and sauce is reduced to ⅔ cup. Stir in sage.
3. While sauce cooks, heat a large nonstick skillet over medium-high heat. Coat pan with cooking spray. Add pork to pan; cook 4 minutes on each side or until done. Serve pork with sauce. Yield: 4 servings (serving size: 2 pork medallions and about 3 tablespoons sauce).

CALORIES 202; FAT 4g (sat 1.3g, mono 1.5g, poly 0.6g); PROTEIN 23.8g; CARB 16.4g; FIBER 1.1g; CHOL 73.7mg; IRON 1.1mg; SODIUM 278mg; CALC 9mg

serve with
Sautéed Swiss Chard

Prep: 3 minutes • Cook: 7 minutes

1½ pounds Swiss chard, trimmed
1½ tablespoons unsalted butter
1 tablespoon cider vinegar
1 teaspoon brown sugar
⅛ teaspoon crushed red pepper

1. Cut chard into ½-inch-wide strips to measure 8 cups.
2. Melt butter in a large nonstick skillet over medium-high heat. Add chard. Cook, stirring constantly, 5 minutes or until tender. Stir in vinegar, brown sugar, and crushed red pepper. Cook 1 additional minute or until liquid evaporates. Yield: 4 servings (serving size: about ⅔ cup).

CALORIES 75; FAT 4.7g (sat 2.8g, mono 1.2g, poly 0.3g); PROTEIN 3.1g; CARB 7.5g; FIBER 2.7g; CHOL 11.4mg; IRON 3.1mg; SODIUM 363mg; CALC 89mg

This salad can be served chilled or warm for a summer or fall dinner.

Black and Blue Salad
Prep: 3 minutes • Cook: 7 minutes • Other: 5 minutes

2 (4-ounce) beef tenderloin steaks
Cooking spray
4 cups sliced romaine lettuce hearts
   (1½ romaine hearts)

½ cup vertically sliced red onion
2 plum tomatoes, quartered
Blue Cheese Dressing
½ to 1 teaspoon freshly ground black pepper

1. Heat a medium cast-iron or nonstick skillet over medium-high heat. Coat beef with cooking spray. Add steaks to pan. Cook steaks 2 to 3 minutes on each side or until desired degree of doneness. Remove steaks from pan; let stand 5 minutes. Cut each steak into thin slices.
2. Place 2 cups lettuce on each of 2 large plates. Sprinkle each salad with ¼ cup onion slices. Arrange 4 tomato quarters around edge of each salad. Place 1 sliced steak in center of each salad; drizzle Blue Cheese Dressing evenly over salads. Sprinkle pepper evenly over salads. Yield: 2 servings (serving size: 1 salad and 3 tablespoons dressing).

CALORIES 295; FAT 16.5g (sat 3.8g, mono 8.2g, poly 3.2g); PROTEIN 26.1g; CARB 10.5g; FIBER 3.3g; CHOL 69.9mg; IRON 2.6mg; SODIUM 233mg; CALC 88mg

Blue Cheese Dressing
Prep: 5 minutes

¼ cup nonfat buttermilk
1½ tablespoons canola mayonnaise

⅛ teaspoon hot sauce
1½ tablespoons crumbled blue cheese

1. Combine first 3 ingredients in a small bowl, stirring with a whisk. Stir in cheese. Yield: 2 servings (serving size: 3 tablespoons).

CALORIES 105; FAT 9.8g (sat 1.3g, mono 5.7g, poly 2.7g); PROTEIN 2.3g; CARB 1.9g; FIBER 0g; CHOL 8.4mg; IRON 0mg; SODIUM 177mg; CALC 28mg

Cheesy polenta is a no-fuss alternative to mashed potatoes as a side for this dinnertime classic.

Steak with Creamy Mushroom Gravy

Prep: 3 minutes • Cook: 16 minutes • Other: 5 minutes

1 (1-pound) flat-iron steak, trimmed
½ teaspoon salt, divided
½ teaspoon freshly ground black pepper, divided
1 tablespoon canola oil
1 (4-ounce) package gourmet mushroom blend
½ cup fat-free, lower-sodium beef broth
2 teaspoons chopped fresh rosemary
¼ cup reduced-fat sour cream

1. Sprinkle steak evenly with ¼ teaspoon salt and ¼ teaspoon pepper.
2. Heat 1 tablespoon oil in large nonstick skillet over medium-high heat. Add steak. Cook 5 minutes on each side or until desired degree of doneness. Remove steak from pan. Let stand 5 minutes.
3. Add mushrooms to pan; sauté 3 minutes or until tender. Stir in broth, rosemary, remaining ¼ teaspoon salt, and remaining ¼ teaspoon pepper. Bring to a boil; cover, reduce heat, and simmer 3 minutes.
4. Place sour cream in a medium bowl. Gradually add mushroom mixture, stirring constantly with a whisk.
5. Cut steak diagonally across grain into thin slices. Serve with gravy. Yield: 4 servings (serving size: 3 ounces steak and 3 tablespoons gravy).

CALORIES 221; FAT 12.7g (sat 4.6g, mono 6.5g, poly 1.5g); PROTEIN 24.8g; CARB 2.6g; FIBER 0.3g; CHOL 86.6mg; IRON 3mg; SODIUM 455mg; CALC 46mg

serve with
Gruyère Polenta

Prep: 1 minute • Cook: 9 minutes

1¾ cups fat-free, lower-sodium chicken broth
¾ cup 2% reduced-fat milk
1 cup instant polenta
¼ teaspoon freshly ground black pepper
2 ounces Gruyère cheese, shredded

1. Bring chicken broth and milk to a boil in a medium saucepan. Gradually add polenta and pepper, stirring constantly with a whisk. Cover; reduce heat, and cook, stirring constantly, 3 minutes. Remove from heat; add cheese, stirring until cheese melts. Serve immediately. Yield: 4 servings (serving size: ¾ cup).

CALORIES 189; FAT 6.1g (sat 3.4g, mono 1.8g, poly 0.6g); PROTEIN 9.1g; CARB 24.1g; FIBER 1.2g; CHOL 19.3mg; IRON 10.9mg; SODIUM 613mg; CALC 305mg

Substitute Greek yogurt for the sour cream and omit the vinegar for a more tangy cucumber sauce. Complete this meal with tomatoes, thinly sliced onion, and pita bread, if you wish.

Feta-Lamb Patties with Cucumber Sauce

Prep: 5 minutes • Cook: 9 minutes

1 pound lean ground lamb	¼ cup shredded English cucumber
¼ cup crumbled feta cheese	¾ cup fat-free sour cream
2 teaspoons chopped fresh oregano	1 teaspoon chopped fresh dill
2 garlic cloves, pressed	½ teaspoon red wine vinegar
¼ teaspoon salt, divided	
½ teaspoon freshly ground black pepper, divided	

1. Combine first 4 ingredients, ⅛ teaspoon salt, and ¼ teaspoon pepper in a bowl. Divide lamb mixture into 4 equal portions, shaping each into a ½-inch-thick patty.
2. Heat a large nonstick skillet over medium-high heat. Add patties; cook 4 minutes. Turn patties over; cook 4 minutes or until done.
3. While patties cook, combine remaining ⅛ teaspoon salt, remaining ¼ teaspoon pepper, cucumber, and next 3 ingredients in a small bowl. Serve with patties. Yield: 4 servings (serving size: 1 patty and 3½ tablespoons cucumber sauce).

CALORIES 225; FAT 8.6g (sat 3.9g, mono 2.8g, poly 0.6g); PROTEIN 26.8g; CARB 8.6g; FIBER 0.1g; CHOL 86mg; IRON 2.2mg; SODIUM 362mg; CALC 133mg

use extra ingredients

Feta Cheese	Cucumber	Sour Cream

Feta-Chickpea Salad, page **102**	Barbecue Chicken Banh Mi, page **119**	Sour Cream–Peach Tart, page **372**

weekend suppers

The spices on this broiled salmon give it the same flavors as many tandoori-cooked dishes.

Tandoori Salmon
Prep: 3 minutes • Cook: 9 minutes

1 teaspoon ground ginger	¼ teaspoon freshly ground black pepper
1 teaspoon ground turmeric	4 (6-ounce) salmon fillets
½ teaspoon ground cumin	Cooking spray
¼ teaspoon salt	Cilantro-Yogurt Sauce

1. Preheat broiler.
2. Combine first 5 ingredients in a small bowl; rub over fillets. Place fillets on a broiler pan coated with cooking spray; broil 9 minutes or until fish flakes easily when tested with a fork or until desired degree of doneness. Serve with Cilantro-Yogurt Sauce. Yield: 4 servings (serving size: 1 fillet and ¼ cup sauce).

CALORIES 246; FAT 7.2g (sat 1.6g, mono 2g, poly 2.4g); PROTEIN 37.4g; CARB 5.8g; FIBER 0.3g; CHOL 92mg; IRON 1.8mg; SODIUM 303mg; CALC 141mg

Cilantro-Yogurt Sauce
Prep: 5 minutes

1 cup plain low-fat yogurt	1 teaspoon fresh lime juice
1 tablespoon chopped fresh cilantro	2 garlic cloves, minced
1 teaspoon grated lime rind	

1. Combine all ingredients in a small bowl. Cover and chill until ready to serve. Yield: 4 servings (serving size: ¼ cup).

CALORIES 41; FAT 1g (sat 0.6g, mono 0.3g, poly 0g); PROTEIN 3.3g; CARB 4.9g; FIBER 0g; CHOL 4mg; IRON 0.1mg; SODIUM 43mg; CALC 115mg

serve with
Sautéed Okra
Prep: 2 minutes • Cook: 12 minutes • Other: 5 minutes

1 teaspoon canola oil	¼ teaspoon salt
1 pound okra pods, cut in half lengthwise	¼ teaspoon freshly ground black pepper

1. Heat canola oil in a large nonstick skillet over medium-high heat; swirl to coat. Add okra, and sauté 5 minutes or until lightly browned. Sprinkle with salt and freshly ground black pepper. Yield: 4 servings.

CALORIES 46; FAT 1.3g (sat 0.1g, mono 0.8g, poly 0.4g); PROTEIN 2.3g; CARB 8.1g; FIBER 3.7g; CHOL 0mg; IRON 0.9mg; SODIUM 157mg; CALC 93mg

Serve this Italian meatless main dish over a bed of hot spaghetti, if you like.

Eggplant Parmigiana
Prep: 12 minutes • Cook: 35 minutes

¼ cup canola mayonnaise
1 (1½-pound) eggplant, cut into 12 (½-inch-thick) slices
¾ cup Parmesan-seasoned breadcrumbs
Cooking spray

1½ cups bottled lower-sodium tomato-basil pasta sauce
1½ cups (6 ounces) shredded six-cheese Italian blend cheese
¼ cup fresh basil (optional)

1. Preheat oven to 425°.
2. Thinly spread mayonnaise evenly on both sides of eggplant slices; dip both sides of eggplant in breadcrumbs. Place eggplant on an ungreased baking sheet.
3. Bake at 425° for 15 minutes or until tender and lightly browned. Turn eggplant over. Bake an additional 5 minutes. Reduce oven temperature to 375°.
4. Place eggplant slices in a 13 x 9–inch baking dish coated with cooking spray. Spread pasta sauce over eggplant; sprinkle with cheese. Bake at 375° for 15 minutes or until thoroughly heated and cheese melts. Sprinkle with basil, if desired. Yield: 6 servings.

CALORIES 200; FAT 11.4g (sat 4.2g, mono 1.7g, poly 1.1g); PROTEIN 9.9g; CARB 16.3g; FIBER 4.6g; CHOL 20mg; IRON 1mg; SODIUM 653mg; CALC 234mg

use extra basil in

Red Curry Flank Steak with Thai Herb and Tomato Salad, page **315**

Pesto Grilled Cheese Panini, page **152**

Pan-Roasted Salmon and Tomatoes, page **268**

Flavorful green curry, a variety of spices and herbs, and coconut milk provide a fragrant sauce for fresh snapper fillets. Coconut milk adds a rich, velvety texture to the savory dish. If snapper is unavailable, substitute another firm white fish.

Green Curry Snapper

Prep: 4 minutes • Cook: 10 minutes

½   cup coconut milk
1   tablespoon fresh lime juice
2   teaspoons green curry paste
2   teaspoons lemongrass paste
1   teaspoon ginger paste

4   (6-ounce) snapper fillets
⅛   teaspoon salt
2   teaspoons olive oil
2   garlic cloves, minced
¼   cup chopped fresh cilantro

1. Combine first 5 ingredients in a small bowl. Sprinkle fillets evenly with salt.
2. Heat oil in a large nonstick skillet over medium-high heat; swirl to coat. Add garlic; sauté 30 seconds. Add fillets. Cook 2 to 3 minutes on each side. Pour coconut milk mixture over fillets. Cover; bring to a simmer. Simmer 2 minutes or until fish flakes easily when tested with a fork or until desired degree of doneness. Carefully place 1 fillet on each of 4 plates. Spoon curry sauce evenly over fillets; sprinkle evenly with cilantro. Yield: 4 servings (serving size: 1 fillet, 1 tablespoon sauce, and 1 tablespoon cilantro).

CALORIES 260; FAT 11.2g (sat 6.2g, mono 2.5g, poly 1.3g); PROTEIN 35.6g; CARB 3.1g; FIBER 0g; CHOL 63mg; IRON 1.4mg; SODIUM 337mg; CALC 66mg

serve with
Tropical Jasmine Rice

Prep: 2 minutes • Cook: 12 minutes • Other: 5 minutes

¾   cup water
½   cup jasmine rice
2   teaspoons butter
¼   teaspoon salt

⅓   cup finely chopped fresh pineapple
2   tablespoons diagonally cut green onions
2   tablespoons flaked sweetened coconut, toasted

1. Combine first 4 ingredients in a small saucepan. Bring to a boil; reduce heat, cover, and simmer 10 minutes. Remove pan from heat; let stand, covered, 5 minutes. Add pineapple, green onions, and coconut; fluff gently with a fork. Yield: 4 servings (serving size: ½ cup).

CALORIES 117; FAT 2.7g (sat 1.9g, mono 0.5g, poly 0.1g); PROTEIN 1.7g; CARB 21.4g; FIBER 1.1g; CHOL 5mg; IRON 0.3mg; SODIUM 173mg; CALC 15mg

Sriracha, orange, and hoisin give halibut a slightly sweet, Asian flavor. Use another firm white fish in place of the halibut, if you can't find it.

Grilled Halibut with Hoisin Glaze
Prep: 4 minutes • Cook: 6 minutes

2 tablespoons fresh orange juice, divided
4 (6-ounce) halibut fillets
¼ teaspoon salt
¼ teaspoon freshly ground black pepper
2 tablespoons hoisin sauce
2 teaspoons Sriracha (hot chile sauce)
Cooking spray
Grated orange rind (optional)

1. Preheat grill to medium-high heat.
2. Brush 1 tablespoon orange juice evenly over fillets; sprinkle evenly with salt and pepper. Combine hoisin sauce, Sriracha, and remaining 1 tablespoon orange juice in a small bowl.
3. Place fillets on grill rack coated with cooking spray. Brush fillets with hoisin mixture. Grill 3 minutes on each side or until fish flakes easily when tested with a fork or until desired degree of doneness, basting occasionally with hoisin mixture. Garnish with orange rind, if desired. Yield: 4 servings (serving size: 1 fillet).

CALORIES 179; FAT 2.6g (sat 0.5g, mono 0.9g, poly 0.6g); PROTEIN 31.9g; CARB 4.9g; FIBER 0.3g; CHOL 84mg; IRON 0.4mg; SODIUM 443mg; CALC 16mg

serve with
Grilled Baby Bok Choy
Prep: 5 minutes • Cook: 11 minutes

4 baby bok choy, halved lengthwise
(about 1 pound)
2 tablespoons water
1 tablespoon dark sesame oil
¼ teaspoon salt
¼ teaspoon freshly ground black pepper
Cooking spray
2 teaspoons toasted sesame seeds

1. Preheat grill to medium-high heat.
2. Place bok choy halves and 2 tablespoons water in a microwave-safe dish. Cover dish with heavy-duty plastic wrap; vent. Microwave at HIGH 5 minutes or until tender. Drain.
3. Drizzle bok choy with sesame oil, and sprinkle with salt and pepper. Place on grill rack coated with cooking spray. Grill 3 minutes on each side or until bok choy begins to char. Sprinkle with toasted sesame seeds. Yield: 4 servings (serving size: 2 bok choy halves).

CALORIES 54; FAT 4.5g (sat 0.6g, mono 1.8g, poly 1.9g); PROTEIN 2.1g; CARB 2.3g; FIBER 1.3g; CHOL 0mg; IRON 1.3mg; SODIUM 187mg; CALC 107mg

Change this Indian-inspired dish to suit your taste: You can substitute chicken or firm white fish for the shrimp.

Shrimp Tikka Masala

Prep: 3 minutes • Cook: 5 minutes

Tikka Masala Sauce
24 large shrimp, peeled and deveined
  (about 1½ pounds)
Cooking spray
¼ teaspoon salt

1 (8.5-ounce) package microwaveable precooked basmati rice
3 tablespoons chopped fresh cilantro
¼ teaspoon coriander

1. Preheat broiler.
2. Prepare Tikka Masala Sauce through step 1.
3. While sauce cooks 5 minutes, arrange shrimp on a broiler pan coated with cooking spray. Sprinkle shrimp with salt, and coat with cooking spray. Broil 2 minutes on each side or until shrimp are done.
4. While shrimp cook, microwave rice according to package directions. Place rice in a medium bowl; stir in cilantro and coriander.
5. Complete step 2 of Tikka Masala Sauce recipe. Stir shrimp into sauce. Spoon rice into each of 4 shallow bowls. Spoon Shrimp Tikka Masala evenly over rice. Yield: 4 servings (serving size: 6 shrimp, ½ cup sauce, and ½ cup rice).

CALORIES 383; FAT 8.9g (sat 2g, mono 3.5g, poly 1.9g); PROTEIN 40.3g; CARB 34.5g; FIBER 2.6g; CHOL 262.7mg; IRON 6.2mg; SODIUM 648mg; CALC 169mg

Tikka Masala Sauce

Prep: 3 minutes • Cook: 12 minutes

1 tablespoon olive oil
½ cup finely chopped onion
2 teaspoons grated peeled fresh ginger
2 teaspoons garam masala
2 garlic cloves, minced

2 hot red chiles, finely chopped
1 (14.5-ounce) can diced tomatoes, undrained
2 tablespoons tomato paste
¼ teaspoon salt
½ cup plain yogurt

1. Heat oil in a large nonstick skillet over medium heat; swirl to coat. Add onion to pan. Cook 4 minutes or until tender, stirring frequently. Add ginger and next 3 ingredients; cook 2 minutes or until fragrant. Stir in tomatoes, tomato paste, and salt. Cook 5 minutes or until slightly thickened. Remove from heat.
2. Stir in yogurt. Serve immediately. Yield: 4 servings (serving size: ½ cup).

CALORIES 103; FAT 4.6g (sat 1.1g, mono 2.8g, poly 0.5g); PROTEIN 3.1g; CARB 12.9g; FIBER 2.1g; CHOL 4mg; IRON 1.2mg; SODIUM 242mg; CALC 70mg

"Saltimbocca" means "jump in the mouth" in Italian, and with the bold flavors of prosciutto, sage, and Marsala, this chicken entrée certainly lives up to its name. Serve with thin spaghetti or mashed potatoes on the side.

Chicken Saltimbocca

Prep: 8 minutes • Cook: 19 minutes

4 (6-ounce) skinless, boneless chicken
   breast halves
¼ teaspoon freshly ground black pepper
18 large fresh sage leaves, divided

4 (½-ounce) thin slices prosciutto
1.1 ounces all-purpose flour (about ¼ cup)
Cooking spray
1 cup dry Marsala wine

1. Preheat oven to 350°.

2. Sprinkle chicken evenly with pepper. Place 4 sage leaves on top of each chicken breast. Top each with 1 slice prosciutto, pressing lightly to adhere. Place flour in a shallow dish. Carefully dredge each chicken breast in flour, patting to adhere flour to chicken and shaking off any excess.

3. Heat a large nonstick skillet over medium-high heat. Coat pan with cooking spray. Add chicken; cook 3 to 4 minutes on each side or until golden. Place on a rack coated with cooking spray set in a rimmed baking sheet.

4. Bake at 350° for 8 minutes or until done.

5. Add wine to drippings in skillet, scraping pan to loosen browned bits. Add remaining 2 sage leaves. Bring to a boil over medium-high heat. Reduce heat; simmer, uncovered, 5 minutes or until reduced to 2 tablespoons. Remove sage from sauce. Serve sauce over chicken. Yield: 4 servings (serving size: 1 chicken breast and 1½ teaspoons sauce).

CALORIES 293; FAT 6.1g (sat 1.5g, mono 2.1g, poly 0.8g); PROTEIN 41.1g; CARB 10.1g; FIBER 0.2g; CHOL 120mg; IRON 1.2mg; SODIUM 579mg; CALC 24mg

use extra ingredients

Chicken Breast Halves	Sage	Prosciutto

Grilled Chicken Salad with Dried Cherries and Goat Cheese, page **169**	Pork Medallions with Cranberry Sauce, page **285**	Frittata with Mascarpone and Prosciutto, page **87**

Veal and pork are excellent substitutes for the chicken.

Schnitzel Chicken
Prep: 5 minutes • Cook: 12 minutes

1.1 ounces all-purpose flour (about ¼ cup)
1 large egg, beaten
1 cup whole-wheat panko (Japanese breadcrumbs)
4 (¼-inch-thick) chicken breast cutlets
⅜ teaspoon salt
¼ teaspoon freshly ground black pepper
2 teaspoons olive oil, divided
Cooking spray
4 lemon wedges

1. Place flour, egg, and panko each in a shallow dish. Sprinkle chicken cutlets evenly with salt and pepper. Dredge each chicken cutlet in flour. Dip in egg; dredge in panko.
2. Heat 1 teaspoon oil in a large nonstick skillet over medium-high heat; swirl to coat. Add half of chicken to pan. Cook 3 minutes or until golden; coat chicken with cooking spray. Turn chicken over. Cook an additional 3 minutes or until chicken is done. Transfer to a plate; cover and keep warm. Repeat procedure with 1 teaspoon oil, chicken, and cooking spray. Serve with lemon wedges. Yield: 4 servings (serving size: 1 chicken cutlet and 1 lemon wedge).

CALORIES 268; FAT 7g (sat 1.4g, mono 3.1g, poly 1.2g); PROTEIN 29.5g; CARB 20.8g; FIBER 2.4g; CHOL 119mg; IRON 1.8mg; SODIUM 394mg; CALC 16mg

serve with
Pan-Fried Slaw
Prep: 1 minute • Cook: 5 minutes

Cooking spray
2 (10-ounce) packages angel hair slaw
⅓ cup rice vinegar
½ teaspoon caraway seeds
¼ teaspoon freshly ground black pepper
⅛ teaspoon salt

1. Heat a large nonstick skillet over medium-high heat. Coat pan with cooking spray. Add slaw. Coat slaw with cooking spray. Sauté 3 minutes or until wilted and beginning to brown. Add vinegar and remaining ingredients; sauté 1 minute. Yield: 4 servings (about 1 cup).

CALORIES 37; FAT 0.2g (sat 0.1g, mono 0g, poly 0g); PROTEIN 1.9g; CARB 8.4g; FIBER 3.7g; CHOL 0mg; IRON 0.7mg; SODIUM 100mg; CALC 59mg

Buy shelled pistachios to save time. You can also use other nuts in this recipe: Try almonds, pine nuts, cashews, or peanuts.

Pistachio-Crusted Chicken

Prep: 3 minutes • Cook: 22 minutes

¾ cup pistachios
2 large egg whites, lightly beaten
4 (6-ounce) skinless, boneless chicken breast halves
¼ teaspoon salt
¼ teaspoon freshly ground black pepper
Cooking spray

1. Preheat oven to 400°.
2. Place pistachios in a food processor. Process until finely chopped; transfer to a shallow bowl. Place egg whites in a shallow bowl. Sprinkle chicken with salt and pepper. Dip chicken into egg whites; dredge in pistachios, pressing lightly to adhere.
3. Heat a large nonstick ovenproof skillet over medium-high heat. Coat pan with cooking spray. Add chicken to pan; cook 4 minutes. Coat chicken with cooking spray. Turn chicken over; cook 4 minutes. Place pan in oven.
4. Bake, uncovered, at 400° for 14 minutes or until done. Cut chicken crosswise into slices. Yield: 4 servings (serving size: 3 ounces chicken).

CALORIES 329; FAT 13g (sat 1.9g, mono 6.2g, poly 3.7g); PROTEIN 46g; CARB 6.6g; FIBER 2.4g; CHOL 99mg; IRON 2.3mg; SODIUM 286mg; CALC 46mg

serve with
Strawberry Salad

Prep: 5 minutes

1 (6-ounce) package fresh baby spinach
1½ cups quartered strawberries
¼ cup thinly sliced red onion
¼ teaspoon freshly ground black pepper
3 tablespoons blush wine vinaigrette
1 tablespoon chopped fresh mint (optional)
2 ounces goat cheese, crumbled

1. Combine first 5 ingredients and mint, if desired, in a large bowl; toss. Sprinkle with cheese. Yield: 4 servings (serving size: about 1⅔ cups).

CALORIES 124; FAT 5.8g (sat 2.3g, mono 1.7g, poly 0.6g); PROTEIN 4.1g; CARB 15.4g; FIBER 3.4g; CHOL 7mg; IRON 1.9mg; SODIUM 278mg; CALC 62mg

Two skillets will go a long way in helping you quickly prepare this dish. The pork cooks while you sauté the cabbage.

Orange-Ginger Pork Chops

Prep: 5 minutes • Cook: 12 minutes

1 navel orange
2 tablespoons lower-sodium soy sauce
2 teaspoons grated peeled fresh ginger
½ teaspoon freshly ground black pepper

4 (4-ounce) boneless center-cut loin pork
chops (about ½ inch thick)
Cooking spray

1. Grate 2 teaspoons rind and squeeze ¼ cup juice from orange. Combine orange rind, orange juice, soy sauce, ginger, and pepper in a shallow dish. Add pork, turning to coat.
2. Heat a medium nonstick skillet over medium heat. Coat pan with cooking spray. Remove pork from marinade, reserving marinade. Add pork to pan; cook 5 minutes on each side or until done. Remove from pan and keep warm. Add marinade to pan. Bring to a boil; boil 1 minute. Spoon sauce evenly over pork. Yield: 4 servings (serving size: 1 pork chop and 1½ teaspoons sauce).

CALORIES 157; FAT 5.8g (sat 1.7g, mono 2.1g, poly 0.7g); PROTEIN 21.8g; CARB 2.7g; FIBER 0.2g; CHOL 66mg; IRON 0.7mg; SODIUM 347mg; CALC 23mg

serve with
Sweet and Sour Cabbage

Prep: 3 minutes • Cook: 10 minutes

Cooking spray
2 cups thinly sliced red cabbage
2 cups thinly sliced green cabbage
1½ cups sliced Granny Smith apple (1 medium)
1 cup thinly sliced sweet onion

¼ cup cider vinegar
1 tablespoon honey
½ teaspoon salt
½ teaspoon freshly ground black pepper

1. Heat a large nonstick skillet over medium-high heat. Coat pan with cooking spray. Add red cabbage and next 3 ingredients to pan. Cook, uncovered, 8 minutes or until tender, stirring frenquently. Stir in vinegar and remaining ingredients. Cook, stirring constantly, 2 minutes. Yield: 4 servings (serving size: ¾ cup).

CALORIES 78; FAT 0.2g (sat 0g, mono 0g, poly 0.1g); PROTEIN 1.7g; CARB 18.6g; FIBER 3.2g; CHOL 0mg; IRON 0.7mg; SODIUM 320mg; CALC 53mg

Grilled beef tenderloin steaks become decadent when drizzled with fig-studded port sauce, which is also delicious served with lamb and game.

Beef Tenderloin with Peppery Fig-Port Sauce

Prep: 5 minutes • Cook: 15 minutes • Other: 5 minutes

4 (4-ounce) beef tenderloin steaks (about ¾ inch thick)
½ teaspoon salt
½ teaspoon freshly ground black pepper, divided

Cooking spray
1 cup tawny port or other sweet red wine
1½ tablespoons finely chopped shallots
8 small dried Mission figs, quartered
1 rosemary sprig

1. Preheat grill to medium-high heat.
2. Sprinkle steaks with salt and ¼ teaspoon pepper. Place steaks on grill rack coated with cooking spray. Grill 3 minutes on each side or until desired degree of doneness. Let stand 5 minutes.
3. While steaks cook, combine remaining ¼ teaspoon black pepper, port, and remaining 3 ingredients in a small saucepan. Bring to a boil; boil 15 minutes or until reduced to ½ cup. Remove rosemary sprig. Spoon port sauce over steaks. Yield: 4 servings (serving size: 1 steak and 2 tablespoons sauce).

CALORIES 302; FAT 7.5g (sat 2.8g, mono 3g, poly 0.4g); PROTEIN 25.7g; CARB 16.8g; FIBER 1.3g; CHOL 76mg; IRON 2.3mg; SODIUM 361mg; CALC 55mg

serve with
Grilled Fennel and Red Onion

Prep: 5 minutes • Cook: 12 minutes

¼ cup balsamic vinegar
1 tablespoon olive oil
¼ teaspoon salt
¼ teaspoon freshly ground black pepper
1 large red onion, cut into 4 (½-inch-thick) slices

2 medium fennel bulbs with stalks (about 2 pounds), trimmed and cut into ¼-inch-thick slices
Cooking spray

1. Preheat grill to medium-high heat.
2. Combine first 4 ingredients in a large bowl. Add onion and fennel, tossing to coat.
3. Place onion and fennel on grill rack coated with cooking spray. Grill 12 minutes or until tender, turning once. Yield: 4 servings (serving size: ¾ cup).

CALORIES 127; FAT 4.1g (sat 0.5g, mono 2.6g, poly 0.4g); PROTEIN 3.3g; CARB 22.4g; FIBER 7.7g; CHOL 0mg; IRON 1.9mg; SODIUM 269mg; CALC 125mg

A slathering of blue cheese spread dotted with bits of crisp bacon sends this burger right over the top. Serve with a side of baked potato wedges, if desired.

Pub Burgers

Prep: 5 minutes • Cook: 10 minutes

1 pound ground sirloin
¼ teaspoon salt
¼ teaspoon freshly ground black pepper
Cooking spray

4 (¼-inch-thick) slices red onion
Blue Cheese–Bacon Spread
4 (1.8-ounce) white-wheat hamburger buns
4 green leaf lettuce leaves (optional)

1. Preheat grill to high heat.
2. Combine first 3 ingredients in a medium bowl. Divide mixture into 4 equal portions, shaping each into a ½-inch-thick patty. Place burgers on grill rack coated with cooking spray. Grill 5 minutes. Turn patties over. Coat onion slices with cooking spray; place on grill rack. Grill patties and onion 5 minutes or until patties are done, turning onion halfway through cooking time.
3. While patties and onion slices cook, prepare Blue Cheese–Bacon Spread.
4. Spread Blue Cheese–Bacon Spread on cut sides of each bun; top each bun bottom with 1 lettuce leaf, if desired, 1 patty, and 1 onion slice. Cover with bun tops. Yield: 4 servings (serving size: 1 burger).

CALORIES 230; FAT 13.8g (sat 5.7g, mono 4.3g, poly 1.3g); PROTEIN 28.4g; CARB 27.2g; FIBER 4.8g; CHOL 71mg; IRON 4.7mg; SODIUM 570mg; CALC 300mg

Blue Cheese–Bacon Spread

Prep: 4 minutes

¼ cup (2 ounces) tub-style ⅓-less-fat cream cheese
2 tablespoons nonfat buttermilk

2 tablespoons crumbled blue cheese
1 bacon slice, cooked and crumbled
¼ teaspoon freshly ground black pepper

1. Combine first 3 ingredients in a small bowl, stirring until smooth. Stir in bacon and pepper. Yield: 4 servings (serving size: 1½ tablespoons).

CALORIES 58; FAT 4.7g (sat 2.7g, mono 1.3g, poly 0.2g); PROTEIN 2.8g; CARB 1.2g; FIBER 0g; CHOL 16mg; IRON 0mg; SODIUM 136mg; CALC 36mg

A quick-to-make marinade takes flank steak from ordinary to extraordinary in this Thai-inspired grill recipe. Although it is unlikely that there will be any leftovers, the steak is delicious served cold over salad greens or in a sandwich.

Red Curry Flank Steak

Prep: 5 minutes • Cook: 10 minutes • Other: 8 hours and 5 minutes

2 tablespoons red curry paste
2 tablespoons rice vinegar
2 tablespoons canola oil
3 tablespoons finely chopped crystallized ginger

1 tablespoon sambal oelek (ground fresh chile paste)
1 (1-pound) flank steak, trimmed
¼ teaspoon salt
Cooking spray

1. Combine first 5 ingredients in a large heavy-duty zip-top plastic bag; add steak. Seal bag. Marinate in refrigerator 8 hours, turning occasionally.
2. Preheat grill to medium-high heat.
3. Remove steak from bag, discarding marinade. Sprinkle steak with salt. Place steak on grill rack coated with cooking spray. Grill 5 minutes on each side or until desired degree of doneness. Let stand 5 minutes. Cut steak diagonally across grain into thin slices. Yield: 4 servings (serving size: 3 ounces steak).

CALORIES 276; FAT 13.5g (sat 2.9g, mono 6.7g, poly 2.3g); PROTEIN 24.7g; CARB 12.4g; FIBER 0g; CHOL 70mg; IRON 4.2mg; SODIUM 850mg; CALC 48mg

serve with
Thai Herb and Tomato Salad

Prep: 8 minutes • Other: 5 minutes

3 large vine-ripened tomatoes, each cut into 12 wedges (about 1½ pounds)
¾ cup fresh bean sprouts
⅓ cup thinly sliced red onion
2 tablespoons coarsely chopped fresh mint
2 tablespoons coarsely chopped fresh basil

2 tablespoons coarsely chopped fresh cilantro
1 tablespoon rice vinegar
1 tablespoon fresh lime juice
½ teaspoon salt
¼ teaspoon freshly ground black pepper

1. Place all ingredients in a large bowl; toss well. Cover and let stand 5 minutes before serving. Yield: 4 servings (serving size: 1½ cups).

CALORIES 210; FAT 0.4g (sat 0.1g, mono 0.1g, poly 0.2g); PROTEIN 2.3g; CARB 9.2g; FIBER 2.7g; CHOL 0mg; IRON 0.8mg; SODIUM 158mg; CALC 27mg

Garam masala—a blend of cumin, coriander, cinnamon, clove, and peppercorns—easily adds Indian spice to these lamb chops.

Grilled Spiced Lamb Chops with Chickpea Relish

Prep: 3 minutes • Cook: 10 minutes

2 tablespoons chili garlic sauce
1 tablespoon garam masala
2 teaspoons fresh lemon juice
¼ teaspoon salt

8 (4-ounce) lean lamb loin chops, trimmed
Cooking spray
Chickpea Relish

1. Preheat grill to medium-high heat.
2. Combine first 4 ingredients; rub evenly over lamb chops. Place lamb on grill rack coated with cooking spray. Grill lamb 5 minutes on each side or until desired degree of doneness.
3. While lamb cooks, prepare Chickpea Relish. Serve Chickpea Relish with lamb chops. Yield: 4 servings (serving size: 2 lamb chops and ½ cup relish).

CALORIES 421; FAT 17.8g (sat 5.2g, mono 8g, poly 2.2g); PROTEIN 50.9g; CARB 14.5g; FIBER 3.1g; CHOL 150mg; IRON 5.7mg; SODIUM 609mg; CALC 62mg

Chickpea Relish

Prep: 4 minutes

1 (16-ounce) can reduced-sodium chickpeas (garbanzo beans), drained
¼ cup chopped fresh flat-leaf parsley
2 tablespoons chopped pitted green olives

2 tablespoons chopped red onion
2 tablespoons fresh lemon juice
2 teaspoons olive oil
½ teaspoon freshly ground black pepper

1. Combine all ingredients in a medium bowl, tossing well to coat. Yield: 4 servings (serving size: ½ cup).

CALORIES 90; FAT 4.1g (sat 0.3g, mono 2.2g, poly 0.4g); PROTEIN 3.5g; CARB 12.8g; FIBER 3g; CHOL 0mg; IRON 1.3mg; SODIUM 203mg; CALC 34mg

Greek yogurt lends moisture to these lamb patties, keeping them tender and juicy as they cook. If you can't find ground lamb, substitute ground beef.

Spiced Lamb

Prep: 7 minutes • Cook: 9 minutes

1 pound ground lamb
¼ cup chopped onion
½ teaspoon garam masala
¼ teaspoon salt

½ cup plain fat-free Greek yogurt, divided
Cooking spray
1 tablespoon chopped fresh cilantro

1. Combine first 4 ingredients and 1 tablespoon yogurt; shape into 12 (½-inch-thick) oblong patties.
2. Heat a large nonstick skillet over medium-high heat. Coat pan with cooking spray. Add patties to pan. Cook 4 to 5 minutes on each side or until done.
3. While patties cook, combine remaining yogurt and cilantro in a small bowl. Serve yogurt mixture with patties. Yield: 4 servings (serving size: 3 lamb patties and about 2 tablespoons yogurt mixture).

CALORIES 179; FAT 6.3g (sat 2.2g, mono 2.5g, poly 0.6g); PROTEIN 25.8g; CARB 3.3g; FIBER 0.5g; CHOL 74mg; IRON 2.2mg; SODIUM 232mg; CALC 38mg

serve with
Fruited Couscous

Prep: 5 minutes • Cook: 2 minutes • Other: 5 minutes

1 cup water
1 cup uncooked couscous
3 tablespoons coarsely chopped dried apricots
3 tablespoons golden raisins

2 tablespoons slivered almonds, toasted
1 tablespoon chopped fresh mint
1 tablespoon fresh lemon juice
1 tablespoon olive oil
½ teaspoon salt

1. Bring 1 cup water to a boil in a medium saucepan; gradually stir in couscous. Remove from heat; cover and let stand 5 minutes. Add apricots and remaining ingredients. Fluff with a fork. Yield: 4 servings (serving size: ¾ cup).

CALORIES 253; FAT 5.3g (sat 0.6g, mono 3.5g, poly 0.9g); PROTEIN 6.6g; CARB 44.5g; FIBER 3.4g; CHOL 0mg; IRON 1mg; SODIUM 306mg; CALC 30mg

Veal Piccata

Prep: 18 minutes • Cook: 8 minutes

4 (4-ounce) veal cutlets (about ¼ inch thick)
¼ teaspoon salt
¼ teaspoon freshly ground black pepper
2 tablespoons all-purpose flour
Olive oil-flavored cooking spray
1 garlic clove, minced

½ cup dry white wine
¼ cup fat-free, lower-sodium chicken broth
2 tablespoons fresh lemon juice
2 tablespoons drained capers
1 tablespoon butter

1. Sprinkle veal with salt and pepper. Combine veal and flour in a large zip-top plastic bag; seal bag, and shake to coat with flour.
2. Heat a large nonstick skillet over medium-high heat. Coat pan with cooking spray. Add veal; cook 2 minutes on each side or until browned. Remove veal from pan; keep warm.
3. Recoat pan with cooking spray. Add garlic; sauté 30 seconds. Add wine and next 3 ingredients. Bring to a boil; reduce heat, and simmer, uncovered, 3 minutes or until reduced by half, stirring occasionally. Stir in butter; pour sauce over veal. Yield: 4 servings (serving size: 1 veal cutlet and ¼ cup sauce).

CALORIES 248; FAT 13.9g (sat 6g, mono 5.1g, poly 0.9g); PROTEIN 19.7g; CARB 4.9g; FIBER 0.3g; CHOL 81mg; IRON 1mg; SODIUM 379mg; CALC 23mg

serve with

Herbed Parmesan Capellini

Prep: 5 minutes • Cook: 8 minutes

4 ounces uncooked capellini or
  angel hair pasta
1 tablespoon olive oil
1 tablespoon chopped fresh parsley

2 teaspoons chopped fresh oregano
⅛ teaspoon salt
⅛ teaspoon freshly ground black pepper
¼ cup shredded fresh Parmesan cheese

1. Cook pasta according to package directions, omitting salt and fat. Drain pasta, and place in a large bowl. Add olive oil and next 4 ingredients; toss to coat. Divide pasta evenly among 4 serving plates. Sprinkle evenly with cheese. Yield: 4 servings (serving size: ½ cup pasta and 1 tablespoon cheese).

CALORIES 176; FAT 6.5g (sat 2.3g, mono 3.4g, poly 0.6g); PROTEIN 7.7g; CARB 21.7g; FIBER 0.9g; CHOL 7mg; IRON 1.1mg; SODIUM 317mg; CALC 135mg

The lemon-caper pan sauce can do double duty in moistening both the veal and the herbed pasta, if you place the veal cutlet on top of the pasta before pouring the pan sauce over it. Chicken cutlets can easily stand in for the veal.

desserts

Use firm, ripe nectarines instead of soft for the best results. Firm fruit will slice easily and stand up to cooking. You can dress these mini tarts with a bit of crème fraîche, whipped cream, or ice cream, and some chopped or sliced toasted nuts.

Mini Nectarine Galettes

Prep: 12 minutes • Cook: 25 minutes • Other: 10 minutes

½ (14.1-ounce) package refrigerated pie dough
1 large egg white, lightly beaten
2 tablespoons turbinado sugar, divided

3 firm ripe nectarines, pitted and sliced
2 tablespoons apple jelly

1. Preheat oven to 425°.
2. Roll dough into a 13-inch circle; cut into 8 (4¼-inch) circles, rerolling dough as necessary. Place circles on a baking sheet lined with parchment paper. Brush circles with egg white; sprinkle evenly with 1 tablespoon turbinado sugar. Arrange nectarine slices evenly in centers of circles, leaving a ½-inch border. Fold edges over fruit. (Dough will only partially cover fruit.)
3. Brush remaining egg white over dough edges; sprinkle evenly with remaining 1 tablespoon turbinado sugar. Bake at 425° for 25 minutes or until crust browns.
4. Place jelly in a microwave-safe bowl. Microwave at HIGH 1 minute or until melted. Brush jelly evenly over fruit. Let stand at least 10 minutes before serving. Yield: 8 servings (serving size: 1 galette).

CALORIES 147; FAT 6.7g (sat 2.8g, mono 2.5g, poly 0.9g); PROTEIN 1.9g; CARB 22.3g; FIBER 0.9g; CHOL 3mg; IRON 0.2mg; SODIUM 136mg; CALC 4mg

From clarifying butter to managing paper-thin phyllo sheets, making baklava is labor intensive. These bite-sized treats simplify the process while staying true to the traditional flavors.

Baklava Bites

Prep: 6 minutes • Cook: 10 minutes

⅓ cup finely chopped walnuts
⅓ cup finely chopped pistachios
2 tablespoons butter, melted
2 tablespoons honey

1 teaspoon grated orange rind
¼ teaspoon ground cinnamon
⅛ teaspoon ground cloves
1 (1.9-ounce) package mini phyllo shells

1. Preheat oven to 425°.

2. Combine first 7 ingredients in a medium bowl. Place phyllo shells on an ungreased baking sheet. Spoon nut mixture evenly into phyllo shells.

3. Bake at 425° for 10 minutes or until golden. Yield: 15 servings (serving size: 1 filled shell).

CALORIES 71; FAT 5.3g (sat 1.3g, mono 1.9g, poly 1.9g); PROTEIN 1g; CARB 5.3g; FIBER 0.5g; CHOL 4.1mg; IRON 0.4mg; SODIUM 36mg; CALC 7mg

use extra oranges in

Ladyfingers with Mascarpone Cream and Fresh Orange Sauce, page **355**

Arugula-Orange Salad with Fig-Bacon Dressing, page **135**

Grilled Halibut with Hoisin Glaze and Grilled Baby Bok Choy, page **298**

Leave the peaches unpeeled, if you desire.
Substitute amaretto for the peach brandy in the mascarpone for an almond-flavored twist.

Balsamic Peach Melba Parfaits with Spiked Mascarpone

Prep: 9 minutes • Other: 10 minutes

1½ tablespoons sugar
1½ teaspoons white balsamic vinegar
 2 small peaches, peeled, pitted, and each cut
   into 12 wedges (about ¾ pound peaches)

¾ cup raspberries
Spiked Mascarpone

1. Place first 3 ingredients in a medium bowl; toss gently until sugar dissolves. Gently stir in raspberries. Let stand 10 minutes.
2. Spoon half of peach mixture evenly into 4 parfait glasses. Top evenly with half of Spiked Mascarpone. Repeat layers with remaining peach mixture and Spiked Mascarpone. Chill until ready to serve. Yield: 4 servings (serving size: ½ cup fruit and about 1½ tablespoons sauce).

CALORIES 154; FAT 6.8g (sat 3.5g, mono 1.9g, poly 0.4g); PROTEIN 2.6g; CARB 19.7g; FIBER 2.4g; CHOL 17.8mg; IRON 0.3mg; SODIUM 20mg; CALC 58mg

Spiked Mascarpone

Prep: 4 minutes

 2 tablespoons mascarpone cheese
 ¼ cup plain fat-free yogurt

1½ tablespoons peach brandy
1½ tablespoons sugar

1. Combine all ingredients in a medium bowl, stirring with a whisk until smooth. Cover and chill until ready to use. Yield: 4 servings (serving size: about 1½ tablespoons).

CALORIES 98; FAT 6.5g (sat 3.5g, mono 0g, poly 0g); PROTEIN 1.8g; CARB 5.8g; FIBER 0g; CHOL 17.8mg; IRON 0mg; SODIUM 19mg; CALC 48mg

You will dream of your grandmother's kitchen
when you smell this cake baking.

Banana Pound Cake
Prep: 10 minutes • Cook: 1 hour • Other: 10 minutes

Cooking spray
1 teaspoon all-purpose flour
7.5 ounces all-purpose flour (about 1⅔ cups)
1 teaspoon baking powder
½ teaspoon salt

1¼ cups light brown sugar
½ cup butter, softened
2 large egg whites
1 cup mashed ripe banana
(2 medium bananas)

1. Preheat oven to 350°.
2. Coat an 8 x 4–inch loaf pan with cooking spray; dust with 1 teaspoon flour.
3. Weigh or lightly spoon 7.5 ounces (about 1⅔ cups) flour into dry measuring cups; level with a knife. Combine 7.5 ounces flour, baking powder, and salt in a medium bowl, and stir with a whisk. Place light brown sugar and butter in a large bowl; beat with a mixer at high speed until blended and fluffy (about 5 minutes). Add egg whites, 1 at a time, beating well after each addition. Beat flour mixture into sugar mixture alternately with banana, beginning and ending with flour mixture. Pour batter into prepared pan.
4. Bake at 350° for 1 hour or until a wooden pick inserted in center comes out clean. Cool 10 minutes in pan on a wire rack; remove from pan. Cool completely on wire rack. Yield: 10 servings (serving size: 1 slice).

CALORIES 289; FAT 9.5g (sat 5.9g, mono 2.4g, poly 0.5g); PROTEIN 3.3g; CARB 49g; FIBER 1.2g; CHOL 24.4mg; IRON 1.3mg; SODIUM 273mg; CALC 40mg

This trifle is a quick take on classic Black Forest cake. Use thawed frozen cherries when fresh cherries are not in season. You can prepare the trifle in individual dishes, or in a 2-quart trifle dish or glass bowl.

Black Forest Trifle

Prep: 15 minutes • Other: 10 minutes

2½ cups pitted dark sweet cherries, halved
6 tablespoons sugar, divided
3 tablespoons kirsch (cherry brandy)
½ cup heavy whipping cream

1 (11-ounce) frozen chocolate cake, thawed and cut into 1-inch cubes
1 ounce shaved bittersweet chocolate (optional)

1. Combine cherries, 3 tablespoons sugar, and kirsch in a medium bowl. Let stand 10 minutes.
2. While cherry mixture stands, place whipping cream and 3 tablespoons sugar in a medium bowl. Beat with a mixer at medium-high speed until soft peaks form.
3. Divide half of cake cubes evenly among 8 small bowls or individual serving dishes. Spoon half of cherry mixture over cake, and top with half of whipped cream mixture. Repeat layers. Sprinkle with chocolate shavings, if desired. Cover and chill until ready to serve. Yield: 8 servings.

CALORIES 256; FAT 9.8g (sat 3.5g, mono 3.6g, poly 2.2g); PROTEIN 2.1g; CARB 39.1g; FIBER 1g; CHOL 20.5mg; IRON 0.9mg; SODIUM 98mg; CALC 16mg

Use ripe bananas with lots of brown spots on the skins. When the bananas get to this point, peel them, dice them, toss them in a heavy-duty zip-top plastic bag, and freeze them. You'll always have frozen bananas ready to go for this creamy, frosty treat.

Chocolate-Flecked Peanut Butter–Banana Freeze

Prep: 8 minutes

1½ cups diced banana (2 medium bananas), frozen
2 tablespoons creamy peanut butter

1 ounce semisweet chocolate, grated, or 2 tablespoons semisweet chocolate minichips

1. Place frozen diced banana and peanut butter in a food processor; process until smooth, scraping sides of bowl occasionally. Stir in grated chocolate. Serve immediately. Yield: 2 servings (serving size: ½ cup).

CALORIES 247; FAT 11.6g (sat 3.5g, mono 4.4g, poly 2g); PROTEIN 5.7g; CARB 36.1g; FIBER 4.6g; CHOL 0mg; IRON 1mg; SODIUM 77mg; CALC 9mg

use extra bananas in

Tropical Waffles with Pineapple-Orange Syrup, page **82**

Banana-Blueberry Smoothies, page **31**

Banana Bread Muffins, page **34**

Keep the dough wrapped tightly in the refrigerator for up to two weeks. Then it's easy to slice and bake for fresh cookies whenever the craving hits.

Chocolate-Cranberry Refrigerator Cookies

Prep: 10 minutes • Cook: 12 minutes • Other: 1 hour and 10 minutes

4.5 ounces all-purpose flour (about 1 cup)
⅓ cup unsweetened cocoa
½ teaspoon baking soda
¼ teaspoon salt
⅓ cup unsalted butter, softened
⅔ cup sugar
2 tablespoons ice water
½ cup chopped sweetened dried cranberries

1. Weigh or lightly spoon flour into a dry measuring cup; level with a knife. Combine flour, cocoa, baking soda, and salt in a medium bowl; stir with a whisk. Place butter and sugar in a medium bowl; beat with a mixer at medium speed until fluffy. Add flour mixture, beating at low speed until crumbly. Add 2 tablespoons ice water, 1 tablespoon at a time, beating until thoroughly moistened. Beat in cranberries.
2. Shape dough into an 8-inch log. Wrap dough in plastic wrap; chill 1 hour.
3. Preheat oven to 350°.
4. Cut dough into 24 (¼-inch-thick) slices. Place slices 1 inch apart on a baking sheet lined with parchment paper. Bake at 350° for 12 minutes or until set. Cool cookies on pan 10 minutes. Remove from pan; cool completely on a wire rack. Yield: 24 servings (serving size: 1 cookie).

CALORIES 75; FAT 2.6g (sat 1.5g, mono 0.6g, poly 0.1g); PROTEIN 0.8g; CARB 12.3g; FIBER 0.5g; CHOL 7mg; IRON 0.4mg; SODIUM 51mg; CALC 1mg

Crushed crisp granola thins put the crunch on top of this easy sundae.

Chocolate Granola Yogurt Crunch
Prep: 6 minutes

2 cups vanilla frozen fat-free yogurt
3 (0.6-ounce) dark chocolate granola thins, coarsely crushed

½ cup sliced strawberries
2 tablespoons honey

1. Divide frozen yogurt evenly among 4 bowls. Sprinkle granola thin crumbs over frozen yogurt. Top with strawberries, and drizzle with honey. Serve immediately. Yield: 4 servings (serving size: ½ cup frozen yogurt, 2 tablespoons crumbs, 2 tablespoons strawberries, and 1½ teaspoons honey).

CALORIES 191; FAT 3.1g (sat 1.1g, mono 1.5g, poly 0.4g); PROTEIN 3.9g; CARB 38.3g; FIBER 0.4g; CHOL 0mg; IRON 0.4mg; SODIUM 102mg; CALC 103mg

use extra strawberries in

Morning Wheat Berry Salad, page **45**

Strawberry-Ginger Yogurt Pops, page **210**

Mixed Berry, Flaxseed, and Yogurt Parfait, page **45**

This sandwich cookie highlights the timeless pairing of chocolate and raspberry.

Chocolate-Raspberry Chews

Prep: 22 minutes • Cook: 10 minutes • Other: 15 minutes

1.9 ounces almond flour (about ½ cup)
1¼ cups powdered sugar, divided
3 tablespoons Dutch process cocoa

⅛ teaspoon salt
2 large egg whites
3 tablespoons low-sugar raspberry preserves

1. Preheat oven to 325°.

2. Weigh or lightly spoon almond flour into a dry measuring cup; level with a knife. Sift together almond flour, ¾ cup powdered sugar, and cocoa.

3. Place salt and egg whites in a medium bowl; beat with a mixer at high speed until foamy. Gradually add ½ cup powdered sugar, 1 tablespoon at a time, beating until stiff peaks form. Sift cocoa mixture over egg mixture; fold cocoa mixture into egg mixture. (Mixture should be smooth and shiny.)

4. Spoon dough into a pastry bag fitted with a ½-inch round tip. Pipe dough into 24 (1½-inch) rounds onto baking sheets lined with parchment paper. Sharply tap pan once on counter to remove air bubbles. Let stand 15 minutes or until surfaces of cookies begin to dry slightly.

5. Bake at 325° for 10 minutes or until cookies are crisp and firm. Cool completely on pans on wire racks.

6. Spoon ¾ teaspoon preserves onto flat side of each of 12 cookies. Top with remaining cookies. Yield: 12 servings (serving size: 1 sandwich cookie).

CALORIES 88; FAT 2.4g (sat 0.2g, mono 1.4g, poly 0.5g); PROTEIN 1.8g; CARB 15.7g; FIBER 0.7g; CHOL 0mg; IRON 0.6mg; SODIUM 36mg; CALC 10mg

Prepare the rice ahead so it can chill, or use leftover plain cooked rice for this tropical dessert.

Coconut Rice Pudding
Prep: 5 minutes • Cook: 45 minutes

2 cups 1% low-fat milk	1 (13.5-ounce) can light coconut milk
1½ cups cooked rice, chilled	1 teaspoon vanilla extract
⅓ cup sugar	½ cup flaked sweetened coconut, toasted
⅛ teaspoon salt	(optional)

1. Bring first 5 ingredients to a boil in a medium saucepan. Reduce heat to medium and simmer, uncovered, 45 minutes or until thickened, stirring frequently. Remove from heat; stir in vanilla. Let cool to warm, stirring occasionally. Spoon evenly into 8 dessert dishes. Sprinkle evenly with toasted coconut, if desired. Yield: 8 servings (serving size: about ½ cup).

CALORIES 128; FAT 3.4g (sat 2.8g, mono 0.3g, poly 0g); PROTEIN 3.5g; CARB 21g; FIBER 0.1g; CHOL 3mg; IRON 0.4mg; SODIUM 73mg; CALC 79mg

Keep this indulgent treat on hand to satisfy your sweet tooth. A small bite of antioxidant-rich dark chocolate with heart-healthy almonds is an alternative to sugar- and fat-filled candy bars.

Dark Chocolate–Cherry Almond Bark
Prep: 10 minutes • Other: 30 minutes

8 ounces dark chocolate (70% cocoa), chopped
¼ teaspoon almond extract
½ cup dried cherries, chopped and divided

½ cup whole natural almonds, toasted, coarsely chopped, and divided
¼ teaspoon coarse sea salt

1. Line a baking sheet with parchment paper.
2. Place chocolate in a microwave-safe bowl. Microwave at HIGH 1 minute, stirring after 30 seconds. Stir until smooth. Add almond extract, stirring until blended. Stir in half of cherries and almonds.
3. Spread mixture onto prepared baking sheet. Sprinkle with remaining almonds and cherries, pressing lightly to adhere. Sprinkle with salt. Chill 30 minutes or until firm. Break into 14 pieces. Yield: 14 servings (serving size: 1 piece).

CALORIES 144; FAT 9.5g (sat 4.2g, mono 3.7g, poly 0.8g); PROTEIN 2.6g; CARB 12.2g; FIBER 2.8g; CHOL 0mg; IRON 2.2mg; SODIUM 45mg; CALC 28mg

Dulce de leche, a milk caramel, combines with low-fat milk to create a rich, silky ice cream.

Dulce de Leche Ice Cream
Prep: 6 minutes • Cook: 5 minutes • Other: 5 hours

    3   cups 1% low-fat milk
    1⅔ cups canned dulce de leche

    ⅛   teaspoon vanilla extract
    ⅛   teaspoon salt

1. Bring milk to a boil in a medium saucepan over medium heat. Gradually add dulce de leche, stirring with a whisk. Remove from heat. Stir in vanilla and salt. Place pan in a large ice-filled bowl until mixture cools to room temperature (about 30 minutes), stirring occasionally. Cover and refrigerate 3 hours or until thoroughly chilled.
2. Pour mixture into the freezer can of an ice-cream freezer; freeze according to manufacturer's instructions. Spoon ice cream into a freezer-safe container; cover and freeze 1 hour or until firm. Yield: 12 servings (serving size: ½ cup).

CALORIES 159; FAT 3.4g (sat 2g, mono 1.1g, poly 0.1g); PROTEIN 4.3g; CARB 26.3g; FIBER 0g; CHOL 14.1mg; IRON 0mg; SODIUM 129mg; CALC 165mg

use extra 1% low-fat milk in

Philly Cheese Steak
Sandwiches, page **182**

"Sausage" Gravy on Grilled
Toast Slabs, page **81**

Ice Cream Crepes with
Chocolate-Hazelnut Sauce,
page **353**

Pecans and bourbon add an extra kick to these fudge brownies. You can also substitute your favorite liqueur.

Fudgy Bourbon-Pecan Brownies
Prep: 8 minutes • Cook: 18 minutes

Cooking spray
4.5 ounces all-purpose flour (about 1 cup)
⅓ cup unsweetened cocoa
¼ teaspoon salt
1 cup sugar
¼ cup canola oil
¼ cup bourbon
2 large eggs
¼ cup chopped pecans

1. Preheat oven to 350°.
2. Coat bottom of an 8-inch square baking pan with cooking spray.
3. Weigh or lightly spoon flour into a dry measuring cup; level with a knife. Combine flour, cocoa, and salt in a medium bowl; stir with a whisk. Combine sugar and next 3 ingredients in another medium bowl; stir in flour mixture. Stir in pecans. Spread batter into prepared pan.
4. Bake at 350° for 18 minutes or until a wooden pick inserted in center comes out almost clean. Cool completely on a wire rack. Cut into squares. Yield: 16 servings (serving size: 1 brownie).

CALORIES 139; FAT 5.6g (sat 0.6g, mono 3.2g, poly 1.5g); PROTEIN 2.1g; CARB 20g; FIBER 0.7g; CHOL 23mg; IRON 0.8mg; SODIUM 46mg; CALC 6mg

Select peaches that are juicy and ripe yet still firm; they will be easier to peel and chop. If you like, save the juices from the grilled fruit to drizzle over the ice cream.

Grilled Fruit Sundaes

Prep: 9 minutes • Cook: 6 minutes

4 (½-inch-thick) fresh pineapple slices
2 firm ripe peaches, halved and pitted
2 plums, halved and pitted

Cooking spray
1½ cups vanilla light ice cream
12 cinnamon sugar pita chips

1. Preheat grill to medium-high heat.
2. Lightly coat fruit with cooking spray. Place fruit on grill rack coated with cooking spray. Grill 3 minutes on each side. Remove skins from peaches. Finely chop fruit; drain. If desired, cool fruit to room temperature.
3. Spoon ½ cup fruit into each of 6 serving dishes. Scoop ¼ cup ice cream onto each serving. Serve each with 2 pita chips. Yield: 6 servings (serving size: 1 sundae).

CALORIES 135; FAT 2.9g (sat 1.1g, mono 0.9g, poly 0.3g); PROTEIN 3g; CARB 26.4g; FIBER 2.2g; CHOL 10mg; IRON 0.5mg; SODIUM 44mg; CALC 40mg

use extra ingredients

Pineapple

Pineapple Parfait,
page **46**

Peaches

White Cranberry–Peach
Spritzers, page **250**

Peaches

Grilled Peach and Granola
Salad, page **150**

With warm, caramelized pineapple and cool, creamy coconut sorbet, this dessert will leave you dreaming of the islands.

Grilled Rum Pineapple with Coconut Sorbet
Prep: 4 minutes • Cook: 7 minutes • Other: 5 minutes

1 small pineapple, peeled and cored
¼ cup packed dark brown sugar
2 tablespoons dark rum
Cooking spray

1 cup coconut sorbet
2 tablespoons flaked sweetened coconut, toasted

1. Preheat grill to high heat.
2. Cut pineapple into 8 (½-inch-thick) rings; place in a medium bowl. Combine brown sugar and rum; pour over pineapple. Let stand 5 minutes.
3. Place pineapple on grill rack coated with cooking spray. Grill 3 minutes. Turn pineapple over; grill 4 minutes or until caramelized, basting frequently with remaining brown sugar mixture. Place 2 pineapple slices on each of 4 plates; top each with ¼ cup coconut sorbet and 1½ teaspoons toasted coconut. Serve immediately. Yield: 4 servings.

CALORIES 275; FAT 5.5g (sat 4.2g, mono 0.4g, poly 0.2g); PROTEIN 1.8g; CARB 54.9g; FIBER 0.3g; CHOL 0mg; IRON 0.9mg; SODIUM 21mg; CALC 40mg

To keep the ice cream from melting while you prepare all 10 servings, place the filled crepes on a wax paper–lined baking sheet in the freezer. Once you have filled all the crepes, plate the crepes, drizzle with sauce, and sprinkle with hazelnuts. If you don't need 10 servings, prepare what you need and store the remaining ingredients. Then, you can fill the additional crepes as needed.

Ice Cream Crepes with Chocolate-Hazelnut Sauce
Prep: 15 minutes

¼ cup chocolate-hazelnut spread
1 tablespoon Frangelico (hazelnut-flavored liqueur)
1½ teaspoons 1% low-fat milk

5 cups chocolate or coffee light ice cream
1 (5-ounce) package refrigerated prepared crepes
5 teaspoons chopped hazelnuts

1. Combine first 3 ingredients in a small bowl; stir with a whisk until smooth.
2. Spread ½ cup ice cream down center of each crepe. Fold sides of crepes over ice cream. Arrange crepes, seam sides down, on dessert plates.
3. Drizzle about 1½ teaspoons sauce over each crepe; sprinkle each crepe with ½ teaspoon hazelnuts. Serve immediately. Yield: 10 servings (serving size: 1 crepe).

CALORIES 201; FAT 7g (sat 4.2g, mono 1.6g, poly 0.1g); PROTEIN 4.6g; CARB 28.2g; FIBER 1.5g; CHOL 25mg; IRON 0.4mg; SODIUM 98mg; CALC 70mg

Vanilla bean paste is a perfect addition: It has no alcohol to compete with the Grand Marnier, and it adds attractive vanilla seeds to the cheese. Find vanilla bean paste at specialty food stores.

Ladyfingers with Mascarpone Cream and Fresh Orange Sauce

Prep: 15 minutes

½ cup sugar, divided
2 tablespoons Grand Marnier (orange-flavored liqueur)
2 large navel oranges
1½ cups fat-free cottage cheese

¼ cup (2 ounces) mascarpone cheese
1 teaspoon vanilla bean paste
1 (3-ounce) package ladyfingers (12 ladyfingers), split
2 tablespoons sliced almonds, toasted

1. Combine ⅓ cup sugar and liqueur in a medium bowl, stirring well. Peel oranges; cut each orange in half lengthwise. Cut each half crosswise into thin slices to measure 2 cups. Add oranges to sugar mixture in bowl; toss gently to coat. Let stand at room temperature while preparing cream mixture.

2. Place remaining sugar, cottage cheese, mascarpone, and vanilla bean paste in a food processor; process until smooth.

3. Arrange 4 ladyfinger halves in each of 6 dessert bowls. Spoon cheese mixture evenly into center of ladyfingers (about ¼ cup each). Top each serving with about ⅓ cup orange sauce, allowing syrup to soak into cake. Sprinkle 1 teaspoon almonds over each serving. Yield: 6 servings (serving size: 1 dessert).

CALORIES 247; FAT 6.2g (sat 2.7g, mono 2.3g, poly 0.5g); PROTEIN 9.4g; CARB 38.3g; FIBER 1.4g; CHOL 44.3mg; IRON 0.3mg; SODIUM 321mg; CALC 102mg

Champagne mangoes are also labeled Ataulfo, Honey, and Manila mangoes. They ripen to a golden yellow and have velvety smooth flesh, a small pit, and almost no fibrous texture, making them ideal for a smooth pudding.

Mango-Lime Pudding
Prep: 25 minutes • Cook: 8 minutes • Other: 4 hours

4 cups cubed peeled ripe champagne mango
   (8 champagne mangoes)
⅓ cup sugar
¼ cup cornstarch
¾ cup evaporated low-fat milk

½ cup water
¼ cup fresh lime juice
½ cup diced champagne mango (optional)
2½ thin lime slices, quartered (optional)

1. Place 4 cups mango in a food processor; process until smooth. Press mango puree through a sieve into a bowl, using the back of a spoon. Discard solids.
2. Combine sugar and cornstarch in a medium saucepan, stirring with a whisk. Stir in mango puree, evaporated milk, water, and lime juice. Bring to a boil; cook, stirring constantly, 1 minute or until thick. Remove from heat. Pour into a bowl; cover surface of pudding with plastic wrap. Chill 4 hours.
3. Spoon pudding into dessert dishes. Sprinkle puddings evenly with diced mango and garnish with quartered lime slices, if desired. Yield: 10 servings (serving size: ½ cup).

CALORIES 94; FAT 0.6g (sat 0.1g, mono 0.2g, poly 0g); PROTEIN 1.8g; CARB 21.8g; FIBER 1.1g; CHOL 3mg; IRON 0.1mg; SODIUM 22mg; CALC 56mg

use extra limes in

Mango Mo-rita, page **247**

Asian Fresh Tuna Salad, page **116**

Melon Kebabs with Lime and Chiles, page **205**

Cool, refreshing, and decadently rich, this sorbet will leave you begging for more on a warm afternoon.

Mint-Chocolate Sorbet
Prep: 4 minutes • Cook: 10 minutes • Other: 4 hours

2 cups water
1 cup sugar
⅓ cup Dutch process cocoa

3 ounces semisweet chocolate, finely chopped
½ cup fresh mint leaves

1. Bring 2 cups water to a boil in a medium saucepan. Combine sugar and cocoa. Gradually add sugar mixture to boiling water; reduce heat, and simmer, uncovered, 5 minutes, stirring frequently. Remove from heat; add chocolate, stirring until chocolate melts. Stir in mint leaves. Cover and let steep 30 minutes. Refrigerate 2 hours or until thoroughly chilled.

2. Pour chocolate mixture through a sieve into freezer can of an ice-cream freezer; discard mint leaves. Freeze according to manufacturer's instructions. Spoon sorbet into a freezer-safe container; cover and freeze 1 hour or until firm. Yield: 5 servings (serving size: about ½ cup).

CALORIES 264; FAT 6g (sat 3.3g, mono 2g, poly 0g); PROTEIN 2.4g; CARB 53.6g; FIBER 2.5g; CHOL 0mg; IRON 2.9mg; SODIUM 1mg; CALC 7mg

This adult dessert is a take on the usual
orange-slice accompaniment to a Belgian-style wheat ale.

Orange-Beer Floats

Prep: 3 minutes

2 (12-oz) bottles Belgian-style wheat ale
1 cup orange sherbet

2 orange slices

1. Pour 1 beer into each of 2 frozen mugs. Scoop ½ cup sherbet into each mug. Serve with orange slices. Yield: 2 servings (serving size: 1 float).

CALORIES 289; FAT 1.5g (sat 0.9g, mono 0.4g, poly 0.1g); PROTEIN 3.4g; CARB 38.7g; FIBER 1.7g; CHOL 1mg; IRON 0.2mg; SODIUM 38mg; CALC 67mg

use extra oranges in

Citrus-Ginger Salad, page **39**

Kentucky Mule, page **244**

Cranberry-Orange Turkey Salad
Sandwiches, page **124**

Store the sweet, chewy almond cookies—with a hint of orange and slight bitterness from chocolate—in an airtight container to keep them from drying out.

Orange-Scented Almond Cookies with Chocolate

Prep: 10 minutes • Cook: 16 minutes

1 (7-ounce) tube marzipan (almond paste)
¾ cup sugar
2 tablespoons all-purpose flour

1 teaspoon grated orange rind
2 large egg whites
2 ounces bittersweet chocolate, chopped

1. Preheat oven to 350°.
2. Line 2 large baking sheets with parchment paper.
3. Place first 4 ingredients in a food processor; process until mixture is crumbly. Add egg whites; process until smooth.
4. Spoon batter, 1 tablespoon at a time, 2 inches apart onto prepared pans. Bake at 350° for 12 minutes or until puffed and lightly golden. Cool cookies completely on pan on a wire rack.
5. Place chocolate in a microwave-safe bowl. Microwave at HIGH 30 seconds; stir. Microwave 30 additional seconds; stir until smooth. Drizzle melted chocolate over cooled cookies. Yield: 23 servings (serving size: 1 cookie).

CALORIES 80; FAT 2.6g (sat 0.8g, mono 1.4g, poly 0.3g); PROTEIN 1.2g; CARB 13.4g; FIBER 0.7g; CHOL 0mg; IRON 0.5mg; SODIUM 6mg; CALC 12mg

Pull these flourless cookies out of the oven
while they are still soft. They firm up slightly as they cool.

Peanut Butter Cookies
Prep: 8 minutes • Cook: 16 minutes • Other: 2 minutes

1 cup creamy peanut butter
1 cup sugar

1 large egg
½ cup dry roasted peanuts, chopped

1. Preheat oven to 350°.
2. Line 2 baking sheets with parchment paper.
3. Place first 3 ingredients in a medium bowl. Beat with a mixer at medium speed until smooth. Roll dough into 16 (1¼-inch) balls; roll each ball in peanuts. Place balls 2 inches apart on prepared pans, flattening balls slightly with fingers.
4. Bake at 350° for 16 minutes or until bottoms of cookies are lightly browned. Cool cookies on pans 2 minutes. Transfer cookies to wire racks; cool completely. Yield: 16 servings (serving size: 1 cookie).

CALORIES 175; FAT 10.6g (sat 1.9g, mono 4.5g, poly 2.6g); PROTEIN 5.5g; CARB 17.1g; FIBER 1.4g; CHOL 12mg; IRON 0.5mg; SODIUM 80mg; CALC 4mg

use extra peanut butter in

Protein-Packed Oatmeal,
page **49**

Peanut-Sesame Noodles,
page **110**

Peanut Butter–Banana Dip,
page **205**

Some supermarkets carry shelled pistachios; if yours does not, buy unshelled nuts and shell them yourself.

Pistachio Milkshakes
Prep: 14 minutes

⅔ cup unsalted pistachios
¼ cup sugar
3 cups vanilla low-fat ice cream

1½ cups 1% low-fat milk
½ teaspoon vanilla extract
Chopped pistachios (optional)

1. Place pistachios and sugar in a blender; process until nuts are finely ground.
2. Add ice cream, milk, and vanilla; process until smooth. Sprinkle chopped pistachio nuts on top of each shake, if desired. Serve immediately. Yield: 6 servings (serving size: ⅔ cup).

CALORIES 236; FAT 10.2g (sat 3.1g, mono 4.4g, poly 1.9g); PROTEIN 7.9g; CARB 30.5g; FIBER 1.3g; CHOL 23mg; IRON 0.6mg; SODIUM 73mg; CALC 151mg

use extra pistachios in

Pistachio-Crusted Chicken and Strawberry Salad, page **307**

Turkey, Apricot and Pistachio Salad, page **131**

Apricot-Stilton Bites, page **221**

We used ice cream cones in place of pastry shells in this Sicilian-style dessert. Enjoy it after Veal Piccata and Herbed Parmesan Capellini (page 320) for an Italian feast.

Quick Cannoli
Prep: 20 minutes

1 ounce semisweet chocolate, melted
1 tablespoon chopped pistachios

4 sugar cones
Marsala-Ricotta Filling

1. Place chocolate in a small bowl. Place pistachios in a small shallow dish. Dip rims of sugar cones in chocolate; dip in pistachios. Place cones on a parchment paper–lined baking sheet; freeze while preparing Marsala-Ricotta Filling.
2. Spoon or pipe ¼ cup Marsala-Ricotta Filling into each cone. Serve immediately. Yield: 4 servings (serving size: 1 filled cone).

CALORIES 227; FAT 11.6g (sat 6g, mono 3.4g, poly 0.8g); PROTEIN 6.5g; CARB 24.7g; FIBER 0.7g; CHOL 29.2mg; IRON 0.9mg; SODIUM 187mg; CALC 69mg

Marsala-Ricotta Filling
Prep: 5 minutes

4 ounces ⅓-less-fat cream cheese, softened
¼ cup powdered sugar
⅓ cup part-skim ricotta cheese

1 tablespoon sweet Marsala wine
1 teaspoon grated orange rind

1. Place cream cheese and powdered sugar in a bowl; beat with a mixer at medium speed until smooth. Add remaining ingredients, beating just until combined. Yield: 4 servings (serving size: ¼ cup).

CALORIES 130; FAT 7.9g (sat 4.6g, mono 2g, poly 0.4g); PROTEIN 4.6g; CARB 10.1g; FIBER 0.1g; CHOL 29.2mg; IRON 0.1mg; SODIUM 123mg; CALC 67mg

The butter and sugar caramelize on the bottom of the pan while the pears roast, forming the base of a flavorful sauce for this simple dessert.

Roasted Pears with Amaretto and Crème Fraîche

Prep: 8 minutes • Cook: 40 minutes

1 tablespoon unsalted butter, softened
5 tablespoons sugar, divided
3 Bosc pears, peeled, halved, and cored
3 tablespoons amaretto (almond-flavored liqueur), divided
½ cup water
⅛ teaspoon salt
6 tablespoons crème fraîche
⅓ cup toasted sliced almonds (optional)

1. Preheat oven to 425°.
2. Spread butter over bottom of a 15 x 10–inch pan; sprinkle ¼ cup sugar over butter. Arrange pear halves, cut sides up, in pan. Brush pears with 1 tablespoon amaretto.
3. Bake, uncovered, at 425° for 25 minutes or just until tender. Add ½ cup water, 1 tablespoon amaretto, and salt to baking pan; brush pears with pan juices. Bake, uncovered, an additional 15 minutes or until pears are glazed, basting twice with syrup.
4. Combine crème fraîche, remaining 1 tablespoon sugar, and remaining 1 tablespoon amaretto. Place 1 pear half, cut side up, on each of 6 dessert plates. Drizzle pears evenly with sauce. Spoon about 1 tablespoon crème fraîche mixture onto each pear half. Sprinkle evenly with almonds, if desired. Yield: 6 servings (serving size: 1 pear half, about 1 teaspoon sauce, and 1 tablespoon crème fraîche mixture).

CALORIES 180; FAT 7.4g (sat 4.7g, mono 2g, poly 0.3g); PROTEIN 0.5g; CARB 25.7g; FIBER 3g; CHOL 25.1mg; IRON 0mg; SODIUM 55mg; CALC 21mg

Other summer fruits work well, too. Try cherries, berries, nectarines, apricots, or plums.

Sour Cream–Peach Tart
Prep: 5 minutes • Cook: 20 minutes • Other: 10 minutes

1 sheet frozen puff pastry dough, thawed
¼ cup (2 ounces) ⅓-less-fat cream cheese, softened

½ cup light sour cream
3 tablespoons brown sugar
1½ cups sliced peeled ripe peaches

1. Preheat oven to 400°.
2. Line a large baking sheet with parchment paper.
3. Place dough on prepared pan. Roll dough into a 14 x 8–inch rectangle. Lightly score dough along each edge, ¾ inch from edges. Brush scored edges lightly with water, and fold over onto remaining dough, creating a border. Press gently to adhere. Pierce bottom of tart shell with a fork. Freeze 10 minutes.
4. Bake at 400° for 20 minutes or until browned. Cool completely on pan on a wire rack.
5. While tart shell bakes, combine cream cheese, sour cream, and brown sugar in a medium bowl, stirring until smooth. Spread sour cream mixture on bottom of tart shell. Arrange peach slices over sour cream mixture. Cut into 8 rectangles. Serve immediately. Yield: 8 servings (serving size: 1 piece).

CALORIES 90; FAT 4.3g (sat 2g, mono 1.7g, poly 0.2g); PROTEIN 2.3g; CARB 10.8g; FIBER 0.5g; CHOL 10mg; IRON 0.3mg; SODIUM 60mg; CALC 44mg

A touch of orange liqueur balances the bright flavor of watermelon and keeps the sorbet from freezing until it's too firm to scoop. Instead, it is slightly soft and light.

Watermelon-Mint Sorbet

Prep: 8 minutes • Other: 2 hours

4 cups cubed seedless watermelon
½ cup sugar

¼ cup packed fresh mint leaves
¼ cup Cointreau (orange-flavored liqueur)

1. Place all ingredients in a blender; process until smooth.
2. Pour mixture into the freezer can of an ice-cream freezer; freeze according to manufacturer's instructions. Spoon sorbet into a freezer-safe container; cover and freeze 1 hour and 30 minutes or until firm. Yield: 7 servings (serving size: ½ cup).

CALORIES 115; FAT 0g (sat 0g, mono 0g, poly 0g); PROTEIN 0.3g; CARB 26.2g; FIBER 0.6g; CHOL 0mg; IRON 0.3mg; SODIUM 4mg; CALC 8mg

use extra mint in

Mint Vodka and Iced Green Tea, page **247**

Feta-Mint Dip, page **199**

Spiced Lamb and Fruited Couscous, page **319**

You don't need an ice-cream maker for this dessert: Freeze in a square or rectangular baking pan. Scraping the mixture with a fork gives it a flaky, melt-in-your mouth texture.

White Grape–Champagne Granita

Prep: 15 minutes • Other: 3 hours

2 pounds green seedless grapes
1 cup Champagne or sparkling white wine
2 tablespoons fresh lemon juice
3 tablespoons sugar

1. Place grapes in a food processor; process until pureed. Pour grape puree through a fine sieve into an 8-inch square baking dish, pressing with the back of a spoon to remove as much liquid as possible. Discard solids. Add wine, lemon juice, and sugar, stirring until sugar dissolves.

2. Freeze 3 hours or until firm, stirring every hour. Remove mixture from freezer; scrape entire mixture with a fork until fluffy. Yield: 8 servings (serving size: ½ cup).

CALORIES 122; FAT 0.2g (sat 0.1g, mono 0g, poly 0.1g); PROTEIN 0.9g; CARB 26.3g; FIBER 1g; CHOL 0mg; IRON 0.5mg; SODIUM 4mg; CALC 14mg

Nutritional Analysis

How to Use It and Why

Glance at the end of any *Cooking Light* recipe, and you'll see how committed we are to helping you make the best of today's light cooking. With chefs, registered dietitians, home economists, and a computer system that analyzes every ingredient we use, *Cooking Light* gives you authoritative dietary detail like no other magazine. We go to such lengths so you can see how our recipes fit into your healthful eating plan. If you're trying to lose weight, the calorie and fat figures will probably help most. But if you're keeping a close eye on the sodium, cholesterol, and saturated fat in your diet, we provide those numbers, too. And because many women don't get enough iron or calcium, we can help there, as well. Finally, there's a fiber analysis for those of us who don't get enough roughage.

Here's a helpful guide to put our nutritional analysis numbers into perspective. Remember, one size doesn't fit all, so take your lifestyle, age, and circumstances into consideration when determining your nutrition needs. For example, pregnant or breast-feeding women need more protein, calories, and calcium. And women older than 50 need 1,200mg of calcium daily, 200mg more than the amount recommended for younger women.

In Our Nutritional Analysis, We Use These Abbreviations

sat	saturated fat	**CHOL**	cholesterol
mono	monounsaturated fat	**CALC**	calcium
poly	polyunsaturated fat	**g**	gram
CARB	carbohydrates	**mg**	milligram

Daily Nutrition Guide

	Women ages 25 to 50	Women over 50	Men over 24
Calories	2,000	2,000 or less	2,700
Protein	50g	50g or less	63g
Fat	65g or less	65g or less	88g or less
Saturated Fat	20g or less	20g or less	27g or less
Carbohydrates	304g	304g	410g
Fiber	25g to 35g	25g to 35g	25g to 35g
Cholesterol	300mg or less	300mg or less	300mg or less
Iron	18 mg	8mg	8mg
Sodium	2,300mg or less	1,500mg or less	2,300mg or less
Calcium	1,000mg	1,200mg	1,000mg

The nutritional values used in our calculations either come from The Food Processor, Version 8.9 (ESHA Research), or are provided by food manufacturers.

Metric Equivalents

The information in the following charts is provided to help cooks outside the United States successfully use the recipes in this book. All equivalents are approximate.

Cooking/Oven Temperatures

	Fahrenheit	Celsius	Gas Mark
Freeze Water	32° F	0° C	
Room Temperature	68° F	20° C	
Boil Water	212° F	100° C	
Bake	325° F	160° C	3
	350° F	180° C	4
	375° F	190° C	5
	400° F	200° C	6
	425° F	220° C	7
	450° F	230° C	8
Broil			Grill

Liquid Ingredients by Volume

¼ tsp			=		1 ml
½ tsp			=		2 ml
1 tsp			=		5 ml
3 tsp	= 1 tbl		= ½ fl oz	=	15 ml
	2 tbls	= ⅛ cup	= 1 fl oz	=	30 ml
	4 tbls	= ¼ cup	= 2 fl oz	=	60 ml
	5⅓ tbls	= ⅓ cup	= 3 fl oz	=	80 ml
	8 tbls	= ½ cup	= 4 fl oz	=	120 ml
	10⅔ tbls	= ⅔ cup	= 5 fl oz	=	160 ml
	12 tbls	= ¾ cup	= 6 fl oz	=	180 ml
	16 tbls	= 1 cup	= 8 fl oz	=	240 ml
1 pt	= 2 cups	= 16 fl oz	=		480 ml
1 qt	= 4 cups	= 32 fl oz	=		960 ml
		33 fl oz	= 1000 ml	=	1l

Dry Ingredients by Weight

(To convert ounces to grams, multiply the number of ounces by 30.)

1 oz	=	¹⁄₁₆ lb	=	30 g
4 oz	=	¼ lb	=	120 g
8 oz	=	½ lb	=	240 g
12 oz	=	¾ lb	=	360 g
16 oz	=	1 lb	=	480 g

Length

(To convert inches to centimeters, multiply the number of inches by 2.5.)

1 in	=		2.5 cm
6 in	= ½ ft	= 15 cm
12 in	= 1 ft	= 30 cm
36 in	= 3 ft	= 1 yd	= 90 cm
40 in	=	100 cm	= 1m

Equivalents for Different Types of Ingredients

Standard Cup	Fine Powder (ex. flour)	Grain (ex. rice)	Granular (ex. sugar)	Liquid Solids (ex. butter)	Liquid (ex. milk)
1	140 g	150 g	190 g	200 g	240 ml
¾	105 g	113 g	143 g	150 g	180 ml
⅔	93 g	100 g	125 g	133 g	160 ml
½	70 g	75 g	95 g	100 g	120 ml
⅓	47 g	50 g	63 g	67 g	80 ml
¼	35 g	38 g	48 g	50 g	60 ml
⅛	18 g	19 g	24 g	25 g	30 ml

index

Grilled (continued)

Sauces (continued)